World War II on Film

Recent Titles in Hollywood History

The Vietnam War on Film
David Luhrssen

The American West on Film
Johnny D. Boggs

The Civil War on Film
Peg A. Lamphier and Rosanne Welch

World War II on Film

David Luhrssen

Hollywood History

BLOOMSBURY ACADEMIC
NEW YORK • LONDON • OXFORD • NEW DELHI • SYDNEY

BLOOMSBURY ACADEMIC
Bloomsbury Publishing Inc
1385 Broadway, New York, NY 10018, USA
50 Bedford Square, London, WC1B 3DP, UK
29 Earlsfort Terrace, Dublin 2, Ireland

BLOOMSBURY, BLOOMSBURY ACADEMIC and the Diana logo
are trademarks of Bloomsbury Publishing Plc

First published in the United States of America by ABC-CLIO 2021
Paperback edition published by Bloomsbury Academic 2024

Copyright © Bloomsbury Publishing Inc, 2024

For legal purposes the Acknowledgments on p. xiii constitute
an extension of this copyright page.

Cover photo: George C. Scott and Karl Malden, *Patton*, 1970.
(20th Century Fox/AF archive/Alamy)

All rights reserved. No part of this publication may be reproduced or
transmitted in any form or by any means, electronic or mechanical,
including photocopying, recording, or any information storage or retrieval
system, without prior permission in writing from the publishers.

Bloomsbury Publishing Inc does not have any control over, or responsibility for,
any third-party websites referred to or in this book. All internet addresses given
in this book were correct at the time of going to press. The author and publisher
regret any inconvenience caused if addresses have changed or sites have
ceased to exist, but can accept no responsibility for any such changes.

Library of Congress Cataloging-in-Publication Data
Names: Luhrssen, David, author.
Title: World War II on film / David Luhrssen.
Other titles: World War Two on film
Description: Santa Barbara, California : ABC-CLIO, An Imprint of ABC-CLIO, LLC, [2021] |
Series: Hollywood history | Includes bibliographical references and index.
Identifiers: LCCN 2020008730 (print) | LCCN 2020008731 (ebook) |
ISBN 9781440871580 (hardcover) | ISBN 9781440871597 (ebook)
Subjects: LCSH: World War, 1939-1945—Motion pictures and the war. | World
War, 1939-1945—Mass media and the war. | War films—United
States—History and criticism. | Motion pictures and history.
Classification: LCC D743.23 .L84 2021 (print) | LCC D743.23 (ebook) |
DDC 791.43/658—dc23
LC record available at https://lccn.loc.gov/2020008730
LC ebook record available at https://lccn.loc.gov/2020008731

ISBN: HB: 978-1-4408-7158-0
PB: 979-8-7651-3095-7
ePDF: 978-1-4408-7159-7
eBook: 979-8-2161-6878-2

Series: Hollywood History

To find out more about our authors and books visit www.bloomsbury.com
and sign up for our newsletters.

Contents

Series Foreword	vii
Preface	ix
Acknowledgments	xiii
Introduction	xv
Chronology	xxv
1. *Saboteur* (1942)	1
2. *Casablanca* (1942)	17
3. *Twelve O'Clock High* (1949)	31
4. *From Here to Eternity* (1953)	43
5. *The Bridge on the River Kwai* (1957)	59
6. *Judgment at Nuremberg* (1961)	73
7. *Patton* (1970)	91
8. *Das Boot* (1981)	103
9. *Saving Private Ryan* (1998)	117
10. *Enemy at the Gates* (2001)	131
11. *Flags of Our Fathers* and *Letters from Iwo Jima* (2006)	145
12. *Dunkirk* (2017)	163
Bibliography	175
Index	183

Series Foreword

Just exactly how accurate are Hollywood's film and television portrayals of American history? What do these portrayals of history tell us, not only about the events they depict but also the time in which they were made? Each volume in this unique reference series is devoted to a single topic or key theme in American history, examining 10–12 major motion pictures or television productions. Substantial essays summarize each film, provide historical background of the event or period it depicts, and explain how accurate the film's depiction is, while also analyzing the cultural context in which the film was made. A final resources section provides a comprehensive annotated bibliography of print and electronic sources to aid students and teachers in further research.

The subjects of these Hollywood History volumes were chosen based on both curriculum relevance and inherent interest. Readers will find a wide array of subject choices, including American Slavery on Film, the Civil War on Film, the American West on Film, Vietnam on Film, and the 1960s on Film. Ideal for school assignments and student research, the length, format, and subject areas are designed to meet educators' needs and students' interests.

Preface

World War II is America's most popular war. When the country finally plunged into the fray after Japan's attack on Pearl Harbor (December 7, 1941), Americans supported the war with a unity and enthusiasm that exceeded any previous conflict and remains unmatched in the years since. The war was almost universally embraced as a fight worth almost any cost.

One measure of World War II's popularity is the number of movies it inspired during and after the conflict. Tabulating Hollywood productions from the exhaustive roster of war movie titles shows that the U.S. movie industry released nearly 200 World War II films from 1942 through 1945 alone. The numbers shrank to only 10 in the late 1940s, probably the result of war and war movie fatigue. However, interest revived during the 1950s, a decade that saw some 90 releases and diminished only slightly in the 1960s with nearly 70 films. However, in the 1960s, television took up the slack with several weekly series. With the unpopular Vietnam War (1955–1975) on the minds of producers and audiences alike, and a rebellious attitude against the older generation, World War II productions slowed to less than two dozen in the 1970s and rose only slightly in the 1980s. Perhaps a renewed interest in the survivors of World War II, and a revival of respect for the military and America's role in the world, explains the resumption of interest in movies about that war. Their number climbed to some 26 in the 1990s and over 40 in the 2000s.

The best seller *The Greatest Generation* (1998) registered and amplified that shift in attitude. World War II was very much on the mind of the book's author, NBC news anchor Tom Brokaw (1940–). He was inspired to write his account of the generation that grew up during the Great Depression of the 1930s and went to war in the 1940s while covering the 50th anniversary of the D-Day landing (June 6, 1944). He found himself "deeply moved and profoundly grateful" for the men and women who fought or worked for victory. "They answered the call to help save the world," he wrote, adding that they "faced great odds and a late start [in the war], but they did not protest" (Brokaw 1998, viii–ix).

The World War II movies produced by Hollywood should not be confused with documentaries. However, even when the war was still a living memory for millions of Americans, it was often remembered less for what happened in reality than for how it was represented on film. During his presidency, Ronald Reagan famously liked to inspire listeners by recounting how a B-17 bomber commander comforted a wounded crew member as their plane was going down by saying, "Never mind, son, we'll ride it down together." Unconsciously or not, Reagan borrowed the story from a World War II movie, *A Wing and a Prayer* (1944) (Gabler 1998, 110–111). A Hollywood actor during the war era, Reagan understood the engrossing power of a medium that tells stories in sound and moving images. That power alarmed thoughtful people even before images on screen became as pervasive as they are in the twenty-first century. As long ago as 1961, historian Daniel J. Boorstin worried that Americans lived in a "world where fantasy is more real than reality" with "illusions so vivid, so persuasive, so 'realistic'" that we can easily live inside the fantasy (Boorstin 1961, 37, 240).

Movies might be "realistic," but "realism" is not necessarily the driving factor of their appeal. "The power of movies cannot be identical to the power of seeing the real event; the movie's power must lie in what *distinguishes* it from seeing real events," wrote philosopher Colin McGinn (McGinn 2005, 6). Not unlike other forms of visual art, film has the power to transform reality into something larger than itself, not only by adding details that might not be present in reality but also by subtracting extraneous elements for a sharper focus on the ideas being represented.

Arguably, the primary job of movie directors and screenwriters is to entertain. It falls to historians to sift fact from legend and sort through memories real or false. The historians' responsibility is to assemble a true picture of events. Working from that directive, *World War II on Film* seeks to find the facts behind the films by contrasting and comparing reality to its representation on screen. Arranged chronologically, each of the 12 chapters of *World War II on Film* is devoted to a particular feature-length movie that renders the war primarily through dramatization and storytelling as opposed to documentary footage and interviews. Each chapter will evaluate how closely those dramatizations reflect or how far they depart from the truth. Some films were chosen for their role in defining public memory and discourse about the war and others for their focus on particular aspects of the war. All of the selections continue to tell us something about the meaning of that war.

World War II on Film opens with a movie produced and released in the early months after America's entry into World War II. Alfred Hitchcock's *Saboteur* (1942) is suffused with anxiety over the possibility that traitors might surrender their country to the enemy. Released only a few months later, *Casablanca* (1942) reflects on America's prewar tendency toward isolationism and the moral necessity of joining the world in a common cause against the enemies of humanity. Neither film is a "war movie" in the narrow sense of depicting combat. There would be many of those movies in the months and years to come.

From the immediate postwar years came *Twelve O'Clock High* (1949), still the most vivid depiction of the Allied air campaign against Germany. *From Here to Eternity* (1953) climaxes with a different sort of air strike, the Japanese raid on Pearl Harbor that brought America into the war. A British-U.S. coproduction, *The Bridge on the River Kwai* (1957) dramatizes the poor treatment of Allied prisoners of war by the Japanese. *Judgment at Nuremberg* (1961) weighs the guilt of German society and individuals in the postwar trials of that country's leaders.

Patton (1970) follows America's flamboyant General George S. Patton through his campaigns in North Africa, Italy, and his thrust into Germany. The international acclaim for *Das Boot* (1981) flips the usual perspective by showing the war through the eyes of a German submarine crew. Steven Spielberg's *Saving Private Ryan* (1998) plunges viewers into the pivotal D-Day invasion. *Enemy at the Gates* (2001) offers the viewpoint of Soviets defeating German invaders at Stalingrad, another of the war's turning points. With the coupled release of *Flags of Our Fathers* and *Letters from Iwo Jima* (2006), director Clint Eastwood explores both the way depictions of the war were falsified in the United States and the lives of Japanese soldiers preparing to die during an American assault. In *Dunkirk* (2017), British filmmaker Christopher Nolan recreates one of his country's finest hours in the early stages of the war.

Of course, even in its vast number, the catalog of World War II movies doesn't include every story from those years. The race riot that tore apart Detroit in 1943 and was put down by the U.S. Army never received its cinematic debut. The factories, mines, and railroads seized by order of President Franklin D. Roosevelt to halt wartime strikes has not been the subject of a major motion picture nor has the wartime sedition trial against right-wing agitators. The race riots in Southern California between GIs and Chicano youths were the subject of one little seen film, *Zoot Suit* (1981). The mass internment of Japanese civilians, including U.S. citizens, was not filmed by Hollywood at the time and has seen recognition in barely a handful of films (Jeansonne and Luhrssen 2014, 29).

Few American filmmakers have chosen to record the war's negative undertones. The prevailing spirit for depicting the war is heard in the popular tune "Ac-Cent-Tchu-Ate the Positive," which won the Oscar for Best Song in the wartime comedy *Here Come the Waves* (1944). The lyrics called on listeners to "eliminate the negative," and the movie industry had no trouble obliging. After all, the progress of the war coincided with Hollywood's love of happy endings. The enemy was reprehensible and vanquished after titanic struggles.

In truth as well as on screen, Americans had many reasons to remember World War II as "the good war." Aside from island possessions in the Pacific and submarines in the coastal waters, the United States was not invaded or even attacked. The nation's cities were not devastated by ground combat or air raids. Although the United States suffered more than 405,000 military deaths, the total was proportionately lower than the war's other major combatants. Most of "the boys" came home, although some lost limbs or were injured in ways less apparent. Unlike many nations in Europe and Asia, the United States did not need to rebuild after it was over.

Hollywood helped to maintain the positive spirit that fueled the war effort. "At least we were the good guys in that war," says Steve Carell's protagonist in *Welcome to Marwen* (2018), a psychologically damaged man who lives in a heroic fantasy based on World War II movies and comic books. Not unlike the character he plays, much of what Americans remember about the war is based on what the entertainment industry fashioned from the material of reality. *World War II on Film* is a close examination of 12 such fantasies with the objective of finding the truth beneath the stories that we tell of the world's greatest war.

FURTHER READING

Boorstin, Daniel J. 1961. *The Image: A Guide to Pseudo-Events in America*. New York: Harper & Row.
Brokaw, Tom. 1998. *The Greatest Generation*. New York: Random House.
Gabler, Neil. 1998. *Life the Movie: How Entertainment Conquered Reality*. New York: Alfred A. Knopf.
Jeansonne, Glen, and David Luhrssen. 2014. *War on the Silver Screen: Shaping America's Perception of History*. Lincoln, NE: Potomac Books.
McGinn, Colin. 2005. *The Power of Movies: How Screen and Mind Interact*. New York: Pantheon.

Acknowledgments

Even though 15 years had already passed between my birth and the surrender of Germany and Japan, I grew up in a culture thoroughly permeated by World War II. Movies and TV shows set during that war were unavoidable on broadcast television, and adult family members spoke often of their formative experiences in "the war," as if Korea had never happened and Vietnam was a distant skirmish. World War II had shaped their lives irrevocably. In my neighborhood, boys my age played World War II much more than the cowboys and Indians favored by earlier generations, and since I was considered the "foreign kid," I was often given the unpleasant role of Axis commander.

In a sense, *World War II on Film* is a book I've been writing all of my life. Although distant from my own experience, the war and its various meanings and outcomes continued to be part of my life. As a graduate student at the University of Wisconsin (UW)-Milwaukee, I was a teaching assistant for the late Dr. William Renzi's course on World War II, perhaps the most popular course in the college's history department. One of my students, John Jahn, remains a World War II buff, and while I was writing this book, he lent me materials from his personal library. My thesis committee at UW-Milwaukee included professors who specialized in political aspects of the war.

As I began to explore film more widely and deeply as a fan, critic, and historian, movies about that conflict were inescapable. The list of people who accompanied or sometimes spurred me on that journey into film is long. I particularly want to cite Patricia Mellencamp, whose Hollywood film course at UW-Milwaukee first showed me that there is more to a movie than meets the eye. I discovered many films that influenced my thinking on the subject with friends such as Cathy Miller, Beth Baer, Anthe Rhodes, and Bob Popkoff. I especially want to acknowledge Mary Manion, who shared with me the movies that comprise the present book, *World War II on Film*.

Introduction

World War II (1939–1941) was the largest and deadliest conflict in history. The fighting spread across Europe, Asia, Africa, the Middle East, and the Pacific islands and spilled across all the world's oceans. Virtually every nation took part in the war whether overtaken or threatened by conquering armies or coming to the aid of allies. Even unswervingly neutral countries such as Portugal, Ireland, and Switzerland became sites of financial transactions, espionage, and refugee settlement. A dozen nations, including Turkey, Saudi Arabia, and several Latin American states, remained neutral through most of the war and committed themselves only in the final months when the outcome was certain. The resources of the colonial empires were also marshaled, leaving no inhabited corner of the earth uninvolved, even those areas untouched by fighting.

The casualties of World War II can never be precisely counted. Perhaps 20 million military personnel were killed. The death toll among prisoners of war would raise the total even higher (Ellis 1993, 253–254). In the European theater, some 20 million civilians may have died in air raids and ground fighting, or were lost at sea, or lost their lives as refugees fleeing the war zones. For many countries impacted by the war, especially in Eastern Europe, exact numbers are impossible to determine (Bullock 1991, 987). At least 20 million civilians died from malnutrition as a result of the war, many of them in areas distant from combat (Collingham 2012, 1). The most notorious massacre of civilians during World War II, the Nazi Holocaust against the Jews, claimed six million victims. The Nazis also killed 200,000 Roma (gypsies), targeting them as "racially inferior," but they were not alone in turning conquered lands into killing fields. Estimates of civilians killed by the Japanese in China vary, but a recent figure puts the number at 20 million (Anderson 2011).

The principal aggressor nations were Germany, Japan, and Italy, bound together in a military pact known as the Axis. The nations opposed to them were called the Allies. The Allied victory was principally led by the United States, Great Britain, and the Soviet Union. The United States and Great Britain were representative democracies with capitalist economies while the Soviet Union was a Communist regime under the brutal dictatorship of Josef Stalin (1878–1953). The agendas of the Allies were often contradictory, but they were united by the necessity of defeating the Axis.

THE ROOTS OF THE WAR

The origins of World War II are often traced to the unsatisfactory conclusion of World War I (1914–1918). Although Italy and Japan were among the victors at the postwar peace conference that resulted in the Treaty of Versailles (1919), both nations left unsatisfied. As payment for entering the war against Germany and Austria-Hungary, Italy had been promised Austrian land by Great Britain and France. Because many of those areas had no Italian inhabitants, the promise was rolled back at Versailles by U.S. president Woodrow Wilson (1856–1924), who stood for the "self-determination" of peoples. As a result, Italy received a smaller portion of the spoils than anticipated. Japan received the territory it desired but was angered because the United States vetoed any discussion of racial equality at the Versailles conference (Andelman 2008, 270).

As the leader of the nations defeated in World War I, Germany was singled out for punishment at Versailles. Under the peace treaty, Germany lost its colonies as well as provinces on its western and eastern borders. As payback for the damage it caused during the war, Germany was also forced to pay enormous reparations to the victors, which weakened its economy and left it vulnerable to unrest. The country's military, which had occupied a place of pride in German life, was drastically reduced.

One of the Versailles conference's more farsighted delegates spotted trouble ahead. Economist John Maynard Keynes (1883–1946), a British representative, resigned in protest and wrote a scathing account, *The Economic Consequences of the Peace* (1920). In his introduction to a recent edition, former Federal Reserve chairman Paul A. Volcker (1927–) emphasized the book's enduring importance and summarized Keynes, who believed Versailles "would dismantle the German economy, impoverish its citizens, and ultimately undermine prospects for peace and reconciliation" (Keynes 2007, xi). His worst predictions came true.

In Germany, the harsh terms of the Versailles Treaty sparked a culture of resentment that enabled the rise of militant right-wing groups, including the Nazi Party. Versailles was less significant as a political issue in Italy and had little influence on the Japanese public. Each of the three belligerent nations took a distinctive path, but they shared important characteristics that help explain why their people accepted dictatorships bent on conquest.

Italy was the first to lurch in that direction by abandoning its parliamentary system for rule by Benito Mussolini (1883–1945) and his Fascist Party. Although many of the party's original members were disgruntled World War I veterans, the rise of Fascism had more to do with economic hardship, widespread fatigue with the existing political order, and thwarting the threat of a Communist-inspired revolution than with Versailles. Italian authorities could easily have defeated Mussolini's paramilitary March on Rome (1922), but in "a remarkable case of collective liberal suicide," the government retreated and vacillating King Victor Emanuel III appointed Mussolini as prime minister (Gilmour 2011, 301).

Mussolini's party introduced the word "fascism" to the world and the stiff-armed "Roman salute" adopted by the German Nazis. In inception, Italian Fascism was a left-wing nationalist movement with strong roots in the radical fringe of socialism. Mussolini's intellectual roots link him with Marxism; however, his emotional fervor was drawn from the powerful attraction of nationalism. Unlike Stalin, he had no interest in seeing himself as leader of an international movement. As prime minister, Mussolini accommodated himself to the monarchy, the Roman Catholic Church, and other power centers (Payne 1995, 119).

Japan was an outlier among the Axis powers politically as well as geographically. It was a dictatorship without a dictator, a ruling political party, or a coherent political ideology. Although some Japanese leaders were "enmeshed in a dialogue with European fascism," the motivating belief system was based on the medieval code of the knightly samurai, egged on by a sense of national greatness and coupled with fervent devotion to their god-ruler (Hofman 2015, 2). Regarded as divine, the hands of Emperor Hirohito (1901–1989) seldom touched the levers of power. Not unlike Victor Emanuel III, he was dithering and easily influenced. The parliamentary system continued to operate even as control fell to squabbling military cliques whose members eagerly assassinated liberal opponents as well as each other. Acting on its own authority, an army faction marched into Manchuria (1931) and installed a puppet empire (Johnson 1991, 312–313).

Japanese authoritarianism has been described as "a complex amalgam of state bureaucrats, conservative economic leaders, and military praetorians" (Payne 1995, 335). During World War II, American propaganda focused on General Tojo Hideki (1884–1948), prime minister at the time of Pearl Harbor. However, Tojo was forced out of office in 1944, a year before the war ended, and "held less personal power" than U.S. president Franklin D. Roosevelt (1882–1945) or British prime minister Winston Churchill (1874–1965) (Payne 1995, 335).

Germany was the Axis state most under the dominance of one man. Adolf Hitler (1889–1945), a veteran of World War I, shared his countrymen's dismay at Versailles and rejected the republican government that signed the hated treaty. In the end, economic disruption and fear of Communism was a larger factor behind the rise of the Nazi Party with Hitler as its undisputed führer (leader). His proclamation of a "Third Reich" had mystical connotations of an almost spiritual empire in the minds of his German audience. Not unlike Mussolini, whom he idolized, Hitler accommodated conservative power centers such as the military, industry, and the Roman Catholic Church. However, for Hitler, these were temporary arrangements, and he moved to erode the authority of any rivals for power. Mussolini looked down on Hitler in the German dictator's early years, but by the late 1930s, a shared agenda of conquest brought them together (Johnson 1991, 319). Soon enough, in light of Italy's relative military weakness, Mussolini was the junior partner and Hitler the leader.

Mussolini dreamed of recreating the Roman Empire with Italy dominating the Mediterranean shore. Hitler sought revenge against France for the harsh Versailles Treaty and revived the old Germanic ambition of dominating Eastern Europe but also had a larger ambition of transforming the world along racial lines. In the hierarchy he imagined, the "Aryan" Northern Europeans led by Germany would rule over "inferior races" such as the Eastern European Slavs. In Hitler's world order, the Jews were a rival, the ultimate threat, and had to be eliminated by any means. The plans of Hitler and Mussolini dovetailed well enough with the desire of Japan's military leaders to dominate East Asia and the Pacific Rim. Hitler entertained the hope of coming to terms with Great Britain, allowing the British Empire to rule the far ends of the earth while he concentrated on the Eurasian continent. Hitler and Mussolini agreed that the Soviet Union, the citadel of Communism, needed to be smashed as soon as convenient. Japan had no love for the Soviets, but its leaders, divided on their priorities, concentrated on subjugating China and drawing the Asiatic peoples into its orbit.

THE COURSE OF THE WAR

The aggressor nations were already at war before World War II began. Italy invaded Ethiopia, one of the only independent African nations, in 1935. Receiving complaints but little opposition from the international community, Italy's land grab encouraged the widening of conflict. In that same year, Hitler repudiated the Versailles restrictions and began enlarging and modernizing Germany's military in preparation for war. In 1936, German troops reoccupied the Rhineland province along the French border, which had been demilitarized at Versailles. In the Spanish Civil War (1936–1939), Germany and Italy aided the rebel General Francisco Franco (1892–1975) in his successful bid to topple Spain's Soviet-supported government. In 1938, Germany absorbed Austria into the Third Reich and annexed part of Czechoslovakia inhabited by German speakers as British and French leaders looked on. Britain's prime minister Neville Chamberlain (1869–1940) assumed it was possible to "appease" Hitler by granting him lands to which Germany had a conceivable claim. Hitler's appetite proved too large to appease. Meanwhile in Asia, the Japanese began their advance into the heart of China in 1937.

The stage was set. World War II began on September 1, 1939, when German forces pushed eastward into Poland, triggering that country's alliances with Great Britain and France. In a cynical move, the Soviet Union had just signed a "Non-Aggression Pact" with Germany that divided Eastern Europe into German and Soviet "spheres of influence." Armed with German approval, the Soviets invaded Poland from the west; occupied Estonia, Latvia, and Lithuania; and attacked Finland. The Non-Aggression Pact introduced a temporary division within the Axis, whose alliance was based on opposition to the Soviet Union. The Japanese felt they "had been betrayed and dishonored" by Hitler's move, and Mussolini was taken aback (Bullock 1991, 620, 624). Italy did not join World War II until after Hitler occupied much of Europe in 1940, and Japan weighed options until December 1941, when it attacked Pearl Harbor and other American and European possessions in Asia and the Pacific.

Hitler waited until spring of 1940 before his next move. In April and May, Germany overran Denmark, Norway, Belgium, Luxembourg, the Netherlands, and France. Their successful campaign was based on tactics the Germans called "blitzkrieg" (lightning war). Making use of the latest military technology, blitzkrieg involved swift-moving tank columns backed by mechanized infantry punching holes in enemy lines with dive bombers in close support.

By the summer of 1940, as Hitler absorbed his new empire, Churchill, a politician known for his opposition to appeasement and his willingness to fight, replaced Chamberlain as Britain's prime minister. His sole success in the early months of his tenure was orchestrating a retreat from continental Europe at Dunkirk, France, saving Britain's army and remnants of French and Belgian forces. Despite slim odds of victory and expectations of a German invasion of the British Isles, he was determined to fight on. Churchill's "entire strategic hopes rested upon the presumption of American entry into the war," as happened in World War I (Kershaw 2007, 185).

Churchill had reason for hope. Innately cautious yet capable of bold strokes, Roosevelt inched toward supporting Britain in the face of widespread antiwar and isolationist opposition in the United States. As Poland fell to the Nazis, he told his advisors, "We aren't going into this war" with troops (Kershaw 2007, 195). In reality, Roosevelt had no troops to send. In 1939, the U.S. Army was smaller in size than the Royal Dutch Army and lacked modern equipment. Roosevelt launched an ambitious rearmament program and instituted a peacetime draft under the heading of defending the Western Hemisphere against attack. In December 1940, he declared that America was "the arsenal of democracy"; he swapped aged warships for leases on British bases in the Caribbean and convinced Congress to pass the Lend Lease Act in 1941, allowing him to sell arms overseas if he deemed it essential for "the defense of the United States." "The immediate significance for the British war effort was largely symbolic," wrote British historian Ian Kershaw (1943–) (Kershaw 2007, 233). Although Britain manufactured most of its own armaments during the war, it needed raw material and food to survive. The convoying of supplies by U.S. Navy warships drew America into an active role supporting the British.

In France, the country's new leader, Marshal Henri Philippe Petain (1856–1951), signed an armistice with Hitler that provided for German occupation of the country's northern tier. Petain governed the remnants of his country and its colonies from a town in southern France called Vichy but faced increasing competition from a maverick officer, General Charles de Gaulle (1890–1970), who organized the Free French movement from exile in London. The Free French competed with Vichy for control of the nation's colonies and encouraged a resistance movement within France.

Hitler had hoped to either bomb the British into submission through a massive air campaign, the Battle of Britain (1940–1941), or starve it through submarine warfare against the beleaguered island's sea lanes in the Battle of the Atlantic (1939–1945). Under Churchill's leadership, Britain held firm. In East Africa, British and South African forces seized Italy's colonies. In Libya and Egypt, Britain dueled with Italian forces and Germany's Afrika Korps. Greece thwarted an Italian assault but succumbed to the Germans, who also occupied Yugoslavia. With Germany appearing invincible, the Axis added several smaller Eastern European nations to its membership including Bulgaria, Rumania, Hungary, and Finland.

In 1941, the Axis overextended its reach. In June, Hitler tore up the Non-Aggression Pact and invaded the Soviet Union, advancing deep into the country. Although a lifelong foe of Communism, Churchill announced his support for the Soviets. By December, the overconfident German invaders were bogged down in the Russian winter as Japan bombed U.S. bases at Pearl Harbor. The attack came after the United States froze Japanese assets in response to the empire's ongoing war with China, threatening a fuel shortage. Japan's military saw the necessity of seizing the old fields of Dutch East India (Indonesia), and to do so, it needed to secure control over the American Commonwealth of the Philippines as well as British colonies such as Hong Kong, Malaya, and Singapore (Kershaw 2007, 333–334). The raid on Pearl Harbor was followed by a swift series of successful military operations against the U.S., British, and Dutch interests. Australia was also bombed by Japanese planes and threatened with invasion.

Following the attack on Pearl Harbor, the United States entered the war. Roosevelt, Churchill, and Stalin, the main Allied leaders, began what proved to be a rough road toward a coordinated strategy to bring down the Axis. Roosevelt and Churchill conferred in person seven times during the war. Stalin was present at two of those meetings and China's president Chiang Kai-shek (1887–1975) at one. At their meeting in Casablanca (1943), Roosevelt and Churchill declared that the Allies would accept nothing less than "unconditional surrender" from the Axis. Some historians believe this was done to discourage the untrustworthy Stalin from seeking a separate peace with Hitler (Ward and Burns 2007, 72).

Roosevelt and Churchill agreed on a "Germany first" strategy, focusing on invasions of Southern and Northern Europe to relieve German pressure on the Soviet Union and allow Soviet forces to advance into Axis-held Eastern Europe. Joint military planning was conducted by British and American army and naval officers. America's enormous industrial and financial capacity gave it the lead role in prosecuting the war. U.S. General Dwight D. Eisenhower (1890–1969) became Supreme Commander of Allied forces in Europe and U.S. General Douglas MacArthur (1880–1964) Supreme Commander of Allied forces in the Southwest Pacific. Aside from the extensive American aid it received in the form of military equipment, food parcels, and raw materials, the Soviet Union fought the war largely alone with relatively little coordination with the other Allies. The Axis had no overall joint strategy. After a series of defeats, Italian forces were largely subordinated to German aims. Japan fought with its own resources.

In 1942, American troops landed in North Africa and helped the British expel the Italians and Germans. Invasions of Sicily and Italy's mainland followed in 1943 and resulted in Mussolini's dismissal by King Victor Emanuel III and an armistice with the Allies. However, German commandos rescued Mussolini and installed him as a puppet ruler in northern Italy. German troops on the Italian peninsula fought doggedly to delay the Allied advance. In Eastern Europe, the Axis made a final push into the Soviet Union, but a large German army was trapped and destroyed at Stalingrad. The battle was one of the war's most significant turning points.

Beginning in 1942, Britain's Royal Air Force and the U.S. Army Air Force brought the air war to Axis-occupied Europe, filling the sky with as many as 1,000 bombers on a single mission. Targets were hit across the continent, but German cities were chosen for devastation in a campaign to break German civilian morale the British termed "de-housing" (Burleigh 2000, 745–746). Despite what should have been crippling blows to German industry and transportation networks, the Nazis continued to produce arms and even introduced new weapons such as jet fighters and ballistic missiles, but they were too late and too few in number to change the war's outcome.

On June 6, 1944 (known as D-Day), the expected Allied invasion of northern Europe began in Normandy. With U.S., British, and Canadian troops in the lead roles under massive air cover and support from naval gunnery, the Allies broke Germany's "Atlantic Wall" of fortifications. The Allies (by now including Free French units) pushed across France and into Belgium, the Netherlands, and Luxembourg. By 1945, the Allies pressed westward into Germany as the Soviets overran Eastern Europe and descended on the German capital, Berlin. On April 30, 1945, Hitler committed suicide in his Berlin bunker as Soviet shells rained on the capital. On May 8, Germany surrendered and was divided until 1952 into U.S., British, French, and Soviet occupation zones.

The war in the Pacific was conducted with little reference to events in Europe. The U.S. Navy played the principal role, thwarting the Japanese fleet in the Battle of the Coral Sea (1942) and the Battle of Midway (1942). U.S. Marines were often first on shore in the campaign to retake strategic islands, but forces from Australia and New Zealand were also active. The United States landed and began to retake the Philippines in late 1944, supported by Filipino forces and a squadron from the Mexican air force. Bloody battles were fought as the Japanese desperately tried to hold the islands on the sea lanes toward Japan. The U.S. capture of Iwo Jima (1945), only 760 miles from Tokyo, signaled that the Pacific war was entering its final phase. Plans for the invasion of Japan were underway, but the war was cut short in August 1945 when the United States dropped atomic bombs on the Japanese cities of Hiroshima (August 6) and Nagasaki (August 9). Within days, Emperor Hirohito, speaking to his people by radio for the first time, announced Japan's unconditional surrender to the Allies. On September 2, MacArthur accepted Japan's surrender in Tokyo Bay. The United States occupied the defeated empire until 1952.

LEGACY OF THE WAR

Not only much of Europe and East Asia was left in ruins at the end of World War II, especially Germany and Japan, but also the lands they had conquered. Although victorious, Great Britain and France were weakened by the war and unable to maintain their empires or prestige as world powers. At the war's end, two superpowers were left standing, the United States and the Soviet Union. The U.S. economy boomed during the war, fueled by military spending, and became the engine for rebuilding the postwar world and for American dominance. The Soviet Union was devastated by the Nazi German invasion, but the war strengthened its military and brought its forces forward into the heart of Central Europe. As a Russian historian wrote, the combination of Allied supplies during the war and the lessons learned from battling the Germans resulted in a military of "fantastic strength," in Stalin's mind "the greatest military machine that had ever existed" (Radzinsky

1996, 496). Before long, the Soviets developed their own atomic weapons, and the long stalemate of the Cold War (1947–1991) began.

During the war, the Allies sometimes referred to themselves as the United Nations and by 1944 began discussing plans for a permanent international organization intended to maintain peace in the postwar world. As a formal organization, the United Nations came into existence in 1945 with 50 members and grew in size as the former Axis nations were admitted and formerly colonized states became independent. The UN's highest body, the Security Council, included five seats reserved for the most significant Allies in the war against the Axis: the United States, Great Britain, France, the Soviet Union, and the China. Russia inherited the Soviet seat when the Soviet Union dissolved in 1991.

Allied tribunals that tried German and Japanese leaders for war crimes set a precedent for human rights in international law. Many of the national boundaries that remain in place today resulted from decisions made during World War II. The influx of Jewish refugee survivors from the Holocaust contributed to the creation of the State of Israel. World War II also spurred the development of technology such as radar, sonar, ballistic missiles, computers, and the atomic bomb. Secondary developments built on those breakthroughs include space travel and the miniaturization of technology enabling the electronic devices of the 21st century.

FURTHER READING

Andelman, David A. 2008. *A Shattered Peace: Versailles 1919 and the Price We Pay Today*. Hoboken, NJ: John Wiley & Son.

Anderson, Duncan. 2011. "Nuclear Power: The End of the War Against Japan." BBC, February 17, 2011. http://www.bbc.co.uk/history/worldwars/wwtwo/nuclear_01.shtml

Bullock, Alan. 1991. *Hitler and Stalin: Parallel Lives*. New York: Alfred A. Knopf.

Burleigh, Michael. 2000. *The Third Reich: A New History*. New York: Hill and Wang.

Collingham, Lizzie. 2012. *The Taste of War: World War II and the Battle for Food*. New York: Penguin Press.

Ellis, John. 1993. *The World War II Data Book: The Essential Facts and Figures for All the Combatants*. London: Aurum Press.

Gilmour, David. 2011. *The Pursuit of Italy: A History of a Land, Its Regions, and their Peoples*. New York: Farrar, Straus and Giroux.

Hofman, Reto. 2015. *The Fascist Effect: Japan and Italy, 1915–1952*. Ithaca, NY: Cornell University Press.

Johnson, Paul. 1991. *Modern Times: From the Twenties to the Nineties*. New York: HarperCollins.

Kershaw, Ian. 2007. *Fateful Choices: Ten Decisions That Changed the World 1940–1941*. New York: Penguin Press.

Keynes, John Maynard. 2007. *The Economic Consequences of the Peace*. New York: Skyhorse Publishing.
Payne, Stanley G. 1995. *A History of Fascism, 1914–1945*. Madison: University of Wisconsin Press.
Radzinsky, Edvard. 1996. *Stalin: The First In-Depth Biography Based on Explosive New Documents From Russia's Secret Archives*. New York: Doubleday.
Ward, Geoffrey C., and Ken Burns. 2007. *The War: An Intimate History, 1941–1945*. New York: Alfred A. Knopf.

Chronology

November 11, 1918	Germany signs an armistice with the Allies, ending World War I.
June 28, 1919	Germany reluctantly signs the Versailles peace treaty imposed by the Allies.
October 28, 1922	March on Rome places Fascist leader Benito Mussolini in control of Italy.
November 8, 1923	Failed "Beer Hall Putsch" in Munich elevates Nazi leader Adolf Hitler to international attention.
January 1924	Joseph Stalin, Communist Party General Secretary, begins consolidating control over the Soviet Union.
October 29, 1929	Wall Street Crash initiates the economic downturn that results in the Great Depression.
September 18, 1931	Japanese military invades Manchuria.
January 28, 1932	Fighting erupts between China and Japan in Shanghai. The United States and Great Britain broker a cease-fire.
February 1932	Japan organizes occupied Manchuria into a puppet state, Manchukuo.
January 30, 1933	Hitler is appointed Chancellor of Germany.

March 1933	Dachau concentration camp is established.
March 4, 1933	Inauguration of Franklin D. Roosevelt as U.S. president takes place.
December 29, 1934	Japan renounces the Washington Naval Treaty, limiting the size of its fleet.
March 16, 1935	Germany renounces Treaty of Versailles and begins rearmament.
March 7, 1936	Germany reoccupies the Rhineland.
July 18, 1936	Spanish Civil War begins.
October 25, 1936	German-Italian pact forms the basis of the Axis alliance.
November 25, 1936	Japan joins the Axis by signing the Anti-Comintern Pact with Germany.
July 7–9, 1937	Japan begins invasion of China after the Marco Polo Bridge Incident.
August 13, 1937–November 26, 1937	Battle of Shanghai ends in Japanese victory over Chinese.
November 6, 1937	Italy joins the Axis.
December 12, 1937	Japan sinks USS *Panay* in China, heightening tensions in Asia.
December 1937–January 1938	Japan slaughters the inhabitants of Nanjing, known as the Nanjing Massacre or the Rape of Nanjing.
March 12, 1938	Germany invades Austria.
July 1938	Soviet forces defeat the Japanese in the Battle of Lake Hassan on the Manchurian.
September 29, 1938	Munich Agreement between European powers gives Hitler a free hand in Czechoslovakia.
March 10–16, 1939	Czechoslovakia collapses under German pressure.
March 28, 1939	Spanish Civil War ends with victory for profascist forces.
April 7, 1939	Italy invades Albania.

May 22, 1939	Germany and Italy reinforce their military alliance by signing the Pact of Steel.
July 26, 1939	The United States signals its disapproval by terminating Treaty of Commerce with Japan.
August 23, 1939	Germany and the Soviet Union sign a Non-Aggression Pact.
September 1, 1939	Germany invades Poland, triggering World War II.
September 3, 1939	Prime Minister Neville Chamberlain announces that Great Britain is at war with Germany.
September 5, 1939	The United States declares itself neutral in the European war.
September 6, 1939	German forces seize Krakow as Polish army retreats.
September 17, 1939	Soviet Union invades Poland.
September 28, 1939	Poland surrenders.
November 23, 1939	Polish Jews are ordered to wear the Star of David.
November 30, 1939	Soviet Union invades Finland.
April 9, 1940	Germany invades Denmark and Norway.
May 1940	Auschwitz concentration camp is established.
May 10, 1940	Germany invades France, Belgium, the Netherlands, and Luxembourg. Chamberlain resigns, and Winston Churchill becomes Britain's prime minister.
May 13, 1940	The Netherlands surrender to Germany.
May 25, 1940	Allied forces retreat to Dunkirk.
May 26, 1940– June 4, 1940	Operation Dynamo evacuates Allied troops from Dunkirk.
May 28, 1940	Belgium surrenders to Germany.
June 10, 1940	Italy joins World War II by declaring war on Great Britain and France.
June 15, 1940	Soviet Union occupies Baltic republics of Latvia, Lithuania, and Estonia.

June 16, 1940	Marshal Henri-Philippe Petain is appointed head of the French government.
June 22, 1940	France signs an armistice with Germany, allowing occupation of northern tier of the country.
July 1, 1940	Petain's government sets up headquarters in Vichy.
July 10, 1940	Battle of Britain begins in the air over the English Channel.
August 26, 1940	First British air raid on Berlin takes place.
September 1, 1940	German Jews are ordered to wear yellow Star of David.
September 9, 1940	Italy invades Egypt.
October 3, 1940	Polish Jews are moved into Warsaw Ghetto.
November 5, 1940	Franklin D. Roosevelt is reelected for a third term as U.S. president.
December 1–8, 1940	Greeks drive Italian troops from their country.
December 6–9, 1940	Italian invasion of Egypt is destroyed by British forces.
February 11, 1941	Germany's Afrika Korps arrives in Libya.
February 15, 1941	Deportation of Austrian Jews to Poland begins.
March 11, 1941	U.S. Congress passes Lend-Lease Act, empowering Roosevelt to aid Great Britain.
April 27, 1941	Athens falls to German forces.
May 27, 1941	British sink German battleship *Bismarck*.
June 22, 1941	Germany invades Soviet Union.
August 14, 1941	Roosevelt and Churchill sign the Atlantic Charter, cementing economic and political relations.
September 1, 1941	Germans begin the siege of Leningrad.
October 2, 1941	Germans begin all-out offensive against Moscow.
October 18, 1941	General Hideki Tojo becomes prime minister of Japan.

October 22, 1941	Nazis begin massacring over 30,000 Jews in Odessa.
December 7, 1941	Japan bombs Pearl Harbor and begins invasion of the Philippines, Guam, Hong Kong, and Malaya.
December 8, 1941	The United States declares war on Japan.
December 11, 1941	Germany and Italy declare war on the United States.
December 23, 1941	The United States surrenders Wake Island to the Japanese.
January 2, 1942	Manila falls to the Japanese.
January 20, 1942	German leaders plan the Holocaust at Wannsee Conference.
February 15, 1942	Britain surrenders Singapore to the Japanese.
February 19, 1942	Roosevelt orders the internment of Japanese-American civilians.
February 22, 1942	Roosevelt orders General Douglas MacArthur to evacuate from Corregidor.
February 27, 1942– March 1, 1942	Japan defeats Allied naval forces in the Battle of the Java Sea.
April 9, 1942	Bataan Death March begins.
May 4–8, 1942	Allies thwart Japanese navy in the Battle of the Coral Sea.
May 29, 1942	French Jews are ordered to wear the yellow Star of David.
June 4–7, 1942	The United States defeats Japanese navy at Battle of Midway.
June 12, 1942	Japan occupies Aleutian island of Attu, marking the farthest reach of its conquests.
June 18, 1942	The United States initiates Manhattan Project, tasked with secretly developing the atomic bomb.
June 28, 1942	German forces begin their advance toward Stalingrad.

July 22, 1942	Large-scale deportation of Jews from Warsaw Ghetto to death camps begins.
August 7, 1942	U.S. Marines begin counteroffensive against Japan, landing on Guadalcanal.
September 14, 1942	German forces enter Stalingrad.
November 8, 1942	U.S. forces invade French North Africa.
November 13, 1942	British army retakes Tobruk, Libya.
November 22, 1942	Soviet army encircles Stalingrad, trapping German forces.
December 2, 1942	First nuclear chain reaction is conducted in secret at University of Chicago.
January 14–24, 1943	At Casablanca Conference, Roosevelt and Churchill declare that they will only accept "unconditional surrender" from the Axis.
January 18, 1943	Jews of the Warsaw Ghetto rise up against the Nazis.
	Soviets lift the German siege of Leningrad.
February 2, 1943	German army surrenders at Stalingrad.
February 9, 1943	The United States gains full control over Guadalcanal.
February 19–24, 1943	Axis forces defeat U.S. and British units at Kasserine Pass in Tunisia.
March 18, 1943	General George S. Patton leads U.S. armored division into Tunisia.
April 18, 1943	Admiral Isoroku Yamamoto, architect of the Pearl Harbor attack, is shot down and killed by U.S. planes.
May 8–13, 1943	Italy surrenders in North Africa, and German forces evacuate.
July 5, 1943–August 23, 1943	Soviets defeat the Axis at Kursk, forcing Germany to retreat.
July 10, 1943	Allied forces invade Sicily.

July 25, 1943	Mussolini resigns as Italian prime minister and is arrested.
August 16, 1943	Allies capture Messina, Sicily.
September 2, 1943	Allied forces invade Italian mainland.
September 9, 1943	Italian prime minister Marshall Pietro Badoglio concludes an armistice with the Allies, but German forces seize much of the country.
	Allies land at Salerno, Italy.
September 10, 1943	German troops occupy Rome.
November 22–26, 1943	At Cairo Conference, Roosevelt, Churchill, Stalin, and Chiang Kai-shek discuss the defeat of Japan.
November 28–30, 1943	At Teheran Conference, Roosevelt, Churchill, and Stalin discuss Allied strategy and the invasion of Northern Europe.
January 4, 1944	Soviet army enters Poland.
January 22, 1944	Allied forces land at Anzio near Rome.
January 31, 1944	U.S. Marines land in Japanese-held Marshall Islands.
February 15, 1944	Historic monastery is destroyed during ongoing fighting at Monte Cassino.
June 4, 1944	Allied forces liberate Rome.
June 6, 1944	Allied forces land at Normandy in D-Day invasion.
June 13, 1944	German V-1 rocket, the world's first cruise missile, strikes London.
June 16, 1944	U.S. strategic bombers begin regular raids on Japanese home islands.
June 19–20, 1944	U.S. Navy defeats Japan at Battle of the Philippine Sea.
June 26, 1944	Allied troops liberate Cherbourg.
July 18, 1944	Japanese prime minister Tojo resigns.

July 20, 1944	German military coup fails to topple the Nazi regime.
July 21, 1944–August 11, 1944	U.S. Marines retake Guam from Japan.
July 24, 1944	Allied forces break through enemy lines at St. Lo, Normandy.
August 1, 1944	Warsaw Uprising begins.
August 25, 1944	Allied forces liberate Paris.
September 3, 1944	British troops liberate Belgian capital of Brussels.
September 8, 1944	German V-2 rockets begin to strike British cities.
September 9, 1944	Charles de Gaulle forms Provisional Government of France in Paris.
September 10, 1944	U.S. Army liberates Luxembourg.
September 12, 1944	U.S. Army crosses the German border.
September 17–25, 1944	Operation Market Garden, an ambitious assault by British paratroops on the Netherlands, fails.
October 10, 1944	Soviet troops reach German frontier.
October 13, 1944	Allied forces liberate Athens.
October 18, 1944	Hitler calls up boys and old men for service in the People's Force militia.
October 19, 1944	MacArthur lands on Leyte, beginning the reconquest of the Philippines.
October 23–26, 1944	U.S. Navy defeats Japan at Battle of Leyte Gulf.
November 2, 1944	Allies liberate Belgium.
November 4, 1944	German forces evacuate mainland Greece.
December 16, 1944–January 25, 1945	The United States defeats the final major German offensive on the Western Front in the Battle of the Bulge.
January 13, 1945	Soviet army pushes into East Prussia.
January 17, 1945	Warsaw falls to Soviet army.
January 27, 1945	Soviet troops liberate Auschwitz death camp.

February 7–12, 1945	Roosevelt, Churchill, and Stalin meet at Yalta and decide the fate of postwar Europe.
February 13–14, 1945	U.S. night bombing destroys Dresden, a city of little military importance.
February 16, 1945	U.S. and Philippine troops land at Corregidor.
February 19, 1945–March 17, 1945	U.S. Marines defeat Japanese in the Battle of Iwo Jima.
February 23, 1945	U.S. Marines raise American flag on Mount Suribachi, Iwo Jima.
March 9, 1945	U.S. bombers commence a massive firebombing campaign against Tokyo.
March 29, 1945	Soviet troops cross the border into Austria.
April 7, 1945	Japanese flagship *Yamato* is sunk in the empire's final naval operation.
April 10, 1945	U.S. troops liberate Buchenwald concentration camp.
April 12, 1945	Franklin D. Roosevelt dies and is succeeded by Harry S. Truman.
April 13, 1945	Soviet troops capture Vienna.
April 15, 1945	British troops liberate Bergen-Belsen concentration camp.
April 20, 1945	Soviet army reaches the outskirts of Berlin.
April 21, 1945	Battle of Berlin begins.
April 28, 1945	Italian partisans kill Mussolini.
April 29, 1945	U.S. troops liberate Dachau concentration camp.
April 30, 1945	Hitler dies by suicide in his Berlin bunker.
May 2, 1945	Soviet troops raise their flag over the Reichstag in Berlin as the German capital surrenders.
May 5, 1945	U.S. troops liberate Mauthausen concentration camp.
May 7, 1945	Germany surrenders.

June 5, 1945	Germany is divided into occupation zones administered by the United States, Great Britain, the Soviet Union, and France.
June 21, 1945	U.S. Marines secure the island of Okinawa.
July 5, 1945	General MacArthur announces the liberation of the Philippines.
July 16, 1945	The United States tests the first atomic bomb at Alamogordo, New Mexico.
July 17, 1945–August 12, 1945	Truman, Stalin, and Churchill meet at the Potsdam Conference, in Occupied Germany, to discuss the postwar world.
July 26, 1945	Clement Atlee replaces Churchill as British prime minister.
August 6, 1945	The United States drops an atomic bomb on the Japanese city of Hiroshima, killing more than 100,000 soldiers and civilians.
August 8, 1945	Soviet Union declares war on Japan and invades Manchuria.
August 9, 1945	The United States drops a second atomic bomb, this time on Nagasaki, killing approximately 80,000 people.
August 15, 1945	Emperor Hirohito announces the surrender of Japan.
August 22, 1945	Japanese army in Manchuria surrenders to Soviet Union.
August 31, 1945	MacArthur arrives in Tokyo to begin U.S. occupation of Japan.
September 2, 1945	MacArthur accepts Japan's surrender in Tokyo harbor.
November 20, 1945	International Tribunal at Nuremberg puts surviving Nazi leaders on trial.
April 29, 1946	International Military Tribunal for the Far East convenes in Tokyo to try Japanese war criminals.
	International Military Tribunal for the Far East begins trial of Japanese leaders.

July 29, 1946– October 15, 1946	Paris Peace Conference convenes to formally end the war.
October 1, 1946	Nuremberg Tribunal completes its sentencing of Nazi leaders.
October 15, 1946	Luftwaffe commander Hermann Göring dies by suicide at Nuremberg.
	Several top Nazi officials are executed at Nuremberg for war crimes.
December 23, 1948	Former Japanese prime minister Tojo is executed by International Military Tribunal.

Chapter 1

Saboteur (1942)

Released in the spring of 1942, *Saboteur* debuted in movie theaters before the United States had won a single battle in World War II. Tension over the war's outcome was palpable throughout the production. British-born Alfred Hitchcock (1899–1980), one of the greatest directors in world cinema, worked feverishly with his staff "to keep abreast of the headlines" although the film made few references to specific events (McGilligan 2003, 296). Preparation for *Saboteur* began in August 1941, four months before the United States was thrust into war by the Japanese attack on Pearl Harbor (December 7). Originally titled *U.S.* and then *Sabotage*, the story was conceived against the backdrop of the national emergency declared by President Franklin D. Roosevelt on May 27, 1941, which put the country on a defensive footing against Nazi Germany and drew it closer to Great Britain. In the months following the president's declaration, Americans increasingly contemplated the possibility of war with Germany and the presence of a "fifth column" of pro-Nazi or fascist elements within the country. *Saboteur* reflected the suspicion that Nazi agents might sabotage the country's burgeoning armaments industry that developed quickly in response to Roosevelt's proclamation of America as "the Arsenal of Democracy."

Saboteur begins at an aircraft plant in Glendale, California, the workplace of the protagonist, Barry, played by Robert Cummings (1910–1990). When a fire breaks out, a coworker named Fry tosses Barry a fire extinguisher, and Barry hands it to his best friend. The extinguisher is filled with gasoline, and it engulfs his friend and the plant in flames. The morally vacant heart of *Saboteur*, Fry, is played by novice actor Norman Lloyd (1914–2011). The police identify Barry as the principal suspect. His best friend's mother lies to detectives, telling them that Barry is not at her home while allowing him to slip out the back way. It is the first of Barry's several encounters with ordinary Americans, whose help in his narrow escapes from the law suggests antiauthoritarian solidarity. All authority figures in *Saboteur* are suspect.

To prove his innocence, Barry must track down Fry. Recalling a letter in Fry's possession addressed to "Charles Tobin, Esq." in Springville, California, Barry sets out for the rural town, hoping Tobin can provide information on the perpetrator. He hitches a ride with a jovial truck driver and manages to avoid being recognized when the police pull the truck over.

The trucker brings Barry to the Deep Springs Ranch, Tobin's home. The music and the panoramic scenery prepare the audience for an idyllic American setting, yet while on the property, Barry discovers that Fry is in league with Tobin, played by Otto Kruger (1885–1974). The ranch is a hotbed of treason. When Barry threatens to expose him, Tobin calmly points out that no one will take the word of an "obscure workman," already the subject of a nationwide manhunt, over a pillar of society. Barry tries to escape, using Tobin's beloved granddaughter as a shield. In a parody of the era's B-movie Hollywood Westerns, the villainous cowboys in Tobin's employ give chase and lasso Barry, turning him over to the unsympathetically portrayed sheriff.

Barry escapes from the deputies with the aid of the jovial truck driver and makes his way to a remote cabin. The owner, a blind pianist, is visited by his niece, Pat, played by Priscilla Lane (1915–1995). She is determined to turn Barry over to the authorities, but her uncle disparages the police and asserts that Barry is innocent. She is eventually won over to Barry's side.

Saboteur's hectic pace continues as Barry and Pat stow away on a circus caravan. The circus "freaks" vote by a narrow margin to conceal them from the police when their caravan is stopped and searched. The circus lets the couple off near a ghost town in the Nevada desert referenced in a telegram that Barry spotted at Tobin's ranch. Encountering more members of Tobin's ring, Barry convinces them that he is on their side, pointing to newspaper headlines trumpeting the official line that he is the Glendale saboteur. Pat slips away and reports the incident to the local sheriff, who, it transpires, is part of the fascist conspiracy.

They arrive separately in the New York mansion of one of the key conspirators, a wealthy dowager, Mrs. Sutton, played by Alma Kruger (1868–1960), a familiar face as a woman of authority in 1930s Hollywood movies. In one of *Saboteur*'s pivotal scenes, Barry and Pat are trapped in the mansion's ballroom during a high society charity ball. As in a nightmare, there is danger at every turn and no escape. The exits are blocked by Sutton's armed servants. The partygoers they turn to for help dismiss their pleas as nonsense or are part of the conspiracy. The couple are separated after surrendering. Barry manages to escape and races to the Brooklyn Navy Yard, trying to thwart the plot he overheard to blow up a battleship at its christening. He struggles with Fry for the detonator, and the charge goes off late, damaging but not sinking the warship.

With the police closing in on Tobin's ring, Pat and Barry separately follow Fry to Federal Island, the site of the Statue of Liberty. Fry is pursued up a service ladder to the statue's torch of freedom and falls to his death. The film ends with much left unresolved. The audience never learns if Mrs. Sutton is charged with conspiracy and could surmise that Tobin escaped to Latin America. The war's end is nowhere in sight and victory is uncertain.

The first steps in *Saboteur*'s production were embroiled in Hitchcock's disputes over money and creative freedom with his studio, Selznick International Pictures. On November 7, producer David O. Selznick (1902–1965) sold the rights to *Saboteur* to Universal Studios (Spoto 1983, 249–251). The project came into the hands of two producers at Universal, onetime director Frank Lloyd (1886–1960) and Jack H. Skirball (1896–1985), the only ordained rabbi working as a Hollywood executive. Determined to please Hitchcock, Skirball tried to provide the director with all resources available to Universal, considered "the least endowed, the least prestigious of the major production companies, a studio without A budgets or stars" (McGilligan 2003, 300). The film's patchy moments can be ascribed to financial limitations.

Saboteur had many authors, not all of them fully credited. According to actor John Houseman (1902–1988), assigned by Selznick to supervise the production, Hitchcock "came up with a notion for a picaresque spy story . . . with a transcontinental chase that moved from coast to coast and ended inside the hand of the Statue of Liberty" (Spoto 1983, 251). The first draft was worked up by Houseman; Hitchcock; his wife and lifelong collaborator, Alma Reville (1899–1982); and longtime personal assistant, Joan Harrison (1907–1994). After Harrison left to pursue her own career in Hollywood, Selznick assigned Peter Viertel (1920–2007) to rewrite the screenplay. A novelist who had never written for movies, Viertel confessed his lack of self-confidence to Hitchcock. "I'll teach you, my dear boy, in about twenty minutes," the director told him (McGilligan 2003, 296). After Universal purchased the rights, Skirball hired Dorothy Parker (1893–1967) to finish the screenplay. An acerbic essayist for the *New Yorker* magazine and part of Manhattan's intelligentsia, Parker added a subversive undertow that worked with the film's rally against fascism message while at the same time suggesting that America was not guiltless when it came to oppression. Viertel, Harrison, and Parker were acknowledged in the credits as *Saboteur*'s cowriters.

Until Pearl Harbor, *Saboteur* labored under fears that a film perceived as anti-fascist might draw fire from a bipartisan Congressional investigation. Isolationist senators Burton K. Wheeler (1882–1975), a Democrat from Montana, and Gerald P. Nye (1892–1971), a Republican from North Dakota, loudly denounced "alien" influences in Hollywood and claimed the studios were promoting America's entry into World War II (McGilligan 2003, 294). Once the United States was at war, Hitchcock was free to develop his story about a fascist conspiracy. Even so, the film never mentions Germany or any Axis belligerent by name.

The everyman and woman disposition of the actors playing *Saboteur*'s heroes Barry and Pat, lacking any idiosyncrasy, inadvertently served the film's message. They were believably ordinary Americans of their time—unpretentious, good-hearted, and willing to be drawn into the conflict to save American values from its enemies. The villains were more memorable. Kruger brought his screen persona as a suave man of the world into the role of Tobin, a wealthy and well-connected leader of the conspiracy who smiled warmly as he spoke of treason and the mediocrity of his nation.

Saboteur was a box office hit and earned handsome profits for Hitchcock and Universal (McGilligan 2003, 313). Reviews were largely positive. The *New York Times*' critic Bosley Crowther (1905–1981) praised its frenetic pace, calling it "a swift, high-tension film which throws itself forward so rapidly that it permits slight opportunity for looking back." Regarding the patchy plot elements, including Barry's almost inexplicable escape from the Sutton mansion, Crowther added that *Saboteur* "hurtles the holes and bumps which plague it with a speed that forcefully tries to cover them up." He perceptively recognized that "the casual presentation of the FBI as a bunch of bungling dolts" and the film's "general disregard of authorized agents . . . somewhat vitiates the patriotic implications" (Crowther 1942). In an unsigned roundup of new motion pictures, *Time* magazine praised *Saboteur* for warning Americans, "as Hollywood has so far failed to do, that fifth columnists can be outwardly clean and patriotic citizens, just like themselves" ("The New Pictures" 1942). "Fifth column" was a popular term in the World War II era for conspirators working behind the lines, on the home front, for the enemy.

THE FIFTH COLUMN

During the Spanish Civil War (1936–1939), a rebel general whose forces were advancing on the capital, Madrid, bragged that he had four columns of troops under his command plus a "fifth column" of saboteurs inside the city ready to strike. Ernest Hemingway, covering the war for the American news media, was responsible for circulating the term outside of Spain.

During World War II, Americans feared that a Fifth Column operated inside the United States, engaging in espionage and sabotage and willing to aid enemy forces in the event of an invasion. The suspicion was not entirely unreasonable, given that the Nazis found small groups of supporters in the nations of occupied Western Europe. After Pearl Harbor, the U.S. government interned or restricted the lives of citizens of Axis nations living in the United States. The weight of suspicion fell most heavily on the Japanese. The government forced U.S. citizens of Japanese heritage, alongside resident aliens, into internment camps, often at great personal hardship. No evidence of Japanese-American collusion with the enemy was ever substantiated.

Saboteur occupies an intermediate place in cinema history as a significant film that falls short of greatness. One of America's leading film critics and historians, Andrew Sarris (1928–2012) described it as less than the sum of its many interesting parts. He found the film engaging less for its heroes than for being "peopled with oddly appealing traitors to America" (Sarris 1998, 250). *Saboteur* was not a masterpiece, but, as Hitchcock said, it contains the blueprint for one of its director's later masterpieces, *North by Northwest* (1959), with its international conspiracy, cross-continental chase, and climactic scene staged on a national monument (Truffaut and Scott 1983, 150). *Saboteur* is most remembered for its finale at the Statue of Liberty. As Fry clings desperately to Lady Liberty's hand, where Fry falls after a vain attempt to escape, Barry becomes sympathetic. Hitchcock's camera viewpoint is mainly downward as Fry's face fills with anguished supplication. Barry holds Fry's hand and tries to pull him up, but the audience watches with anticipation as the seam of the saboteur's jacket slowly tears, sending him tumbling to his death. *Saboteur* ends with Barry and Pat embracing at the top of the Statue of Liberty, but as Sarris wrote, "The relieved reunion of the nominal hero and heroine loses any possibility of joyous celebration" (Sarris 1998, 250). The audience that first saw *Saboteur* in 1942 was painfully aware that the end was nowhere in sight.

HISTORICAL BACKGROUND

In Italy, Benito Mussolini (1883–1945) rose to power on the backs of the Fascist Party militia known as the Black Shirts for their uniform. Adolf Hitler (1889–1945) emulated him by organizing the Nazi Party storm troopers, familiarly called the Brown Shirts. America in the years before World War II swarmed with a gaggle of uniformed fascist militias including the White Shirts, the Khaki Shirts, and the Silver Shirts. Unlike their Italian and German models, none of their commanders enjoyed the status of Italy's Duce or Germany's führer. They never got along with each other long enough to form a fully coordinated movement.

While most of the leading figures on America's far right expressed admiration for Hitler, only one group, the German-American Bund (Amerikadeutscher Volksbund), was avowedly Nazi and served as an overseas branch of the German Nazi Party. Although many rightist groups had fascist characteristics, none would have felt entirely at home in Mussolini's Italy. How to categorize these groups puzzled careful pundits and historians even before the United States entered World War II. Perhaps, the most accurate label was coined when those militias were still active. At University of Texas, Austin, political science professor Donald S. Strong (1912–1995) called them the "national radical revolutionary" movement (Strong 1941, 2).

Unlike the Italian fascists who embraced modernity and, despite evoking ancient Rome, looked toward the future, America's national radicals were archconservative and nostalgic for an imaginary White Anglo-Saxon Protestant past. Departing entirely from Hitler or Mussolini, their ideology was based on interpretations of Christianity, especially a militant millenarian doctrine concerning the Antichrist and the second coming of Jesus. Also, Italian fascism was not inherently anti-Semitic; Mussolini counted Jewish adherents and only followed Nazi Germany's path as he fell into Hitler's orbit (Johnson 1991, 319). America's radical nationalists were comparable to the Nazis in their hatred of Jews and proposed various solutions to the "problem" of the Jewish presence in the United States.

The largest national radical militia, the Silver Shirts, peaked at 15,000 uniformed members by 1935. Torn by factionalism and controversy, their number hovered around only 5,000 by 1939. Reliable estimates give the Silver Shirts an additional 75,000 sympathizers through the 1930s based on subscriptions to their publications, attendance at rallies, and other measures (Beekman 2005, 100–101). Members of the Silver Shirts were almost entirely Northern European in heritage, predominantly British and German, and were active mostly on the West Coast and in the industrial cities of the Midwest. The group included a women's auxiliary. Most were middle or working class, but the Silver Shirts caught the interest of some members of the intelligentsia. Prominent modernist poet Ezra Pound (1885–1972) was in contact with the organization and quoted the Silver Shirts' leader favorably in one of his poems (Moody 2014, 240). Pound later served fascist Italy by broadcasting anti-American propaganda during World War II.

The Silver Shirts' founder and "Beloved Chief," William Dudley Pelley (1890–1965), was the focus of national media attention as "one of America's leading 'star-spangled fascists'" (Beekman 2005, xii) and was cited in Sinclair Lewis's popular novel, about an impending right-wing dictatorship in the United States, *It Can't Happen Here* (1935). Described as "well-spoken and intelligent," Pelley enjoyed a successful career as a journalist, award-winning storywriter, and novelist (Beekman 2005, xiii). He worked in Hollywood during the 1920s, where his screenplays were produced with casts including popular stars such as Lon Chaney and Tom Mix. As a proponent of traditional values, Pelley claimed to be appalled by the "glamorous, cockeyed, crazy gang, booze-lit, and money-drunk children in Arabian nights palaces" he encountered (Pelley 1939, 198). Calling out Hollywood's Jewish producers, the emotional force of Pelley's anti-Semitism may have resulted from a need to find scapegoats for his failure to rise to the highest tiers of the movie industry and other professional frustrations.

While continuing to assert Christianity, Pelley had already deviated from the Protestantism of his background before founding the Silver Shirts. Claiming contact with disembodied spirits, Pelley engaged in automatic writing, attended séances, and spoke of the lost continent of Atlantis. Some discounted him as a charlatan and "mail order mystic" peddling fake spirituality. Pelley's consistency in the face of skepticism argues that he believed his own doctrine. A wealthy follower gave him 300 acres at the base of Black Mountain near Asheville, North Carolina, where he established his base. Like most national radical leaders, Pelley was a millenarian, but he tied the second coming of Jesus to astrology and predicted the dawn of the Age of Aquarius decades before the idea took hold in the 1960s counterculture (Beekman 2005, 62–78).

Claiming guidance from unseen voices on the day Hitler became Germany's chancellor (January 30, 1933), Pelley founded the paramilitary Silver Shirts, drawing on the membership of his previous spiritualist society. Around that same time, Pelley made contact with the Nazi representative of a German transatlantic shipping firm, Paul Lilienfeld-Toal, who became the Silver Shirts' "foreign adjunct." As a result, Pelley attended Germany's Erfurt Anti-Comintern Congress (1938), which brought together far-right leaders from around the world (Beekman 2005, 81, 123).

Some of Pelley's spiritualist followers were unwilling to become militiamen and defected to other theosophical organizations. The Silver Shirts' esoteric underpinning proved an obstacle for working with otherwise like-minded American national radicals. Many extremist leaders corresponded with Pelley but balked at giving public support to a fellow anti-Semite "who promoted a spiritualist doctrine they neither agreed with nor completely understood" (Beekman 2005, 114).

Pelley laid out his ideas for a theocratic state, the "Christian Commonwealth," in his book *No More Hunger* (1935). His plans to sweep away existing institutions went far beyond anything accomplished by the German Nazis or Italian fascists in their homelands. The Commonwealth's features included state ownership of manufacturing, private ownership of personal property, universal income for all citizens, and a generous social welfare program. Paper money would be abolished. Cities would be razed (Pelley 1935, 57–58, 73, 201–202).

His racial attitudes were analogous with Hitler's. Under Pelley's Commonwealth, blacks would be wards of the state and treated as a labor pool to be exploited, much like the Slavs in Nazi-occupied Eastern Europe. Jews would be confined to a single ghetto within each of the 48 states. He trumpeted his views in the Silver Shirts' newspaper, *Liberation*, called "the most pro-Nazi and racist publication in the United States" (Grill and Jenkins 1992).

The Silver Shirts provoked trouble in many places but drew national notoriety in San Diego. There the Silver Shirts allegedly purchased rifles stolen from a U.S. Navy armory and drilled for combat at a fortified ranch near El Cajon. They planned to assassinate Jewish public officials and disrupt left-wing marches but were infiltrated by a pair of U.S. Marine Corps drill instructors who reported to Naval Intelligence. The resulting controversy led the U.S. House of Representatives to establish the Special Committee on Un-American Activities, predecessor of the committee that became notorious during the Cold War for investigating Communist subversion in Hollywood. Chaired by John William McCormack (1891–1980), a Democrat from Massachusetts, and Samuel Dickstein (1885–1954), a Democrat from New York, the special committee was empaneled to investigate the Silver Shirts as well as the Communist Party (Goodman 1968, 10–12).

Undeterred by public scrutiny, the Silver Shirts clashed with left-wing protestors in the lead up to World War II, and Pelley stepped up his campaign of abuse against "the Jew stooge" Roosevelt. The Federal Bureau of Investigation (FBI) responded with intimidation by "interviewing" subscribers to *Liberation*. Pelley became a fugitive in 1939, going underground to evade subpoenas from the State of North Carolina and the Un-American Activities Committee. In February 1940, Pelley finally testified before the committee, where he was denounced as a racketeer as well as a fifth columnist (Beekman 2005, 131–135). During the next year and a half, Pelley took steps to avoid prosecution on various charges in North Carolina. He officially disbanded the Silver Shirts (some local units remained active) and moved his headquarters to Indiana. Even then, Pelley remained indiscreet and continued to issue a stream of publications under several names. In an issue of the *Galilean* in late December 1941, he attacked Roosevelt for forcing the Axis to declare war on the United States and called Pearl Harbor "divine justice for our crime" (Beekman 2005, 137).

On April 4, 1942, FBI agents arrested Pelley on charges of sedition. Two of his followers were also indicted. The prosecution never firmly established his direct links to the Nazis. However, at Pelley's trial, Yale political scientist Harold Lasswell (1902–1978) testified that he found 1,195 statements in the *Galilean* that echoed the Nazi line, enough in his mind to make Pelley a German agent. On August 13, Pelley was sentenced to 15 years in prison. His appeals proved futile. Pelley was released in 1950, marginalized but a "martyr" to America's extreme right.

The Silver Shirts were not the only uniformed militia in the spotlight. Drawing on their links to segments of the ethnic German community in cities such as New York, Los Angeles, and Milwaukee, the German-American Bund enrolled as many as 25,000 members wearing swastikas and uniforms modeled after the German storm troopers. The Bund held raucous public rallies as well as church events under the auspices of Lutheran ministers (Higham 1985, 4). In 1936, the organization's leadership passed to a German immigrant, Fritz Kuhn (1896–1951). Kuhn was a chemist at Detroit's Ford Motors, whose founder, Henry Ford (1863–1947), published a scurrilous anti-Semitic newspaper, *The Dearborn Independent*. The widely circulated paper was edited by William J. Cameron (1879–1953), president of the Anglo-Saxon Federation, which claimed northern Europeans as the true descendants of the biblical Hebrews and espoused hatred against Jews (Luhrssen 2015, 136).

Only people of "pure Aryan ancestry" were allowed to join the Bund. However, by declaring that Native Americans were Aryan, the Bund secured an American Indian spokesman, Elwood Towner, who called himself Chief Red Cloud of the River Rouge Tribe. Dressed in buckskins adorned with Native American renditions of the swastika, Towner addressed Bund rallies, condemning Jews and the Roosevelt administration (Bell 1973, 90).

The Bund established a youth branch modeled after the Hitler Youth with camps in Wisconsin, Pennsylvania, Michigan, and Long Island. Weapons drill, marching, and camping were among the activities offered. The Bund's pronounced identification with Germany placed limits on its appeal to Germans and non-Germans alike. "The problem was that many German-Americans or their parents had come to the United States to escape" the authoritarianism of their fatherland (Higham 1985, 6).

Kuhn's greatest triumph was visiting Berlin during the 1936 Olympics and meeting with Hitler. However, a photograph of Kuhn shaking hands with the führer circulated widely in the American media and brought condemnation. As a result, the German embassy in Washington treated Kuhn and his Bund with caution. Their diplomatic mission was to sway the American public toward, not away from, Germany.

Relishing his self-image as America's führer, Kuhn was unrelenting in the face of official disapproval in the United States and Germany. On February 22, 1939, the Bund held a rally in New York's Madison Square Garden honoring George Washington's birthday, "the single most striking display of nazism in the history of the United States" (Higham 1985, 8).

Translating the aesthetics of Nazi German rallies into an American idiom, the stage was dominated by a 30-foot high portrait of Washington in full uniform flanked by swastikas and the Stars and Stripes. Banners from the rafters read: "Wake Up America. Smash Jewish Communism." A drum and bugle corps and a color guard paraded before Kuhn took the podium, calling for "Gentile-controlled labor unions, free from Jewish Moscow-directed domination." The crowd roared approval, shouting "Sieg Heil!" and raising arms in a Nazi salute. Attendance was estimated at 22,000. Outside Madison Square Garden, nearly 2,000 police officers held back some 100,000 protestors, including communists, socialists, Jewish and African American activists, veterans groups, and ordinary citizens (Bernard 2018).

Kuhn had little time to enjoy his performance. He was subpoenaed by the Un-American Activities Committee, sentenced to prison for embezzling Bund funds, and interned as an enemy alien during World War II. Leadership of the Bund passed to a chauffeur from New Jersey, Gerhardt Wilhelm Kunze (1882–1958). Kunze fled to Mexico after Pearl Harbor but was arrested and returned to the United States, where he was convicted and sentenced to prison for espionage.

The thousands of men who marched in colored shirts were neither the only nor the greatest threat from the right to the American political system. At least two leading oppositional figures were clergymen from the nation's heartland. After the assassination of Louisiana's erratic authoritarian Governor Huey P. Long (1893–1935), Long's publicist, Rev. Gerald L.K. Smith (1898–1976), blamed the Great Depression for "a conspiratorial alliance of Jewish bankers, railroad barons, business monopolists and politicians who sold out to their interests" (Jeansonne and Luhrssen 2001). Despite his populist demagoguery, Smith was well connected with industrialists such as Henry Ford as well as far-right Congressmen, who encouraged his unsuccessful yet credible Republican candidacy for a Senate seat in 1942.

More threatening, because he commanded a larger national audience, was Father James Coughlin (1891–1979). The "Radio Priest" enjoyed a coast-to-coast audience in the 1930s for his ethical lessons and criticism of American capitalist greed. The tone grew anti-Semitic. He began to lose radio stations after mid-1940 when he praised the Nazis for "imposing a new moral purity upon Germany." Coughlin continued to speak to followers through his magazine, *Social Justice*. Even after Pearl Harbor, he praised the Axis nations as superior and blamed Roosevelt for the war.

In the spring of 1942, as *Saboteur* arrived in movie theaters, the U.S. Postmaster General Frank C. Walker (1886–1959) banned *Social Justice* from the mail, and Attorney General Francis Biddle (1886–1968) warned the Roman Catholic hierarchy that Coughlin would be arrested for sedition if he continued on his path. "The Radio Priest" finally fell silent (Brinkley 1982, 267–268). In *Saboteur*, however, the greatest danger to America was posed by some of the nation's leading citizens.

DEPICTION AND HISTORICAL CONTEXT

Director Alfred Hitchcock explained the inspiration behind the conspirators depicted in the film. "We were in 1941 and there were pro-German elements who called themselves America Firsters and who were, in fact, American Fascists. This was the group I had in mind when writing the scenario" (Truffaut and Scott 1983, 146).

Hitchcock's characterization was harsh but reflected the feelings of a growing segment of the public in the months before Pearl Harbor. America First began in September 1940 as a coalition of disparate people who opposed American involvement in World War II and Roosevelt's effort to aid Great Britain. It initially included liberals, conservatives, socialists, and pacifists but became an umbrella for anti-Semites and factions inclined to favor an Axis victory or the fascist model. Prominent on America First's executive board was Colonel Charles Lindbergh (1902–1974), the first aviator to cross the Atlantic. Lindbergh considered himself a patriot, yet even a sympathetic biographer conceded that in many respects his "foreign policy views *were* similar to those advanced by Nazi propaganda in the United States" and "German agents were pleased by Lindbergh's noninterventionist efforts, and profascists in the United States applauded him" (Cole 1974, 152). His racial views were in accord with the national radicals. As Hitler's armies moved into Eastern Europe, Lindbergh called on America to "preserve that most priceless possession, our inheritance of European blood" and to guard against "dilution by foreign races" (Lindbergh 1939).

Like the well-dressed guests at Mrs. Sutton's party, America First's leadership came from the top of society. Funding was contributed by a handful of millionaires, including manufacturer William H. Regnery (1877–1954), Vick Chemical Company president H. Smith Richardson (1885–1995), *New York Daily News* publisher Joseph M. Patterson (1879–1946), Sears, Roebuck chairman Brigadier General Robert E. Wood (1879–1969), and *Chicago Tribune* publisher Colonel Robert R. McCormick (1880–1955). America First's founder, Yale Law School student R. Douglas Stuart Jr. (1916–2014), was the son of Quaker Oats' cofounder. Isolationist politicians such as Senator Burton K. Wheeler (1882–1975), Democrat from Montana; Senator David I. Walsh (1872–1947), Democrat from Massachusetts; and Senator Gerald P. Nye (1892–1971), Republican from North Dakota were active in America First. Actress Lillian Gish (1893–1993) and novelist Sinclair Lewis (1885–1951) were among its supporters. America First's 850,000 members also included future distinguished figures from American politics including President John F. Kennedy (1917–1963), President Gerald R. Ford (1913–2006), Peace Corps director Sargent Shriver (1915–2011), and U.S. Supreme Court Justice Potter Stewart (1915–1985) (Kauffman 1995, 18).

America First drew strength from several sources, including bad memories of World War I (1914–1918), a bloody foreign conflict that failed to bring stability to Europe, the strong current of isolationism that had always run deep through American history, and nativists who viewed foreigners and recent immigrants with suspicion. Although it disbanded after Pearl Harbor and some of its leaders aided the U.S. war effort, the organization never escaped suspicion for being pro-Axis as well as pro-American.

Neither America First nor any organization or foreign nation is named in *Saboteur*, but its audience was already suspicious of traitors lurking behind respectable facades like those of the film's wealthy, socially connected villains. Fueling that apprehension were Un-American Activities Committee hearings, the much-publicized campaign against America First by its opponents, and the tireless muckraking by gossip columnist and broadcaster Walter Winchell (1897–1972). In 1940, the powerful media personality regularly included a section in his syndicated features called "The Winchell Column vs. The Fifth Column." In 1941, he also called out anti-Semites, white supremacists, and profascists on his radio show in a segment called

"Some Americans Most Americans Can Do Without" (Gabler 1994, 294). Many Americans felt like Pat, who described the Sutton house party as "a bad dream" because any number of respectable fellow citizens could be traitors. "The room is well sprinkled with them," Barry agreed.

The central figure among *Saboteur*'s conspirators, Charles Tobin, is a suave and charming man at the center of power and wealth. Confronted by Barry in the mansion of his supporter, Mrs. Sutton, Tobin is frank. He sneers at Barry for being "one of the ardent believers . . . plodding along without asking any questions." From Tobin's perspective, Barry belongs to "the great masses, the moron millions." He adds: "There are a few of us in America who desire a more profitable type of government. The competence of totalitarian nations is much higher than ours."

Tobin's words could have been taken directly from Lawrence Dennis (1893–1977), a well-known figure from the nation's East Coast elite at the time of *Saboteur*. Dennis was described by historian Arthur Schlesinger Jr. (1917–2007) as bringing "powers of intelligence and style" to the advocacy of fascism (Schlesinger 1960, 74). According to Anne Morrow Lindbergh, wife of the famed aviator, Dennis's "brilliance carries you along with the greatest of ease," but he was "a man with no love of mankind as such" (Lindbergh 1980, 151–152). Like Tobin, Dennis was frank in private, declaring, "I do not believe in democracy" (Carlson 1943, 154–155). Dennis forecast "the inevitability of the leadership of the elite" whose "acts are not subject to popular control by the ballot" (Dennis 1936, 109–110).

A Harvard graduate, Dennis was on social terms with the Roosevelts, Kennedys, and Coolidges. He was a Foreign Service officer before joining Wall Street firms J&W Seligman and E.A. Pierce. He argued articulately that the American system was doomed and fascism was the only alternative to communism. He became known through essays for prestigious publications such as the *New Republic* and *American Mercury* and testimony before the Senate, where he made many friends. He lunched at New York's Harvard Club and was a familiar face at Manhattan cocktail parties. Dennis's circle of political protégés included Philip Johnson (1906–2005), later America's most prominent modern architect, and Alan R. Blackburn Jr., executive director of the Museum of Modern Art (Brinkley 1982, 275). With his elegant manner, he resembled Tobin for his ease of smiling while making shocking pronouncements.

Dennis traveled in Europe during the 1930s and met with leading politicians. "Hitler didn't impress me," he said (Horne 2006, xv). Dennis found the German-American Bund distasteful, and while anti-Semitic, he stopped short of the extreme positions of the Nazi Party and most American national radicals. He irritated liberals and conservatives alike for calling out American hypocrisy for advocating human rights while depriving African Americans of their rights as citizens. The reason for his unusual position on race became clear in later years. Dennis was a black man "passing" as white.

Avoiding the color shirt militias, Dennis was active in respectable organizations such as America First, appearing onstage at rallies alongside Lindbergh, and the American Fellowship Forum, a New York profascist society whose magazine *Today's Challenges* included prominent contributors such as Senator Earnest Lundeen (1878–1940) of the Minnesota Farmer-Labor Party and Hamilton Fish III (1888–1991), a Republican Congressman from New York (Higham 1985, 55–56).

Dennis also cultivated contacts with the military. The Sutton mansion charity ball was attended by uniformed officers from the army, navy, and marines. Barry and Pat had no way of knowing whether any were part of Tobin's conspiracy, but their presence signaled an undercurrent of public anxiety over the military's higher ranks. During the 1930s, Major General Smedley Butler (1881–1940) claimed he was approached by New York business interests with a plan for a military coup, and in the months before Pearl Harbor, Dennis was not alone on the far right for seeing Major General George Van Horn Moseley "as the solution to America's problems" (Higham 1985, 56). Moseley was General Douglas MacArthur's adjutant and retired after publicly criticizing Roosevelt. He was a "notorious anti-Semite, nativist, and admirer of Hitler," friendly with MacArthur and a circle of army officers (Schaller 1989, 21).

At the dawn of World War II, America's far right extended across class and geography, and so *Saboteur* reflects a conspiracy whose nationwide network extends beyond high society to include men such as the rancher whom Barry encounters in the Soda City ghost town, grousing about his bosses "from out east." The character represents the heartland populism that fed into America First and sometime veered to the far right.

Many elements in *Saboteur* correspond to developments current during production, including the heavily guarded aircraft plant in Glendale, California, where the film begins. The seeds of what became America's West Coast–based aerospace industry grew rapidly in 1941 and 1942. Noticeable among the defense plant's workers are women whose numbers swelled as the war continued. The American Newsreel Company that served as one of Tobin's fronts had a real-life counterpart on Madison Avenue, the Transocean News Service. Funded by Nazi Germany, the agency planted stories and hoped to manipulate public opinion in Germany's favor (Higham 1985, 9).

The tactical objectives of Tobin's ring were likely targets of sabotage. Knocking out Boulder Dam, as one of the conspirators pointed out, would shut off the lights of Los Angeles with its many defense plants. During the filming of *Saboteur*, the French ocean liner *Normandie*, seized after Pearl Harbor by the United States for use as a troopship, was badly damaged by a suspicious fire. Hitchcock shot footage of the *Normandie* lying on its side in New York harbor to represent the battleship damaged by Fry and his cohort in the film. "The Navy raised hell with Universal about these shots because I implied that the *Normandie* had been sabotaged, which was a reflection of their lack of vigilance in guarding it," Hitchcock recalled (Truffaut and Scott 1983, 147).

As his conspiracy unraveled, Tobin blithely spoke of slipping away to Latin America, a region Dennis knew well from his years in the Foreign Service and investment banking. At the time of *Saboteur*'s release, the respectable figures of America's far right were at large although under scrutiny by the FBI, which read their mail, listened to their phone conversations, and questioned their associates. Dennis was indicted for sedition in 1944, but the case ended in a mistrial.

Saboteur released only two months after Roosevelt's February 19, 1942, order authorizing the military to intern all residents of Japanese descent, regardless of their citizenship. They fell under a blanket of suspicion. Other communities were affected on a smaller scale. Individuals of German or Italian heritage suspected of sympathy with Axis nations were ordered to move from "exclusion zones" near the coastline. Interestingly, none of *Saboteur*'s villains have any ethnic ties, and all appear to be White Anglo-Saxon Americans.

Saboteur crackles with the nervous energy of a nation besieged and seeking turncoats within the fortress. At the same time, it upholds a radical insistence on American idealism. Pat's uncle, the blind pianist who helps Barry escape from the police, expresses confidence in "the American heart" and states, "I have my own ideas of my duty as an American citizen. They sometimes include disregarding the law" when confronted by injustice.

FURTHER READING

Beekman, Scott. 2005. *William Dudley Pelley: A Life in Right-Wing Extremism and the Occult*. Syracuse, NY: Syracuse University Press.

Bell, Leland V. 1973. *In Hitler's Shadow: The Anatomy of American Nazism*. Port Washington, NY: Kennikat Press.

Bernard, Diane. 2018. "The Night Thousands of Nazis Packed Madison Square Garden for a Rally—And Violence Erupted." *Washington Post*, December 9, 2018. https://www.washingtonpost.com/history/2018/12/09/night-thousands-nazis-packed-madison-square-garden-rally-violence-erupted/

Brinkley, Alan. 1982. *Voices of Protest: Huey Long, Father Coughlin, and the Great Depression*. New York: Alfred A. Knopf.

Carlson, John Roy. 1943. *Under Cover: My Four Years in the Nazi Underworld of America—The Amazing Revelation of How Axis Agents and Our Enemies Within Are Now Plotting to Destroy the United States*. New York: Dutton.

Cole, Wayne S. 1974. *Charles A. Lindbergh and the Battle against American Intervention in World War II*. New York: Harcourt Brace Jovanovich.

Crowther, Bosley. 1942. "Saboteur." *New York Times*, May 8, 1942. https://www.nytimes.com/1942/05/08/archives/saboteur-alfred-hitchcock-melodrama-starring-priscilla-lane-robert.html

Dennis, Lawrence. 1936. *The Coming of American Fascism*. New York: Harper & Bros.

Gabler, Neil. 1994. *Winchell: Gossip, Power and the Culture of Celebrity*. New York: Alfred A. Knopf.

Goodman, Walter. 1968. *The Committee: The Extraordinary Career of the House Committee on Un-American Activities*. New York: Farrar, Straus and Giroux.

Grill, Johnpeter Horst, and Robert L. Jenkins. 1992. "The Nazis and the American South in the 1930s: A Mirror Image?" *Journal of Southern History* 58 (4): 667–694.

Higham, Charles. 1985. *American Swastika*. Garden City, NY: Doubleday.

Horne, Gerald. 2006. *The Color of Fascism: Lawrence Dennis, Racial Passing, and the Rise of Right-Wing Extremism in the United States*. New York: New York University Press.

Jeansonne, Glen, and David Luhrssen. 2001. "Minister of Hate: Gerald L.K. Smith, Orator of the Far Right." *History Today*, December 2001. https://www.historytoday.com/archive/minister-hate

Johnson, Paul. 1991. *Modern Times: From the Twenties to the Nineties*. New York: HarperCollins.

Kauffman, Bill. 1995. *America First! Its History, Its Culture, and Politics*. Amherst, NY: Prometheus Books.

Lindbergh, Anne Morrow. 1980. *War Within and Without: Diaries and Letters of Anne Morrow Lindbergh, 1939–1944*. New York: Harcourt Brace Jovanovich.

Lindbergh, Charles. 1939. "Aviation, Geography, and Race." *Readers' Digest*, November 1939. https://groups.google.com/forum/#!topic/rec.aviation.piloting/j7aGQa2lQ5I

Luhrssen, David. 2015. *Secret Societies and Clubs in American History*. Santa Barbara, CA: ABC-CLIO.

McGilligan, Patrick. 2003. *Alfred Hitchcock: A Life in Darkness and Light*. New York: Regan Books/HarperCollins.

Moody, A. Donald. 2014. *Ezra Pound: A Portrait of the Man and His Works, Volume II: The Epic Years 1921–1939*. New York: Oxford University Press.

"The New Pictures." *Time*, May 11, 1942. http://content.time.com/time/subscriber/article/0,33009,790443,00.html

Pelley, William Dudley. 1935. *No More Hunger*. Ashville, NC: Pelley Publishing.

Pelley, William Dudley. 1939. *The Door to Revelation*. Ashville, NC: Pelley Publishing.

Sarris, Andrew. 1998. *"You Ain't Heard Nothin' Yet": The American Talking Film, History and Memory, 1927–1949*. New York: Oxford University Press.

Schaller, Michael. 1989. *Douglas MacArthur: The Far Eastern General*. New York: Oxford University Press.

Schlesinger, Arthur, Jr. 1960. *The Age of Roosevelt: The Politics of Upheaval*. Boston, MA: Houghton Mifflin.

Spoto, Donald. 1983. *The Dark Side of Genius: The Life of Alfred Hitchcock*. Boston, MA: Little, Brown.

Strong, Donald S. 1941. *Organized Anti-Semitism in America: The Rise of Group Prejudice during the Decade, 1930–1940*. Washington, D.C.: American Council on Public Affairs.

Truffaut, Francois, with Helen G. Scott. 1983. *Hitchcock*. New York: Simon and Schuster.

Chapter 2

Casablanca (1942)

Casablanca premiered on November 26, 1942, just two weeks after the city of Casablanca, Morocco, fell to U.S. troops under General George S. Patton (1885–1945). The story began as *Everybody Comes to Rick's*, a play by Murray Burnett (1910–1997) and Joan Alison (1901–1992), inspired by Burnett's experiences in 1930s Europe. Burnett traveled to Vienna, Austria, to help his Jewish relatives smuggle some of their wealth out of Nazi-occupied Austria and visited a nightclub in Nice, France, catering to "a mixed clientele made up of refugees and military officials of all political stripes" speaking many languages and entertained by an African American jazz pianist (Isenberg 2017, 4–5).

Rights to the unproduced play were sold to Warner Brothers, the first major studio whose films openly criticized Nazi Germany before the United States entered World War II. The script arrived at Warner's offices on December 8, 1941, one day after the Japanese attack on Pearl Harbor, and the production was given high priority under a new name, *Casablanca*. Many of Burnett and Alison's story elements and characters found their way to the screen, but the screenplay underwent many changes. *Casablanca*'s primary authors were twin brothers Julius J. Epstein (1909–2000) and Philip G. Epstein (1909–1952), credited with the film's humor, and Howard Koch (1901–1995), who emphasized the political message. However, several other hands worked on the screenplay through its production into the summer of 1942 with newly rewritten pages brought to the set each morning (Rode 2017, 319, 326).

Warner Brothers' producer Hal B. Wallis (1898–1986) assigned *Casablanca* to director Michael Curtiz (1886–1965). A Hungarian Jew whose filmmaking career began in his native Budapest, Curtiz was one of the industry's hardest working directors, helming over 180 films in almost every genre. He was a master craftsman in an age when Hollywood functioned as a factory town and "cranked out movies with conveyor-belt precision" (Rode 2017, xvi).

The casting process, like everything else about the production, became the subject of legend. The rumor that Ronald Reagan (1911–2004) was slated for the lead role as Rick was gossip planted by Warner Brothers. Studio head Jack Warner (1892–1978) proposed George Raft (1895–1980) for the part, but Wallis vetoed Raft in favor of the actor who became unforgettable in the role, Humphrey Bogart (1899–1957) (Isenberg 2017, 33–34). Bogart had already established himself as a "tough-guy" actor with a conscience and was well suited for playing a world-weary man who recovers his idealism.

Casablanca is a story of refugees. Aside from Bogart and his African American pianist sidekick, Dooley Wilson (1886–1953) in the role of Sam, the cast was largely foreign born. Costar Ingrid Bergman (1915–1982), cast as the story's love interest, Ilsa, had recently arrived in Hollywood from Sweden. Two actors were British: Claude Rains (1889–1967) as the wily French prefect of police Louis Renault and Sydney Greenstreet (1879–1954) as the criminal kingpin Ferrari. Many actors were actual refugees from Nazism. Paul Henreid (1908–1992), an Austrian actor who fled his homeland, costarred as resistance leader Victor Laszlo. Four cast members had been active in German cinema before the Nazi takeover, including Peter Lorre (1904–1964) as the racketeer Ugarte, Conrad Veidt (1893–1943) as Nazi Major Strasser, Hans Heinrich von Twardowski (1898–1958) as Strasser's adjutant, and Ludwig Stossel (1883–1973) as the German Jewish husband waiting for passage to America. The role of Rick's head waiter went to S. Z. Sakall (1883–1955), a Hungarian Jew who escaped Europe only two years before *Casablanca*'s release.

The movie's action begins with a message on the police radio alerting officers that two German couriers were killed and the valuable documents they were carrying were stolen. The perpetrators are believed to be in Casablanca. "The usual suspects" are rounded up, but the stolen documents, "letters of transit," cannot be located. Those letters, enabling any bearer to exit French North Africa for Lisbon, are the engine driving *Casablanca*'s plot. Many potential buyers of those letters are refugees who gather at Rick's Café Americain, the elegant nightclub operated by the protagonist. Hoping to sell them to refugees but under suspicion by the police, Ugarte passes them to Rick before his capture and death at Renault's hands. Laszlo and his wife, Ilsa, arrive in Casablanca, hoping to gain possession of those letters and escape their Nazi pursuers. Strasser applies pressure on Renault to confine Laszlo; if Renault proves uncooperative, Strasser threatens to have Laszlo killed.

Lazslo does not know at first that Rick and Ilsa had an affair in Paris during the early months of the war, a time when he was presumed dead. A flashback shows their Paris romance before Rick's departure on the last train before Paris fell to the Germans. He is heartbroken by Ilsa's failure to leave with him as planned. Embittered, Rick at first refuses to give or even sell the letters of transit to Ilsa and Laszlo. He eventually changes his mind, disgusted by the Nazis and realizing that Laszlo needs Ilsa's love to sustain his intrepid leadership of European resistance movements against the Nazis.

As Rick puts it, "I'm no good at being noble, but it doesn't take much to see that the problems of three little people don't amount to a hill of beans in this crazy world." He puts aside his personal interests, his desire to either keep or punish Ilsa, and lets her go in the name of defeating Nazism. *Casablanca* dramatizes self-sacrifice, idealism, and hard-earned nobility without succumbing to sentimentality.

Casablanca received mixed reviews upon release. Writing in *The New Republic*, Manny Farber (1917–2008), one of America's most influential critics, called it "hokum" and classed it with other "epic phonies" produced by the movie industry (Farber 1942). However, the *New York Times*' Bosley Crowther (1905–1981) hailed it as "one of the year's most exciting and trenchant films" and added that it "makes the spine tingle and the heart take a leap" for "draping a tender love story within the fold of a tight topical theme" (Crowther 1942). *The Film Daily*, a Hollywood trade paper, predicted that this "smashing melodrama of timely import should click heavily at box-offices everywhere" (Miller 1992, 169).

CASABLANCA CONFERENCE (1943)

On January 24, 1943, the city of Casablanca received top billing on the front pages of newspapers in the United States and Great Britain. On that date, the governments of both nations announced that U.S. president Franklin D. Roosevelt and British prime minister Winston Churchill had been meeting for the past week in a hotel at Fedala, a suburb of Casablanca.

The summit that became known as the Casablanca Conference was intended to work out the common goals of the Western Allies in the struggle against the Axis. The most significant decision made at the conference was the Allied demand for the "unconditional surrender" of the Axis powers. This was a pledge that neither the United States nor Great Britain would consider a "separate peace" or a negotiated settlement to the war. Some historians have praised the declaration as the best way to ensure that the war would uproot Nazism, Italian Fascism, and Japanese imperialism. Others have criticized "unconditional surrender" for prolonging the war by giving dissidents within the enemy camp little room for negotiation.

The Casablanca Conference drew additional attention to the movie *Casablanca*, which was still showing in theaters as news of the summit broke.

The forecast was quickly affirmed. *Casablanca* sold 31,000 tickets in Hollywood during its first week of release. In a 10-week New York run, the film grossed $255,000 ($3.5 million in today's dollars). By the end of 1943, it earned $3.7 million ($52 million today). *Casablanca* also won Oscars for Best Picture and Best Adapted Screenplay.

Television put much of Hollywood's catalogue back in circulation, and *Casablanca* quickly "became one of the most popular 'old movies' shown on TV" (Osborne 2011, 253). However, the unparalleled respect *Casablanca* earned among the movies of Hollywood's golden age, "the *Casablanca* Cult," began in 1957 when the film was shown in an art house cinema near Harvard University and drew a packed house for weeks. The phenomenon spread at a time when college students began to seriously appreciate movies their parents had largely understood as entertainment (Osborne 2011, 257–258). "Imbued with romantic agony, the undergraduates identify with Rick's noble misery as he forsook Ilsa for the Greater Good," Bogart's biographer explained (Kanfer 2011, 229).

The film became a touchstone for 1960s student activism. Typical was the comment recorded by screenwriter Howard Koch while on the lecture circuit that *Casablanca* addressed the need "to have something outside of ourselves that we believe in, that we're willing to come together for and share that sense of brotherhood" (Koch 1973, 222–223). The "*Casablanca* Cult" also inspired popular comedy, including a 1969 stage play by Woody Allen (1935–) transformed into a 1972 movie.

However, *Casablanca* continued to slip the bonds of time and remain, in the 21st century, one of the most beloved and widely known films of its era. It "is still, some seven and a half decades later, considered representative of a real political and historical epoch" (Isenberg 2017, xv). Its romantic idealism is not only nostalgic but also provides heroic models for contemporary problems. As film critic Roger Ebert (1942–2013) put it, *Casablanca* is "one of those rare films that actually improves with repeat viewings" (Ebert 2002). The American Film Institute chose *Casablanca* as the third greatest movie, after *Citizen Kane* (1941) and *The Godfather* (1972); AFI also named Rick as cinema's fourth greatest hero, ranked only behind James Bond, Indiana Jones, and Atticus Finch.

Although it was the product of Hollywood's assembly line, constructed within budget and in haste by a crew and cast with no thought of creating enduring art, *Casablanca* rose on the strength of memorable dialogue, screen chemistry between cast members, and a sense of urgency. The war's outcome was by no means certain during production in the summer of 1942. During the filming of *Casablanca*'s most stirring scene, when the orchestra at Rick's café drowns out the Nazis with a rousing rendition of "La Marseillaise," real tears appeared in the eyes of the cast. Many of them were refugees who had seen Nazism up close (Rode 2017, 325). In 1989, *Casablanca* was one of the first 25 films selected for the Library of Congress's National Film Registry for its historical significance.

HISTORICAL BACKGROUND

The rapid collapse of France in the face of Germany's Spring 1940 Offensive caught even Adolf Hitler by surprise. For the people of France, "confident of a special role in the world," their defeat in six weeks "was a shattering trauma" (Paxton 1975, 5). The French army was considered Europe's strongest, but it rested behind the Maginot Line, a network of fortifications stretching along the length of the border with Germany. Avoiding the hazards of a frontal assault against well-defended positions, the German blitzkrieg shot past the Maginot Line, cutting through neutral Belgium and thrusting with motorized speed and aerial support against the French, whose commanders failed to stay abreast of the changing strategies of war.

The German attack that began on May 10 ended on June 22 with an armistice on terms favorable to Germany. Events raced at a bewildering speed. Only days before the armistice, on June 16, Prime Minister Paul Reynauld resigned, leaving the government in the hands of his recently appointed deputy, Marshal Henri Philippe Petain (1856–1951). Petain was a hero of World War I (1914–1918), who thwarted the Germans at Verdun (1916) and enjoyed a reputation for treating his troops as more than cannon fodder. The armistice that Petain signed reduced the French army to token size, allowing Germany to annex the long-disputed borderland of Alsace-Lorraine and to occupy three-fifths of France, including Paris and the Atlantic shore. The new French government pledged neutrality in Germany's ongoing war for Europe. "Occupied France" would be administered by the French government but with German guns pointed at its officials.

Unwilling to remain in Paris, France's newly formed government moved south to Vichy, a small resort town whose ample hotels accommodated the newly arrived bureaucracy. The town became the capital of "Unoccupied France." On July 11, the French National Assembly convened in Vichy's Grand Casino and gambled everything on Petain's leadership. The Assembly gave him full power as the chief of state. "Strikingly, parliamentarians of all political points of view voted in favor, including 54 per cent of socialists and 66 per cent of radical moderates." Eight of the 14 Communist Party members of the Assembly voted for Petain (Curtis 2002, 68).

Petain was sincere in seeing himself as one of the "natural defenders" of France, determined to stick it out and make the best of a bad situation rather than flee to the colonies and continue the war from overseas, as some members of Renauld's cabinet suggested (Paxton 1975, 16). The only significant figures who took steps to continue the war in 1940 were far away; most of them circled around General Charles de Gaulle (1890–1970), who led the Free French movement from London. In the first few years, de Gaulle had little support in France or in the colonies, aside from French Equatorial Africa. The only officials of the French Republic to side with him had fled to London as their nation collapsed.

The French public agreed with the old marshal's call for unity and order. "Many who would later become the very antithesis of Vichy supporters were still sorting out the wreckage of their lives in the summer of 1940" (Paxton 1975, 17). The regime that assembled at Vichy was also a coalition of opportunity for diverse groups and individuals unhappy with the direction of modernity as well as the French Republic. Vichy drew much of its support from a widespread feeling that French politics had become deadlocked, beholden to special interest and in need of a shake-up. For years, the National Assembly was unable to pass an old-age pension bill. Petain instituted old-age pensions by decree (Paxton 1975, 137). Anti-communism was the common thread that tied together the politics of Vichy and bound the regime to the Nazis.

Fascist parties thrived self-consciously at the margins of French society in the 1930s, but none of their leaders rose to high positions in Vichy until 1944 and then only under pressure from Germany. The most outspoken French fascists gravitated to Paris, where they complained to the German occupiers about Vichy's "old-fashioned clerical, patriotic air and its half-hearted association with the world fascist 'revolution'" (Paxton 1975, 253). Vichy had no overarching ideology and no ruling party. Resembling Japan more than Italy or Germany, Vichy was led by a revered and distant figure surrounded by shifting factions with overlapping yet often conflicting agendas. The "National Revolution" that Vichy proclaimed was largely an evocation of ancient values and past glories.

The most prominent figure in Petain's circle was an odd bedfellow for the old marshal. Pierre Laval (1883–1945), Vichy's on-again, off-again prime minister, was a renegade socialist known for relentless intrigue and few genuine principles "except perhaps a pessimistic pacifism, a dislike of Britain, a dread of war and an aspiration for Franco-German reconciliation" (Curtis 2002, 84). Petain found Laval disagreeable and dismissed him in December 1940. Only German pressure forced his reappointment in 1942. Beholden to his masters in Berlin, Laval championed maximum collaboration, sending French workers to Germany to work in defense plants, urging Frenchmen to volunteer for the Waffen-SS, and handing Jews over to the Nazis with a show of enthusiasm. Petain, sometimes supported by Laval, tried to hold the line against deporting Jews with French citizenship, but both leaders were willing to dispatch Jewish refugees to their death (Curtis 2002, 85). Altogether, some 65,000 Jews were deported from France, only 6,000 of them French citizens. Most perished in the death camps of Eastern Europe. Some 2,800 deportees returned to France after the war (Paxton 1975, 183).

While Vichy included few authentic pro-Germans until the final year of the state's existence, it numbered many who resented Great Britain. The traditional French enmity against the British was aroused after, in what British prime minister Winston Churchill (1874–1965) called a "hateful decision,"

Royal Navy aircraft and warships launched a sneak attack on the French fleet at Mers-el-Kebir, Algeria, on July 3, 1940, sinking or damaging several ships and claiming the lives of over 1,200 French sailors (Lacouture 1991, 246). The attack was motivated by fears that Vichy would surrender the fleet to Germany and was accompanied by the seizure of French ships in British ports. Vichy broke relations with Britain and bombed Gibraltar in response. Vichy continued to be recognized as the legitimate government of France by the United States. In January 1942, Roosevelt dispatched a new ambassador, Admiral William D. Leahy (1875–1959), who sent back favorable reports on meetings with Vichy's foreign and naval minister, Admiral Francois Darlan (1881–1942). After the more pro-German Laval returned to Petain's cabinet in April, Leahy was recalled to Washington (Paxton 1975, 111–112).

The shifting, uncertain wind that blew from Vichy was often a matter of pragmatic calculation. As December 1941 began, the French could reflect that Nazi Germany had defeated not only their own military but also the not inconsiderable armies of Poland, Belgium, and the Netherlands and advanced deep into the Soviet Union. Great Britain was still besieged by air and *sea. By fall 1942, the picture began to change. America had entered the war, the Soviets held on, and Germany began losing the air war over Europe.

The willingness of Vichy officials to accommodate Germany fell along a spectrum from grudging acceptance of a bad situation through dreams of becoming a partner of a new European order to enthusiastic support for Nazi ambitions. Near the start of his regime, Petain announced, "I am today setting out along the road of collaboration." At that time "collaboration" meant participation in a common task, but as the fortunes of war turned, the word assumed negative connotations and implied treasonable cooperation with the enemy (Burrin 1996, 3–4). Darlan hedged his bets on a stalemate in the war with Britain. "If we collaborate with Germany, without necessarily lining up alongside it to make deliberate war on England," France might "play an honorable—or even important—role in the future of Europe," he told Petain (Burrin 1996, 120).

The German occupation of "Unoccupied France" in November 1942 dispelled illusions of Franco-German partnership and prompted many Vichy officials to make covert contact with the resistance or defect to the Free French. As the war continued and support for Vichy crumbled, French fascists became the regime's crutch. The most militant among them, a paramilitary force called the Milice, fought the resistance and aided the Nazis in rounding up Jews.

On D-Day, June 6, 1944, Allied forces landed in Normandy and began to push back the Germans. Vichy's months were numbered. In August 1944, Petain wrote to Laval condemning the brutality of the Milice, but he was no longer in control. A month later, the Nazis evacuated Petain, Laval, and the remnants of their regime to the German village of Sigmaringen, where they squabbled and presided over a nonexistent administration (Curtis 2002, 103–104).

Justice was swift against some of Vichy's leaders. After a six-hour trial, Laval was convicted of treason and executed. Petain was also sentenced to death, but de Gaulle, mindful of the marshal's role in World War I, commuted the sentence to life imprisonment. After a brief frenzy of post-liberation vigilante retribution against collaborators real or suspected, de Gaulle and his successors prioritized national reconciliation, involving a high degree of willful amnesia as well as mythmaking about the heroic resistance. Many lesser known Vichy officials rose to prominence, including President François Mitterand (1916–1996), and they had good reason to forget the past.

DEPICTION AND CULTURAL CONTEXT

Casablanca is set one year before the film's premiere and takes place during the first week of December 1941, just before Japan's attack on Pearl Harbor and America's entry into the war. A large part of the film's message is that neutrality in the face of evil is not a viable path.

At the time of its release, *Casablanca* was understood by the public as a critique of isolationism, the idea that the United States should remain aloof from the problems of the world outside the western hemisphere. The attitude was deeply engrained in American history and geography. In his farewell address, President George Washington counseled, "Our detached and distant situation invites and enables us to pursue a different course." His successor, Thomas Jefferson, memorably warned against "entangling alliances." U.S. intervention in World War I was a break from tradition, but Americans reverted to isolationism in the aftermath, their attitudes hardened by the failure of President Woodrow Wilson's (1856–1924) lofty objective to "make the world safe for democracy."

Until the Japanese attack on Pearl Harbor, many Americans preferred to keep out of the war or prepare only to defend the homeland rather than contemplate intervention in Europe. Isolationism was the issue pursued by America First, an organization that peaked at 800,000 members in 1940 and had many supporters in Congress. The world had already shrunk through technology, and the Atlantic and Pacific oceans were no longer wide enough to preserve the United States against enemies with global agendas, yet the neutrality laws of 1935 and 1939 hampered Roosevelt's ability to aid the Allies in the face of Nazi aggression.

By 1942, most Americans ruefully agreed with Rick's assessment of their country on the eve of Pearl Harbor. "I'll bet they're asleep all over America," he muses. Rick expresses isolationism another way as Vichy police arrest Ugarte in his café. "I stick my neck out for nobody," he says. Bogart's character embodies an update of an American archetype, the "lone wolf" and "frontier renegade" who prefers to chart his own course in the wilderness but is willing to do the right thing when confronted by an obvious wrong (Isenberg 2017, 102–103). Americans of 1942 identified with Rick's refusal to allow a financier from the Deutsche Bank into his café's inner sanctum, the casino. "Your cash is good at the bar," he tells the angry banker, tearing up his business card. Even as he continued to profess neutrality, in his heart, Rick knew who the bad guys were.

Rick's isolationism is complicated by remarks in the screenplay about his previous activities in Ethiopia and Spain. The implication is that Rick was among the minority of Americans in the 1930s who were willing to take a stand against the rising tide of fascism. He apparently violated U.S. neutrality laws by running guns to Ethiopia after Italy attacked the African nation (1935–1937) and by joining the Abraham Lincoln Brigade, a volunteer force fighting with Spain's leftist government against the Nazi-supported right-wing insurgency during the Spanish Civil War (1936–1939). This might explain Rick's mysterious inability to return to America. The penalty for violating the Neutrality Act of 1935 was a fine of up to $10,000 and up to five years in prison or both.

Casablanca opens with a voiceover narrator in the style of the era's newsreels, lending a patina of realism to the introduction's description of the refugee trail from Nazi-occupied Europe that crossed the Mediterranean from Marseilles and wound along the North African coast to Casablanca in French Morocco. The narrative is accompanied by snippets of documentary footage showing people escaping from Europe. According to the narrator, in the city of Casablanca, refugees were kept waiting for the exit visas or money necessary to leave for Lisbon, the last stop on the way to the New World.

The voiceover is truthful in large part. Casablanca was a way station for émigrés; the city was home to consulates from several foreign nations including the United States. Visas issued by a consular authority were necessary for admission to most of the world's nations. Many of those asylum seekers were forced, as the voiceover said, to "wait and wait." What the movie doesn't acknowledge is that one reason for the long wait was the U.S. Immigration Act (1924), which instituted a rigid quota system for applicants based on their national origins. The law, intended to preserve America's White Anglo-Saxon majority, favored immigrants from Northern European nations and discriminated against Asians and Southern and Eastern Europeans. The movie's Bulgarian couple would have had a long wait, given their nation's low placement in the Immigration Act's ranking. Only 100 Bulgarians were admitted annually under the law, and the waiting list was long.

The words "Jew" or "Jewish" never occur in the film's screenplay, in keeping with the long-standing policy of Hollywood's Jewish moguls to maintain a low ethnic profile for fear of drawing ire from anti-Semites. However, the audience of 1942 would have immediately recognized many of the film's refugees as Jewish and that the plight of the Bulgarian couple ("A devil has the people by the throat," the young wife tells Rick) resulted from Nazi-inspired anti-Semitism. The United States did not bend immigration restrictions to accommodate Jewish persecution by Hitler, but ironically, Jews with German citizenship might have taken advantage of Germany's higher rank in the immigration quota. Many other nations behaved similarly and refused to open their gates to Jews fleeing the Nazis. As a result, many Jewish refugees in Casablanca eventually went east instead of west, bound for Palestine with the assistance of Jewish aid groups operating in the city (Osborne 2011, 3–4).

Conditions for Jews who found their way to Casablanca were less restrictive than in Vichy France itself, as seen by their free movement in Rick's café. French Morocco was not a colony but a semi-independent state under the "protection" of France since 1912. French colonists acquired possession of the country's best farmland and dominated international commerce, and French officials were largely responsible for administering the protectorate. However, Morocco's sultan was acknowledged as the nation's sovereign, and the French administration carefully avoided giving him offense or undermining his aura of authority. Morocco's ruler during World War II, Sultan Mohammed V (1909–1961), was mindful of his nation's centuries-old Jewish community and disinclined to enforce Vichy decrees for interning all Jews who lacked French citizenship. "I wish to inform you that, as in the past, the Jews remain under my protection and I refuse to allow any distinction to be made among my subjects," he told French officials (Rosen 2019).

While many refugees counted the United States as their desired destination, Mexico or other Latin American nations offered other possibilities. The number of foreign consulates in Casablanca afforded multiple paths to the New World. However, British travelers like those seen in the movie may have been stranded; unfriendly relations between Great Britain and Vichy resulted in the closure of British consulates in French North Africa (Osborne 2011, 12).

Once a visa was obtained from a consulate, the next step was acquiring an exit visa from French Moroccan authorities. The process gave corrupt officials such as Renault many opportunities for enrichment. The "letters of transit" central to *Casablanca*'s plot have been described as "those fictional golden tickets" and compared to "Dorothy's ruby slippers in *The Wizard of Oz*" (Isenberg 2017, 7). However, they were based on the reality of diplomatic documents called laissez-passer, which allowed individuals to pass through customs and other checkpoints without question. Such documents would have been of great value to refugees, the reason racketeers such as Ugarte and Ferrari wanted them. Rick could have made a good deal of money by selling the letters Ugarte had passed to him. The film's mistake was in stating that the letters of transit were signed by General de Gaulle. At the time of the film's 1941 setting, the bearer of any document signed by the maverick general would have been arrested by Vichy authorities.

Until spring of 1941, French ocean liners continued to sail between Casablanca and the Vichy-held island of Martinique in the Caribbean, but British seizure of French merchant ships cut that channel (Osborne 2011, x). Exit by sea became rare. The main way out of Casablanca was, as the movie stressed, by air to Lisbon, capital of neutral Portugal.

The port of Lisbon remained open, and transatlantic trade proceeded despite threats by German U-boats prowling the waters near Portugal's coast. Wealthy travelers with American visas were able to cross the ocean on the Pan American clipper, a deluxe "flying boat" with sleeper cabins that flew from New York to Lisbon at prices comparable to first class on a luxury liner. Most had to buy passage on Portuguese ocean liners or on freighters that accepted a few passengers. For most refugees, Lisbon was another long stopover. They "had to wait months, or even years, in the city before securing their onward passage" (Lochery 2011, 2–3).

An illicit way out of Morocco is depicted in *Casablanca*'s brief scene at Rick's café, where two men quietly discuss hiring a fishing smack. Slipping out of Morocco on small boats was a way of evading exit visas, but once the smack arrived in Portugal, the passengers faced the same obstacles as every other refugee. If they had no money for accommodations, they were placed in refugee camps outside Lisbon (Lochery 2011, 53).

Casablanca depicts a Free French working underground, supporting de Gaulle operating in the city but subject to arrest if caught by Renault's police. A Norwegian refugee involved in the underground Free French approaches Laszlo's table at Rick's café and flashes a ring bearing de Gaulle's symbol, the Cross of Lorraine, a two-barred cross with patriotic significance from medieval French history. Later in the film, Strasser tells Renault, "We know that every French province in Africa is honeycombed with traitors, waiting for their chance." It was true. Support for the Free French existed throughout the French colonies, but with insufficient strength at the time of *Casablanca*'s 1941 setting to wrest control from Vichy. At the film's conclusion, Renault tells Rick of a "Free French garrison over at Brazzaville," the capital of French Equatorial Africa, the only major colony at the time to throw support behind de Gaulle.

In the film, little is seen of the modern city of Casablanca, a seaport with a multistoried skyline and outdoor cafés; many of the settings focus on the old Moorish city recreated on Warner Brothers' back lot complete with an outdoor bazaar. The city was even thicker with intrigue in reality than is shown in the film. American as well as German civilians and secret agents were at work.

> **CHARLES DE GAULLE (1890–1970)**
>
> Charles de Gaulle was a decorated French army officer but little known outside the ranks until the fall of France in 1940. As a liaison officer with the British, de Gaulle was in London when Marshall Petain agreed to an armistice with Germany. In a series of broadcasts from the British capital in June, he urged France and its colonies to continue resistance, denounced Vichy as an illegitimate regime, and formed the Free French to continue the war. His provisional government-in-exile went unrecognized during its first years by the United States and the Soviet Union; his relations with the British were poor, and he was largely ignored by French officials and citizens. However, as Vichy was reduced to a puppet of Nazi Germany and the war turned in the Allies' favor, de Gaulle gained support at home and the colonies. As Vichy crumbled, most of the overseas empire pledged allegiance to de Gaulle, and as the Germans retreated from France, Free French units were the first Allied forces to enter Paris. However, he was never treated as an equal by U.S., British, and Soviet leaders.
>
> De Gaulle's provisional government administered the country through 1946. When a new constitution was proclaimed, establishing France's Fourth Republic, he retired and wrote his memoirs. With the political unrest that accompanied the disbanding of the French empire and especially the war for Algerian independence, de Gaulle was brought back into government. He became the first president of the new Fifth Republic, granted independence to Algeria, and held office until resigning in 1969 in the wake of new political upheavals that overtook his country. His political philosophy, a socially and economically pragmatic nationalism dubbed Gaullism, remained influential in France long after his death.

Among the Germans stationed in Casablanca were military officers from the armistice commission dispatched to Morocco over Vichy's objections to ensure French compliance with the terms of the cease-fire with Germany. However, Vichy won a concession: the German officers could appear in public only in civilian clothes. Strasser and his associates strutting in full uniform with unfettered access to the city might be counted as one of the film's errors. In reality, the German armistice commission members were kept under close surveillance by Vichy agents, who made life dangerous for locals working for them. The Germans' "Arab contacts were arrested and even shot by French police" (Paxton 1975, 114). The edginess of Vichy-German relations is implied in the film. As Renault warns Strasser, "You may find the climate of Casablanca a trifle warm, Major," Strasser understands the implication. "But perhaps you were not referring to the weather," he replies.

Renault's famous line, "I blow with the wind, and the prevailing wind happens to be from Vichy," anticipated the shift that actually occurred two weeks before the film's debut. On November 8, 1942, U.S. troops landed at multiple points in French North Africa, including Casablanca. Vichy forces fought back for a few days but ceased fire under orders of Admiral Darlan. Darlan happened to be in Algiers; as the ranking Vichy officer in North Africa, he negotiated a deal with the Allies recognizing him as French High Commissioner for the region in a move that undercut both Vichy and the Free French.

A comical Italian officer appears as a minor character in two of *Casablanca*'s scenes. This alludes to Italy's decision to attack France after its army was defeated by the Germans. Italy managed to seize a small border zone in the face of French resistance and with German backing was able to impose its own armistice on Vichy. The Italian in the film belonged to that country's armistice commission in Morocco. German condescension for him and the contempt shown by the French reflects the way Italy's war effort was viewed at the time.

Unlike many products of wartime Hollywood, *Casablanca* strove for accuracy in the uniforms worn by German and French soldiers and police. The screenplay's major military mistake sounds like it might have resulted from a typographical error. In his description of the German artillery barrage audible in Paris, Rick refers to the big guns as 77s. The Germans had no 77mm cannons, but the 88s were among the most efficient weapons in their arsenal. Renault's rebuke to Strasser's arrogant dismissal of the United States, his remark that "we mustn't underestimate American blundering. I was with them when they 'blundered' into Berlin in 1918," could falsely imply that Franco-American forces occupied Germany's capital at the end of World War I. However, Renault might be referring to officers sent to Berlin to oversee details of the recently signed armistice ending the war.

Perhaps, the screenplay's most senseless error occurred during the exchange between Rick and Renault. "I came to Casablanca for the waters," Rick says sarcastically. Renault responds, "Waters? What waters? We're in the desert." The desert is actually some distance from Casablanca, which sits on Morocco's temperate Atlantic shore.

CONCLUSION

Casablanca correctly depicts many details about life in French North Africa under the Vichy regime and the situation faced by refugees from Nazi-occupied Europe, who flocked to the city hoping to find transit to Portugal and from there to the New World. More importantly, the character of Rick served as an allegory of the United States as an idealistic nation that had retreated into isolationism, only to rise to the occasion when the Nazi threat became clear. *Casablanca* called on Americans in the first year of the war to prepare for letting go of personal comfort and objectives in the long struggle ahead. *Casablanca* "demonstrates America's mythological vision of itself—tough on the outside and moral within, capable of sacrifice and romance without sacrificing the individualism that conquered a continent, sticking its neck out for everybody when circumstances demand heroism" (Harmetz 2002, 6).

FURTHER READING

Burrin, Philippe. 1996. *France under the Germans: Collaboration and Compromise.* New York: The New Press.

Crowther, Bosley. 1942. "Casablanca." *New York Times*, November 27, 1942. https://www.nytimes.com/1942/11/27/archives/casablanca-with-humphrey-bogart-and-ingrid-bergman-at-hollywood.html

Curtis, Michael. 2002. *Verdict on Vichy: Power and Prejudice in the Vichy France Regime.* London: Weidenfeld & Nicholson.

Ebert, Roger. 2002. "Audio Commentary for *Casablanca* DVD on Warner Home Video."

Farber, Manny. 1942. "The Warner Boys in Africa." *The New Republic*, December 14, 1942.

Harmetz, Aljean. 2002. *The Making of "Casablanca": Bogart, Bergman, and World War II.* New York: Hyperion.

Isenberg, Noah. 2017. *We'll Always Have* Casablanca: *The Life, Legend, and Afterlife of Hollywood's Most Beloved Movie.* New York: W. W. Norton.

Kanfer, Stefan. 2011. *Tough Guy without a Gun: The Extraordinary Life and Afterlife of Humphrey Bogart.* New York: Alfred A. Knopf.

Koch, Howard. 1973. Casablanca: *Script and Legend.* Woodstock, NY: Overlook Press.

Lacouture, Jean. 1991. *De Gaulle: The Rebel, 1890–1944.* London: W. W. Norton.

Lochery, Neill. 2011. *Lisbon: War in the Shadows of the City of Light, 1939–1945.* New York: PublicAffairs.

Miller, Frank. 1992. Casablanca *as Time Goes by . . . 50th Anniversary Commemorative.* Atlanta, GA: Turner Publishing.

Osborne, Richard E. 2011. *The* Casablanca *Companion: The Movie Classic and Its Place in History.* Indianapolis, IN: Riebel-Roque Publishing.

Paxton, Robert O. 1975. *Vichy France: Old Guard and New Order, 1940–1944.* New York: W. W. Norton.

Rode, Alan K. 2017. *Michael Curtiz: A Life in Film.* Lexington: University Press of Kentucky.

Rosen, Lawrence. 2019. "Victim Enough? The Jews of North Africa during the Holocaust." *Jewish Review of Books*, Spring 2019. https://jewishreviewofbooks.com/articles/5186/victim-enough-the-jews-of-north-africa-during-the-holocaust/

U.S. Department of State. n.d. "The Immigration Act of 1924 (The Johnson-Reed Act)." https://history.state.gov/milestones/1921-1936/immigration-act

Chapter 3

Twelve O'Clock High (1949)

Released in Los Angeles on December 21, 1949, and elsewhere in the United States early the following year by 20th Century Fox, *Twelve O'Clock High* was directed by Henry King (1886–1982), a Hollywood veteran whose career began in silent movies and spanned many genres. *Twelve O'Clock High* is his most acclaimed film. With King's assistance, Sy Barlett (1900–1978) and Beirne Lay Jr. (1909–1982) adapted the screenplay from their 1948 novel, *12 O'Clock High*, an account of the air war over Europe, drawn from their own experience. During the war, Bartlett was an intelligence officer with the Eighth Air Force, the U.S. Army Air Force contingent stationed in Great Britain. Lay commanded the Eighth Air Force Film Unit and copiloted a bomber on the mission that became *Twelve O'Clock High's* climactic combat scene.

The film is the story of how a demoralized bomber unit surmounted many obstacles before conducting damaging daylight raids over Germany. *Twelve O'Clock High* is structured as a long flashback. It begins after the war ends when former Lieutenant Colonel Harvey Stovall, played by Dean Jagger (1903–1991), discovers a battered Toby jug in the window of a London antique shop. Purchasing the jug, which had once decorated the officers' club of his wartime unit, the 918th Bomb Group, he travels to the group's airbase at Archbury, abandoned and already overgrown with weeds. His arrival triggers the flashback of the crucial time in the 918th's story when the unit, dubbed the "hard luck group" for its high casualties and aborted missions, was whipped into shape.

Set in 1942, shortly after the Eighth Air Force arrived in Great Britain, *Twelve O'Clock High's* flashback opens with the return of the 918th from a bombing mission over Nazi-occupied France. They had lost several B-17 bombers from attacks by German Focke-Wulf FW-190 fighters, and surviving crew members were badly shaken. One man taken off a damaged bomber by stretcher is still alive even though the back of his head has been torn away by German bullets. A disembodied arm is all that remains of another crewman. After flying missions four days in a row, most of the 918th's survivors ask to be excused from duty because of illness.

Their commanding officer, Colonel Keith Davenport, played by Gary Merrill (1915–1990), wonders whether the men have been pushed past the edge of endurance. "Somebody's got to give me a policy," replies the medical officer, Major Kaiser, played by Paul Stewart (1908–1986). The medic has no idea what standards to apply to a situation verging on combat fatigue.

The 918th's performance is poor compared to other bomber groups, and the Eighth Air Force commander, Major General Pritchard, played by Millard Mitchell (1903–1953), is concerned that its low morale could spread to other units and wants to sustain a seemingly impossible combat regimen for the bomber squadrons. His main objective appears to be proving the theory that victory will be achieved by the air force through "precision daylight bombing" of German targets. One of the era's leading actors, Gregory Peck (1916–2003), stars as the officer, Brigadier General Frank Savage, who applies Pritchard's hard standards to the men in combat. Savage arrives at the 918th's base at Archbury in the English Midlands, dresses down the MP at the gate for failure to maintain tight security, demotes the office clerk for his sloppy dress, and relieves Davenport of command, convinced that the colonel has become emotionally close, and hence overprotective, to his men. Savage poses as an officer with no use for coddling and is determined to raise the 918th to the highest level of performance or break the men by trying. Savage cancels all leaves, closes the bar at the officers club, and arrests the unit's executive officer, Lieutenant Colonel Ben Gately, played by Hugh Marlowe (1911–1982). He later gives Gately command of the "weakest" members of the 918th and dubs their bomber "The Leper Colony." His objective is to shame them into greater effort. Savage's plan succeeds.

Early on, Savage makes a pair of allies among the largely hostile 918th. Stovall joins his side along with the bravest of the unit's flight commanders, Lieutenant Jesse Bishop, played by Robert Patten (1925–2001). Although initially antagonistic, Major Joe Cobb, played by John Kellogg (1916–2000), accepts the role of the 918th's executive officer. Most of the men request a transfer in response to Savage's browbeating, but he eventually wins them over, instilling pride in the unit and leading by example in flying dangerous missions with them over Europe. Savage's fierce behavior is partly an act; he also cares about the men under his command but is determined to carry out Pritchard's orders by testing the limits of human endurance in the air war.

Enduring casualties, the 918th is sent deep over Germany, first on a bombing run over the port of Wilhelmshaven and then striking at the heart of the German armaments industry by bombing its ball bearing plants. By the time of the Wilhelmshaven raid, unit pride swells to the point where the 918th's chaplain, medical officer, and other ground crew stow away on B-17s in order to share in the achievement. Savage learns that Gately had been flying with a painful injury to prove his worth as an officer. However, during the follow-up raid against the ball bearing plant, many of the 918th's planes are shot down by thickets of enemy fighters and clouds of bursting antiaircraft artillery. When ordered on a second raid against the same facility, Savage is unable to board his plane, losing control of his arms and his orientation, shouting, "Stop it! They can't go!" in realization that the mission will cost many more American lives. He finally cracks under the strain. Despite his contempt for weakness, Savage reaches his breaking point.

Twelve O'Clock High was made with the full cooperation of the U.S. Air Force. The chief of staff, General Hoyt Vandenberg (1899–1954), helped find locations to stand in for the film's wartime British airfield. Many scenes were shot at Ozark Army Airfield near Daleville, Alabama, and Duke Field outside Eglin Air Force base in western Florida. *Twelve O'Clock High*'s technical advisors, Colonel John deRussy and Major Johnny McKee, had served in the Eighth Air Force with the men who were the basis for the film's characters. In exchange for air force assistance, Vandenberg demanded only one change in the screenplay. Instead of Savage descending into utter hysteria during his breakdown, the scene was rewritten with a "much more subdued approach." The stoicism of men under fire could be questioned only up to a point (Fishgall 2002, 140). The air force provided surplus B-17s, including several that had taken part in the Bikini Atoll atomic test. The planes were contaminated with radiation and could fly only for short periods. One of the radioactive B-17s was deliberately crash-landed in an early scene to simulate the forced landing of a damaged bomber returning from mission, air force personnel were used as extras in several scenes (Correll 2011).

Hollywood largely curtailed making war movies at the end of World War II, fearing public exhaustion with the topic. Along with a slightly earlier film about the Eighth Air Force, *Command Decision* (1948), and a pair of 1949 releases, *Sands of Iwo Jima* and *Battleground*, *Twelve O'Clock High* helped to launch a second wave of World War II movies, which continued almost unabated for two decades. However, few of the previous or the forthcoming pictures were as convincing to the men who served in the war. The *New York Times* called *Twelve O'Clock High* "tremendously vivid" and declared that no previous World War II film could compare with it for "rugged realism and punch" (Crowther 1950).

In 1950, *Twelve O'Clock High* ended as the year's 10th highest grossing film with revenue of $3.2 million (Fishgall 2002, 142). It was nominated for four Academy Awards and earned Oscars in the categories of Best Sound Recording and Best Actor in a Supporting Role for Dean Jagger. The New York Film Critics Circle awarded Gregory Peck its Best Actor prize for his role. In 1998, *Twelve O'Clock High* was added to the Library of Congress's

National Film Registry for its historical significance. Aviation veterans have called it the "best movie ever made about the Air Force" and "a cult film for several generations of Air Force members" (Correll 2011).

HISTORICAL BACKGROUND

Although the first heavier-than-air aircraft was flown in the United States (1903), invented by bicycle repairmen Orville Wright (1871–1948) and Wilbur Wright (1867–1912), America lagged behind other nations in developing an air force until World War II. The Wright brothers refused an offer from Great Britain to purchase their technology, hoping instead to interest their own government. However, the Wrights had to overcome much homegrown skepticism about their invention, including the refusal by the U.S. Army to acknowledge the evidence that flying machines actually flew. Although the military potential for aviation was apparent, it took until the end of 1907 before the Wright brothers finally convinced the army that there was a future in aircraft (Anderton 1981, 13–14).

In December 1907, the U.S. Army announced it would purchase an airplane that could reach speeds of 40 mph, carry a two-man crew, and be transportable on a mule-drawn wagon. By 1909, the Wright brothers had finally developed a flying machine meeting those specifications and sold a handful to the Signal Corps (Anders 1966, 27–28). The Signal Corps was chosen because it had been the branch of the army that was responsible for manning reconnaissance balloons during the Civil War (1861–1865), but the Corps had enjoyed less success in recent years. The one balloon it launched during the Spanish-American War (1898) was brought down by enemy fire. Afterward, the Corps was unable to keep a working dirigible in service (Anderton 1981, 13–14).

The Signal Corps entered the age of aircraft with reluctance, and its newly formed Aeronautical Service was seen as "the ugly stepchild of the military establishment" (Anders 1966, 29). Although airplanes were used effectively during the Balkan Wars (1912–1913), the U.S. embrace of military aviation continued to be marked by hesitation. The rickety planes deployed for the 1916 "Punitive Expedition" into Mexico, led by Brigadier General John J. Pershing (1860–1948), suffered from heat and turbulence and proved ineffective. While Pershing was a cavalry officer and no supporter of aviation, he praised the daredevil pilots who "risked their lives in old and often useless machines" (Anderton 1981, 20).

Meanwhile in Europe, with World War I (1914–1918) underway, British, French, and German fighter planes dueled in the sky over the Western Front; German zeppelins bombed London's docks; and Russia deployed the world's first four-engine heavy bombers against Germany. In 1916, some two dozen ambitious American aviators volunteered to fight the Germans in a French air squadron, the Lafayette Escadrille. When the United States finally entered World War I in 1917, the renamed Army Aviation Service numbered only 100 pilots with 125 planes, none suitable for combat (Anderton 1981, 22).

The Aviation Service's European commander, Colonel (later Brigadier General) William "Billy" Mitchell (1879–1936), was determined to show that America could fight in the air alongside its allies despite budgetary limitations and lack of interest from his superior officer, Pershing, back from Mexico to lead the American Expeditionary Force in Europe. The Aviation Service was given cast-off British and French planes, most of them obsolete, but his pilots flew bravely into action.

Mitchell listened eagerly to the lessons of his British counterparts and was impressed by the potential of aerial bombardment after a nighttime German raid damaged the French town of Chalon where he was billeted (Mitchell 1960, 83). In August 1918, Mitchell coordinated a major offensive involving 1,500 French, British, and American planes, "the greatest concentration of air power the world had seen" (Anders 1966, 34). Mitchell targeted not only German forward positions near St. Mihiel but also demonstrated the strategic potential of air power by bombing railroads, communication lines, and logistics centers. However, the U.S. military refused to follow up on the lessons of that mission. For much of the war, "American air power was subordinated to the ground armies and their immediate needs" (Anderton 1981, 23).

Mitchell returned home after the war and became America's apostle of airpower, testifying before Congress and badgering his superiors in an environment of postwar budget cutbacks and a public sentiment favoring isolationism and pacifism. At Mitchell's urging, the navy conducted test bombing runs in 1921 on captured German warships, proving to the dismay of some commanders that even an "unsinkable" battleship was vulnerable to air strikes.

However, the Army General Staff refused to consider establishing an independent air force and resented Mitchell's much-publicized criticism of traditional military strategy. "Today, armies and navies are entirely incapable of insuring a nation's defense," he wrote (Mitchell 1960, 5). After several notorious crashes of naval aircraft, Mitchell's strident advocacy for creating what became the third branch of the service crossed the line of permissible military behavior when he accused the army and navy of "almost treasonable administration of the national defense" (Sharp 1977, 430–433). After his conviction in a court martial for "conduct unbecoming an officer," Mitchell left the army but continued to speak out on the inadequacy of American military aviation when compared to the air forces of other nations. World War II vindicated most of his ideas, beginning with Germany's deployment of dive bombers and paratroops and continuing through the Japanese attack on the U.S. fleet at Pearl Harbor and the Allies' reliance on strategic bombing in Europe and the Pacific.

Despite the rebuke he received from his superior officers, Mitchell's call for a third branch continued to circulate. The first significant development occurred in 1926 with the elevation of the Aviation Service into a separate Army Air Corps responsible to a newly created office, the Assistant Secretary of War for Air. Despite budget limitations, the Army Air Corps mastered new skills such as aerial refueling and slowly upgraded its arsenal. By the late 1930s, modern single-wing fighter planes replaced biplanes, and a long-range heavy bomber, the B-17, was introduced, which became the warhorse of the air war in Europe. Production was slow in the prewar years. In 1939 as World War II began, only 13 B-17s were in service; the Air Corps totaled 800 combat-ready planes compared to 2,000 for Britain's Royal Air Force and 4,000 for Germany's Luftwaffe. Urged on by President Franklin D. Roosevelt (1882–1945), the United States began to rearm in 1940 and increase the size of the Air Corps in preparation for the defense of the western hemisphere against a possible Axis attack. Although long-range operations in Europe and Asia were not contemplated, Roosevelt turned a blind eye to the American volunteer squadrons led by Lieutenant General Claire L. Chennault (1890–1958). His "Flying Tigers" fought against Japan as part of China's air force until the United States entered the war.

LUFTWAFFE

During World War I, German airpower was formidable. Zeppelins conducted long-range bombing raids, and speedy fighter planes contested the Allies over the Western Front. So concerned were the Allies over German air superiority that the Treaty of Versailles (1919) specifically prohibited Germany from reestablishing an air force. However, the German military secretly evaded the rules, training pilots in the Soviet Union and establishing supposedly civilian "flying clubs."

When Hitler tore up the Versailles Treaty (1935), Germany's air force, the Luftwaffe, rapidly became the most technically sophisticated in the world. When World War II began (1939), the Luftwaffe's Stuka dive bombers provided pinpoint combat support for advancing troops, and its fighter planes, the Messerschmidt Me109 and Focke-Wulf Fw 190, were among the best in the air. The Luftwaffe's commander, the World War I ace-turned-Nazi politician Hermann Göring, believed he could defeat the British through a bombing campaign and defend German airspace against all intruders. He was proven wrong on both counts.

By the start of 1943, American factories had turned out aircraft in enormous numbers, as German factories, continually subject to bombardment, struggled to keep pace. By the time of the D-Day landing (June 7, 1944), Allied air superiority was assured. However, the Luftwaffe continued to harass Allied aircraft until the war's end. The first operational jet fighter, the Me-262, could have thwarted Allied bombers if they had been produced in sufficient numbers.

The United States stepped toward establishing a separate branch of the service when the Army Air Corps was reconfigured in June 1941 as the Army Air Forces and prepared for its growing role by establishing the structure for the numbered "air forces" that would fight in particular regions during the coming war. For the Army Air Forces, the war began with Pearl Harbor (December 7, 1941). Most of its planes on Hawaiian airfields were destroyed on the ground, but a few fighters managed to pursue the Japanese and shoot down several enemy planes.

In April 1942, Lieutenant Colonel James J. Doolittle (1896–1993) led a flight of B-25s launched from the deck of an aircraft carrier for a bombing raid against Tokyo. They caused little damage, and the crews were forced to crash-land in China, but their gesture was a morale-lifter during the uncertain early months of the war. U.S. Navy carrier-born planes fought the air war in the Pacific, but army bombers and transport planes eventually proved indispensable for victory over Japan. The Tenth Air Force helped turn back Japan's threat to India and aided the British reconquest of Burma. The Fourteenth Air Force lifted supplies to China over the "hump" of the Himalayas. By 1944, B-24 Superfortress bombers from the Seventh Air Force based on Guam and Saipan conducted devastating raids against Japanese cities. In August 1945, two of the Twentieth Air Force's bombers ended the war by dropping atomic bombs on Hiroshima and Nagasaki.

The Army Air Forces played a role in every theater of combat, including North Africa and Europe. As World War II continued, the air forces operated with greater independence from the army and proved not only its ability to support forces on land and sea but also demonstrated its capacity to carry the war to enemy homelands. With the National Security Act of 1947, the U.S. Air Force finally became a fully independent branch of the military on equal footing with the army and navy.

DEPICTION AND HISTORICAL CONTEXT

The written message displayed at the start of *Twelve O'Clock High* is correct. The Eighth Air Force crews were the "only Americans fighting in Europe in the fall of 1942." The Eighth began to arrive in Great Britain in the summer of 1942 on troopships, including the mighty British ocean liner *Queen Mary*. The Eighth (joined in 1943 by the Ninth) Air Force was scattered across 100 bases in England. *Twelve O'Clock High*'s air base was typical in appearance, with prefabricated Quonset huts and wooden structures hastily erected on fields that often turned to mud in the rainy English climate. No thought was given to permanence; they were temporary wartime accommodations and, as shown in the movie's opening scene when Lieutenant Colonel Stovall visits the site, would have fallen to weed and ruin within a few years after the war.

Twelve O'Clock High was widely understood in air force circles at the time of its release as "based on actual persons and events. Very little of it was pure fiction" (Correll 2011). Coauthor Beirne Lay was one of a handful of officers who arrived in Britain in February 1942 under Bomber Command's Brigadier General Ira Eaker (1896–1987) to establish the advance element of the Eighth Air Force. His collaborator, Sy Bartlett, arrived around the same time as aide to Major General Carl Spaatz (1891–1974), commanding officer of the Eighth Air Force. Lay eventually flew combat missions as copilot of a B-17 called Piccadilly Lily, the name of Savage's plane in *Twelve O'Clock High*.

According to an air force historian, the actual unit that inspired the film's "hard luck," 305th Bomb Group, was based not at Archbury but at Thurleigh in Bedfordshire. When Bartlett accompanied Eaker and Spaatz on an inspection of that base in November 1942, they went unchallenged by MPs, and on finding "sloppy conditions and loose policies," the group commander was relieved. Eaker placed Colonel Frank Armstrong Jr. in charge of the outfit. Like Savage in the movie, Armstrong turned the bomb group around under a "strong, disciplinary hand" (Correll 2011).

Twelve O'Clock High focuses on the 305th Bomb Group's officers and accurately represents the physical setting of their quarters and officers club. The film ignores the servicemen's club, the PX, and the makeshift theater for screening Hollywood movies. "Each base was a self-contained little America," complete with an endless supply of Coca-Cola and amply provisioned with supplies shipped from the states. Nothing, not even garbage cans, was purchased in Britain (Ward and Burns 2007, 117).

Arguably, the men of the Eighth Air Force were handed America's most difficult combat mission in the war. As noted in *Twelve O'Clock High*'s screenplay, the airmen were scheduled to fly only 25 missions before returning to the United States to train the next wave of bomber crews (Anders 1966, 244). As late as the fall of 1943, only one in three airmen made it home. Statistically, it was safer to be a marine landing on a heavily defended Japanese-held island in the Pacific than to fly on bombing raids over Nazi territory. The military suppressed those facts from the public and tried to hide them from their own men. Andy Rooney, a reporter during the war for the army's *Stars and Stripes* newspaper, recalled that the Army Air Force command did not "want to discourage the crews with the details of the carnage" (Rooney 1995, 78). The men in the air were not fooled by the silence over casualties. According to a navigator on a B-17, "one did not have to be a brain surgeon to figure out one's odds of finishing a combat tour" (Fleming and Hall 1992, 49). From 1944 to 1945 with the Luftwaffe increasingly diminished and Allied control of the sky assured, the odds of survival increased dramatically. Altogether 26,000 Eighth Air Force crewmen died during the war, 40,000 more were shot down and taken prisoner (Ward and Burns 2007, 117).

Brigadier General Savage, like all Army Air Force bomber command officers, was committed to the doctrine of the "combat box." Developed by Colonel (later General) Curtis E. LeMay (1906–1990), the combat box was a tight formation of bombers stacked and spread to provide maximum defense by their gunners against enemy fighter planes in a kind of aerial phalanx (Anders 1966, 241, 250). The box worked as depicted in *Twelve O'Clock High*; when one bomber was lost, the remaining planes closed ranks and tried to hold formation. Coupled with the dogma of "high altitude precision bombing," which supposedly kept the B-17s just above the reach of ground artillery, the Eighth Air Force began the war with a confidence that was soon confronted by reality. Sometimes the B-17s dropped to 17,000 feet or lower, putting them in range of antiaircraft guns. Luftwaffe pilots were well trained and motivated, charging in fast maneuverable craft toward the bombers at 600 mph from below, above, front, and rear, hence the "o'clock" designations used by B-17 gunners.

Attacks by German fighters took a heavy toll on bomber missions, especially when long-range runs went beyond the range of fighter escorts. However, the ruggedly-built B-17s could absorb a great deal of punishment and often returned to base after sustaining heavy damage, as shown in the film's first wartime scene.

Although the effect of Nazi propaganda on U.S. servicemen was negligible, the officers of the 305th Bomb Group are seen listening to an English-language broadcast from Berlin. The speaker is Lord Haw-Haw, the radio name for the British traitor William Joyce (1906–1946), whose primary mission was to demoralize the British public by convincing them that their government was inept and their military unable to win. In *Twelve O'Clock High*, Lord Haw-Haw also taunts the Eighth Air Force, saying that while the cowardly Royal Air Force bombs Europe under cover of night, the United States plays a fool's game by bombing during daylight when aircraft are more vulnerable.

Lord Haw-Haw's monologue correctly identifies the complementary strategies of Britain and America. The Royal Air Force was tasked with blindly bombing German cities by night and the United States with hitting military targets with "precision" by day. Despite the alleged accuracy of the top-secret Norden bomb sight and U.S. assertions of avoiding civilian centers, it was impossible to avoid massive casualties and destruction of homes. Civilians across Nazi-occupied Europe suffered from the inherent inaccuracy of American bombing raids. Beginning in 1942, French coastal towns were reduced to rubble without seriously disrupting German shipping or putting a dent into the reinforced concrete pens that sheltered U-boats from attack.

"They said you could drop a bomb into a pickle barrel," a B-17 gunner recalled, referring to the vaunted Norden bomb sight. "We would fly over, drop tons of bombs," but many landed in "some muddy field. And the minute they hit, they went down in the mud" (Ward and Burns 2007, 120). An unsympathetic British historian charged that false claims about daylight bombing enabled America "to claim the moral high ground, always important when the Republic makes war, even as their bombs rained down indiscriminately through dense clouds from a vast height" (Burleigh 2000, 745). Those dense clouds sometimes caused missions to be scrubbed or flights delayed. *Twelve O'Clock High* accurately cites the challenge of the North Sea climate, which reduced visibility for daylight missions and grounded planes many days in a row.

In the movie, the 305th had the reputation for being "a hard luck group." That was not merely a metaphor. While the airmen valued their operational skills, they inevitably pondered the vagaries of fate when discussing who returned from their missions and who was lost. "Everyone knew that without luck you weren't going to make it," recalled a B-17 waist gunner from the Second Bomb Group (McGuire and Hadley 1993, 309). Sometimes particular planes or individuals were deemed as ill fated; sometimes entire crews "without obvious skill weaknesses" were considered a "jinx crew" after a succession of problems (Mackenzie 2017, 58–59).

The command structure of a bomber group was accurately reflected in *Twelve O'Clock High* with the group commander piloting the front plane. "The man whose plane was most vulnerable to the Germans' head-on fighter attacks" led the way. The pilot was absolute commander of his plane regardless of rank (Anders 1966, 239, 241).

The B-17 in flight was not a comfortable or secure position from which to conduct a war. Flying at 20,000 feet necessitated wearing oxygen masks in the unpressurized cabins exposed to the air from open gun ports on each side of the bomber's belly. In a magazine article written shortly after the mission he describes, Beirne Lay, coauthor of the *12 O'Clock High* novel, wrote, "It was cold in the cockpit, but sweat was running from his [the pilot's] forehead and over his oxygen mask from the exertion of holding his elements with tight formation and the strain of the warnings that hummed over the interphone" (Lay 1943). Because they flew in such close formations, "most crew members had a grandstand view of what could happen to other aircraft when struck by antiaircraft shells—flak—from the ground or cannon and machine-gun fire from attacking fighters" (Mackenzie 2017, 9).

The documentary footage and realistic restaging of *Twelve O'Clock High*'s combat missions give an accurate if not entirely complete picture of war in the air. In his article, Lay described "the cluttered wake of a desperate air battle" that included human and aircraft parts from decimated planes flying past his cockpit. "The spectacle registering on my eyes became so fantastic that my brain turned numb," he wrote. After a while, he "might easily have been watching an animated cartoon in a movie theater" (Lay 1943). Similar sensations were reported by other survivors of bombing missions. "I had a feeling that the planes weren't really falling and burning, the men inside weren't really dying, and everything would turn out happily in the end," a B-17 bombardier told a *New Yorker* writer while on leave (Gill 1944).

Many incidents depicted in *Twelve O'Clock High* correspond to events reported by eyewitnesses other than Lay and Bartlett. A pilot from the 92nd Bomb Group actually returned with the back of his skull blown away; arms were severed by enemy fire; a flight engineer, rapidly losing blood from his injuries, was parachuted over Germany in the hopes that German medics would save his life (Sloan 1946, 48–49). The film showed the effects of war with a graphic realism unusual in its time. Unlike most Hollywood war movies, women and romance did not distract the screenplay of *Twelve O'Clock High* from its mission of depicting the psychology of men in battle and the psychological damage some of them endured. Although Savage's real life model, Colonel Armstrong, did not endure a breakdown, the scene was based on the experience of the commander of another unit. According to Lay, the breakdown had happened to another "very fine commander who had been on four rough missions in a row" (Correll 2011).

The climactic mission in *Twelve O'Clock High* is based on the August 17, 1943, operation deep into Germany against the Messerschmidt fighter plant in Regensburg and a complex of ball bearing factories at Schweinfurt. It was, as depicted on screen, a deadly mission for the Eighth Air Force. Three hundred seventy-six B-17s were sent to hit those targets. Sixty were shot down and 600 crewmen were lost.

Both targets were valuable. The Messerschmidt Me-109 was one of Germany's best fighter planes and was a deadly foe to Allied bombers. The ball bearing factories were vital to Germany's war effort. According to Germany's Armaments Minister Albert Speer, the Regensburg raid had "only minor consequences," but ball bearing production dropped by 38 percent after Schweinfurt was hit, temporarily hampering production of war materials (Speer 1970, 285).

CONCLUSION

Twelve O'Clock High is a vivid, accurate representation of the bombing campaign over Europe from the bomber crews' perspective. The effect of that campaign on the ground is not examined, and whether those strikes were decisive in defeating the Nazis remains disputed and crucial in ongoing arguments over the effectiveness of waging war by air. Speer claimed that, at first, "in spite of the losses of the factories we were producing more, not less," adding that the air raids "spurred us to do our utmost" and increased morale (Speer 1970, 278). Speer responded to the raids by dispersing German industry to the countryside and installing factories underground. Transportation networks were vital and vulnerable to air attack, especially by low-flying fighter bombers.

The Allied air war's greatest achievement might have been diversion of German resources from the front lines to the home front, including the production of antiaircraft shells and the deployment of 800,000 men to the air defense system (Burleigh 2000, 746–747). "Air power did not win World War 2," an Air Force historian admitted. "But it did make a decisive contribution to the final victory" (Anderton 1981, 129).

FURTHER READING

Anders, Curt. 1966. *Fighting Airmen*. New York: G.P. Putnam's Sons.
Anderton, David A. 1981. *The History of the U.S. Air Force*. New York: Crescent Books.
Burleigh, Michael. 2000. *The Third Reich: A New History*. New York: Hill and Wang.
Correll, John T. 2011. "The Real Twelve O'Clock High." *Air Force Magazine*, January 2011. https://www.airforcemag.com/article/0111high/
Crowther, Boseley. 1950. "'Twelve O'Clock High,' Realistic Saga of the Eighth Air Force, Arrives at Roxy Theatre." *New York Times*, January 28, 1950. https://www.nytimes.com/1950/01/28/archives/the-screen-in-review-twelve-oclock-high-realistic-saga-of-the.html
Fishgall, Gary. 2002. *Gregory Peck*. New York: Scribners.
Fleming, Samuel P., and Ed Y. Hall. 1992. *Flying with the "Hell's Angels": Memoirs of a B-17 Flying Fortress Navigator*. Spartanburg, SC: Honoribus.
Gill, Brendan. 1944. "Young Man behind Plexiglass." *The New Yorker*, August 12, 1944. https://www.newyorker.com/magazine/1944/08/12/young-man-behind-plexiglass
Lay, Beirne, Jr. 1943. "I Saw Regensburg Destroyed." *Saturday Evening Post*, November 6, 1943. From *Reporting World War II, Part One: American Journalism 1938–1944*. New York: Library of America, 623.
Mackenzie, S.P. 2017. *Flying against Fate: Superstition and Allied Aircrews in World War II*. Lawrence: University Press of Kansas.
McGuire, Melvin W., and Robert Hadley. 1993. *Bloody Skies: A 15th Army Air Force Combat Crew*. Las Cruces, NM: Yucca Tree.
Mitchell, William. 1960. *Memoirs of World War I: "From Start to Finish of Our Greatest War."* New York: Random House.
Rooney, Andy. 1995. *My War*. New York: Times Books.
Sharp, Harold S. 1977. *Footnotes to American History*. Metuchen, NJ: Scarecrow Press.
Sloan, John S. 1946. *The Route as Briefed: The History of the 92nd Bomb Group, USAAF, 1942–1945*. Cleveland, OH: Argus.
Speer, Albert. 1970. *Inside the Third Reich: Memoirs*. New York: Macmillan.
Ward, Geoffrey C., and Burns, Ken. 2007. *The War: An Intimate History, 1941–1945*. New York: Alfred A. Knopf.

Chapter 4

From Here to Eternity (1953)

Directed by Fred Zinnemann (1907–1997), an Austrian émigré known for high-quality Hollywood films such as *High Noon* (1952), *From Here to Eternity* premiered on August 5, 1953. Columbia Pictures tasked Daniel Taradash (1913–2003), a rising Hollywood writer, with transforming the 800-page novel of the same name by James Jones (1921–1977) into a suitable screenplay. The novel was a best seller and won the National Book Award, making it a tempting prize for Hollywood. However, the graphic depictions of sexuality and army life made a close adaptation for the screen impossible under censorship rules of that time. As a result, Taradash inventively trimmed many of Jones's subplots, scoured the rough language, and skirted many issues altogether without entirely losing the story's sense of realism.

From *Here to Eternity* is an emotionally complicated love story set against army life in Hawaii on the eve of the Japanese attack on Pearl Harbor (December 7, 1941). The eventuality of that raid was foremost in mind for movie audiences at the time of its release; for them, Pearl Harbor was as unforgettable as the assassination of President John F. Kennedy or the terrorist attacks of September 11, 2001, for later generations.

The film begins with protagonist Robert E. Lee Prewitt's (Montgomery Clift, 1920–1966) arrival at Schofield Barracks on the island of Oahu. Although Zinnemann wanted husky, barrel-necked Aldo Ray (1926–1991) for the role, an actor who fit the character as described in the novel, he settled instead for Clift, a moody, inwardly tortured actor who brought an appealing mix of vulnerability and intensity to the part (Thomson 2008, 314).

Prewitt has just been demoted to private and transferred from the Bugle Corps at Fort Shafter in Honolulu to an infantry company stationed at

Schofield. Prewitt soon encounters the key male characters in the story, including the soldier who becomes his only friend in the unit, Private Angelo Maggio, played by Frank Sinatra (1915–1998). At the time he was cast, the hitmaking 1940s singer and Hollywood musical star had faded and was considered a has-been. Sinatra identified with the role as a put-upon Italian American and campaigned hard to win the spot. Rumors persist that the singer used Mafia connections to get a hearing with Columbia's head Harry Cohn. Regardless of how he got the part, Sinatra's terrific performance as the sympathetic, rebellious Italian-American serviceman put him back on top (Levy 1998, 22).

Burt Lancaster (1913–1994), already a star, agreed to a supporting role as the company's adjutant, First Sergeant Milton Warden. The company commander, Captain Dana Holmes, is played by character actor Philip Ober (1902–1982). Holmes is a negligent and lazy officer more interested in impressing his superiors than leading his men. He counts on his company's victory in the upcoming army divisional boxing match as a means of achieving promotion to major and routinely slips away from the barracks to visit his mistress, leaving Warden to run the company's day-to-day tasks. Holmes offers favored treatment to Prewitt, who has the reputation of being a formidable middleweight, if he agrees to represent the company in the contest. Prewitt refuses, and under pressure, he admits to intense guilt over blinding an opponent in a boxing match.

To force him into the boxing ring, Holmes assigns Prewitt hard duty, including scrubbing pots and pans in the kitchen, cleaning latrines, and washing floors. Some men from Prewitt's company harass Prewitt with rough physical and verbal abuse to change his mind about boxing. Warden keeps aloof from the conflict. He comes to like the rebellious Prewitt but, commenting on his resolution and integrity, says that a man in America's pioneer days could go it alone. However, he says, "Today you got to play ball."

The personal lives of the major characters occupy much of the screen time. Before long, Warden begins an affair with Holmes's wife, Karen (Deborah Kerr, 1921–2007), a woman with a reputation for "playing around." In one of Hollywood's most memorable romantic scenes, Warden and Karen make love on the beach at Halona Cove near Honolulu with the ocean waves crashing around them.

While on leave, Prewitt and Maggio visit a "gentleman's club" in Honolulu. Prewitt falls in love with Lorene (Donna Reed, 1921–1986), one of the women ostensibly working there as a dancer. Like Kerr, Reed was usually cast in wholesome roles, but as Lorene, she plays a socially disreputable character. At the club, Maggio gets into a fight with Staff Sergeant James R. Judson (Ernest Borgnine, 1917–2012), sergeant of the guard at the stockade where military prisoners are held. Later, Maggio is court-martialed for leaving his post and sentenced to six months in the stockade. He later dies as a result of injuries inflicted by the sadistic Judson. Confronting Judson on a Honolulu street, Prewitt accidentally kills the staff sergeant and hides in Lorene's house until the attack on Pearl Harbor. Although she begs him to stay, fearing for the punishment he might receive if he returns, Prewitt chooses duty over love and tries to return to Schofield Barracks. In the confusion that follows the Japanese air raid, he is shot dead by an army patrol, who mistakes him for a saboteur or an enemy paratrooper.

The film's success more than fulfilled Hollywood's expectations, grossing $30.5 million at the box office, approximately $278 million in today's dollars. It was one of the top movie attractions of 1953 and one of the 10 best-selling films of the 1950s.

The critics applauded as loudly as the public. The *New York Times* called it "as towering and persuasive" as its source, the novel that had "stirred the post-war reading public," and added that the film's cast and crew convincingly captured "the muscularity of the basically male society with which the book dealt; the poignance and futility of the love lives of the professional soldiers involved, as well as the indictment of commanding officers whose selfishness can break men devoted to soldiering" (Crowther 1953). The entertainment industry trade paper *Variety* praised *From Here to Eternity* as "outstanding" and "an important motion picture from any angle." The reviewer commented that the movie conveyed the essence of the best-selling novel and predicted "very bright prospects" among moviegoers (Brogdon 1953).

From Here to Eternity was honored with 13 Oscar nominations and dominated the 1954 Academy Awards. It captured eight Oscars, including Best Picture. Zinnemann won for Best Director, Sinatra for Best Supporting Actor, Reed for Best Supporting Actress, and Taradash for Best Adapted Screenplay. It also won the Oscars for cinematography, editing, and sound recording. *From Here to Eternity* swept 1954's Golden Globes and New York Film Critics Circle awards and took a Special Award of Merit at the Cannes Film Festival as well as other trophies.

The film has endured as one of the greatest accomplishments of Hollywood at the end of its golden age. It ranks 52nd on the American Film Institute's list of Top 100 Films. Film historian David Thomson placed *From Here to Eternity*'s characters among "the most commanding in American film drama" (Thomson 2008, 314). Critic Roger Ebert included the love scene on the beach between Kerr and Lancaster among his 100 Great Movie Moments (Ebert 1995). In 2002, the Library of Congress added *From Here to Eternity* to its National Film Registry for its historical significance.

HISTORICAL BACKGROUND

For the Japanese, Pearl Harbor was a reckless gamble, a tactical victory but a strategic defeat. For Americans, it became the rallying cry overriding all objections to entering the war. The architect of the attack, Admiral

Yamamoto Isoruku (1884–1943), who had lived in the United States, worried that his superiors had misunderstood the character of the American people and that the raid would only succeed in awakening a sleeping giant. He was proven correct, even before he was targeted and killed by vengeful U.S. Navy fighter pilots in an aerial ambush less than two years later.

Japan's first encounter with the United States occurred in a show of force in Tokyo Bay by Commodore Matthew C. Perry (1794–1858). With persuasion and coercion, Perry obtained Japanese signatures on the 1854 treaty that opened the stubbornly insular empire to the West. As a result, Japan embarked on the program of modernization, militarization, and colonial ambition that would lead, although not inevitably, to Pearl Harbor. Many Japanese dreamed of overtaking the Western nations, whose racism was often undisguised and whose foreign policy seemed determined to hold Japan down. By the 1890s, the new imperial regime in Tokyo had built a modern army and navy and seized Korea, Formosa (Taiwan), and the strategic Manchurian city of Port Arthur during the First Sino-Japanese War (1894–1895). "Most Japanese regarded territorial expansion as an essential element of entry into the modern world," because possession of an overseas empire was deemed important both to a nation's status and from economic necessity in a world without open borders (Johnson 1991, 186).

Japan had little time to savor its victory. Russia, France, and Germany forced Japan to return Port Arthur to China as part of a European scheme to carve up the Chinese mainland. Japanese competition was unwelcome. Japan sought assistance from the United States and Great Britain, but the Anglo-Saxon nations refused to intervene. The Japanese public was "devastated," and talk of revenge was in the air (McClain 2002, 301).

Despite the setback, as the 20th century began, Japan was poised to become the dominant power in East Asia. In 1904, a Japanese squadron sank the Russian fleet at Port Arthur without warning in the opening salvo of a war that extended Japan's political and economic control into Manchuria. The sneak attack set a precedent for Japanese strategic planning that persisted through Pearl Harbor. President Theodore Roosevelt (1858–1919) won the Nobel Peace Prize for negotiating the settlement for the Russo-Japanese War (1905). Under the terms of the treaty, Russia turned over Port Arthur and most of its Manchurian properties to Japan, creating a Japanese zone of administration in the outermost province of China. Russia's defeat reverberated around the world. "By defeating the Russian colossus Japan had destroyed the myth of the White Man's invincibility and the Japanese were quick to turn the situation to their advantage" (Barker 1969, 19).

Although Japan could have remained neutral during World War I (1914–1918), it allied with Britain and used the conflict as an excuse to capture German holdings in China and the Pacific. However, the Japanese were unhappy with the postwar order despite territorial gains. At the Paris Conference (1919) that produced the League of Nations Covenant, the

Japanese delegation tried to insert a clause into that covenant, banning discrimination based on race or nationality. The proposal was turned down, and even if it involved Japanese hypocrisy given their treatment of Koreans and other minorities, the rejection rankled the Japanese. Their emissary to the conference, Prince Konoe Fumimaro (1891–1945), expressed the worries of many Japanese that the League would "condemn the late-coming nations to remain forever subordinate to the advanced nations" (Yoshitake 1992, 12).

Many Japanese were also insulted by the Washington Naval Treaty (1922), which imposed an unequal balance of power in the Pacific based on the number of battleships in the U.S., British, and Japanese fleets. The pact permitted equality for the American and British navies but allowed Japan only three battleships for every five possessed by the United States and Britain. The agreement "virtually relegated Japan to third power status" (Barker 1969, 11). The Washington Naval Treaty was one of various treaties signed during the Washington Conference that included promises of international cooperation in China. The "spirit of the Washington Conference" was much discussed by diplomats in those years, signifying the mindset of international consultation in the Pacific and East Asia rather than unilateral action.

Within the Japanese military, however, many officers had acquired a taste for unilateral action even if this meant operating at cross-purposes to the civilian government in Tokyo and their own high command. They were encouraged by the proliferation of patriotic societies and nationalist intellectuals who castigated the international system for subjugating their empire's sovereignty to the West and compromising its cultural identity. Some dreamed of an army-led "purification" campaign to save Japan from outside influence. Many believed the solution to Japan's growing population and limited resources was to build an empire on the Asian mainland and the South Seas. Strict racially based immigration laws in the United States and Australia aggravated the situation, blocking the outflow of Japanese dissatisfied with the direction of their country. Likewise, high tariffs against Japanese goods thwarted economic expansion goods (Johnson 1991, 188–189). Social and economic imperatives moved Japan's political and business leaders to contemplate a new economic system with Japan as the industrial center and East Asia as the market for its products and the source of raw materials.

Anger at pro-Western politicians grew more heated as the worldwide Great Depression cut Japan's export trade and led to unemployment. In the coming years, ultranationalists within the military killed other officials accused of accommodating foreign interests, including the 1932 assassination of Prime Minister Inukai Tsuyoshi (1855–1932).

Unlike its Axis partners, Germany and Italy, and its eventual opponent, the Soviet Union, Japan in the 1930s and early 1940s was authoritarian but not totalitarian. No individual or group gained unassailable control over the empire. Outwardly resembling Great Britain more than Nazi Germany, Japan's political system boasted of a monarch who symbolized the nation, a peerage sitting in the upper house of parliament, squabbling political parties vying for control of the lower house, a cabinet form of government, and an active if often irresponsible press. The chief difference was that in Japan, the general staff and the admiralty nominated the war and naval ministers, and by withdrawing them, the military could force the government to resign. By increasingly exercising this prerogative, the military gained political ascendance, yet the two services often operated independently of each other and were ridden with factions. In February of 1936, a group of army officers led a coup against the government, which was squashed by naval forces. Although its ringleaders were executed, the high command used the specter of radical elements in its ranks to pressure moderates within the Japanese state.

The turning point on Japan's long road to Pearl Harbor was the clash on September 18, 1931, between Japanese and Chinese forces near the Manchurian town of Mukden, the site of a great victory by Japan in the war against Russia and a place of patriotic resonance. Acting without authority from Tokyo, army officers dynamited a small section of the Japanese-owned South Manchuria Railway to provoke an incident with China. By 1932, Japanese troops had subdued Manchuria, transforming it into a puppet nation called Manchukuo and installing China's dethroned last emperor, Puyi (1906–1967), as its emperor. U.S. president Herbert Hoover (1874–1964) condemned Japan and declared that the United States would "deny recognition to any territory seized by force." He refused to take additional steps, believing that the U.S. military was unready for war in Asia and the Pacific (Jeansonne and Luhrssen 2016, 249). The League of Nations also censored Japan, leading to its withdrawal from the League.

The campaign of aggression on the Asian mainland was spurred at many points by Japanese frontline officers and encouraged at home by ultranationalists. Many of Japan's civilian leaders hoped to end the war, but military conspirators acted with greater dispatch. For the conspirators, the invasion of China was the opening bid in a scheme to achieve complete economic self-determination by dominating East Asia and throwing off the influence of Western powers. They argued that the international status quo inevitably benefited wealthy Western nations and kept Japan in dependence and relative poverty. Dissidents "found it increasingly difficult to speak out," and the vigorous action by the military was contrasted in the minds of many people with the gridlock of parliamentary democracy and "unprincipled party leaders and equally unprincipled leaders of big business" (McClain 2002, 426).

The military conspirators were encouraged in their endeavors by the inaction of an international community preoccupied by the Great Depression and ineffectiveness of the League of Nations. The new U.S. president

Franklin Roosevelt (1882–1945) seldom mentioned the Asian crisis in the early years of his administration; focusing on domestic problems, especially economic recovery, the U.S. president had no incentive to develop a coherent foreign policy beyond the Western Hemisphere until the prospect of a European war in the aftermath of the Munich Conference (1938). Although diplomats from the United States and the leading European nations condemned Japan, little action was taken to isolate the Japanese or aid the Chinese. Ironically, the greatest supporter of China's Nationalist regime under President Chiang Kai-shek (1887–1975) through 1938 was Nazi Germany, which supplied China with weapons and military advisors until the Adolf Hitler regime drew closer to Tokyo and ended the program.

Japan responded to criticism of its China policy by withdrawing from the international community and abrogating treaties in a series of steps that paralleled the diplomatic brinkmanship of Nazi Germany. Japan canceled its naval agreements and announced that it would not look favorably on political or economic intervention in China by foreign nations. Increasingly under the sway of pro-German factions within Japan's army, on November 25, 1936, Japan signed the anti-Comintern Pact with Germany, an alliance whose stated purpose was to thwart the spread of communism. Italy signed the pact nearly a year later, solidifying the Axis alliance.

Having established the ostensibly independent state of Manchukuo along with several other puppet administrations in China's northern provinces, Japan plunged deeper into the Chinese heartland in 1937. Mid-level officers used an easily containable incident at the Marco Polo Bridge near Peking (Beijing) as the justification for an all-out assault against China. Prime Minister Prince Konoye Fuminato opposed the invasion, as did the general staff, who were more concerned with planning for the possibility of war with the Soviet Union or the United States. However, they surrendered to usual pressure from nationalist pundits and vocal super-patriots. On the other side of the dispute, Chiang Kai-shek signaled his intention to stand up to Japan through provocative actions. The skirmish became the Second Sino-Chinese War, ending only with Japan's surrender to the Allies in 1945. It was a savage conflict with a guerilla campaign led by communist leader Mao Zedong (1893–1976) in uncomfortable alliance with Chiang. Japanese soldiers committed wanton atrocities. The brutality of the Japanese army, especially the massacre of civilians during the "Rape of Nanking" that claimed as many as 200,000 lives, drew condemnation from the foreign news media and blackened Japan's reputation in much of the world.

In response, in a speech on October 6, 1937, Roosevelt proposed to "quarantine" those nations promoting "international anarchy and instability." He refrained from naming those nations, yet everyone understood the reference to Germany, Italy, and Japan (Doenecke and Wilz 1991, 70). His proposal went nowhere due to lack of political support and apathy over foreign policy. However, American outrage swelled in December when Japanese warplanes sank a U.S. Navy gunboat, *Panay*, on patrol on the Yangtze River in an unprovoked attack. Although Tokyo apologized for what it called an accident, the sinking was probably a deliberate provocation by Japanese commanders on the ground. The U.S. ambassador to Japan, Joseph C. Grew (1880–1965), feared the incident would lead to a break in diplomatic relations, but Japanese civilians flooded his embassy with letters of apology and support for America, and the Japanese government paid an indemnity to the victims. The American public did not forget the sinking of the *Panay*, but the crisis was defused (Doenecke and Wilz 1991, 73).

In early 1938, against the backdrop of mounting international indignation over its aggression in China, the Japanese general staff, meeting in the presence of Emperor Hirohito (1901–1989), decided on a policy of "passive maintenance" of Japan's position in China, yet the conflict continued to expand under pressure from factions determined to build a new order in Asia. Foreign protests were ignored. In the spring and summer of 1939, Japan's navy seized Hainan Island from China and control over the Spratly Islands, a disputed archipelago of strategic importance.

During the summer of 1939, Roosevelt fired a shot across Japan's bow by nullifying the 1911 commercial treaty between the United States and Japan. Despite his action, Japan continued to purchase substantial stocks of oil, scrap metal, and machine tools from the United States. Within the Roosevelt administration, powerful figures such as Treasury Secretary Henry Morgenthau (1891–1967) and Interior Secretary Harold Ickes (1874–1952) pressed for greater U.S. support for China and tougher sanctions against Japan. During the summer of 1940, the United States imposed an embargo of aviation fuel against Japan, and Roosevelt moved the Pacific Fleet from its usual harbors on the West Coast of the United States to the forward base at Pearl Harbor, Hawaii, positioned to sail in defense of the United States' Pacific Island possessions.

Germany's defeat of France and the Netherlands left its Asian and Pacific colonies vulnerable, and it further encouraged Japanese militarists in their belief that the region was ripe for conquest. Although the United States refused to aid the Vichy regime in opposing the landing of Japanese forces in French Indo-China in July 1941, the move hardened Washington's resolve to halt Japanese expansion. Roosevelt allowed a squadron of volunteer fighter pilots, the famous "Flying Tigers," to fight in China. More significantly, he froze Japan's assets in the United States and made export licenses necessary for the sale of American commodities to Japan. After July 1941, Japan received no oil from the United States.

Although Roosevelt hoped economic sanctions would prevent a war with Japan, they became a rationalization for the prowar party in Tokyo. Japan's navy estimated its reserve of oil could run dry by year's end. The military clamored for possession of the oil fields of the Dutch East Indies as an important step toward achieving self-sufficiency.

> **THE PACIFIC FLEET**
>
> As early as 1820s, the U.S. Navy maintained a Pacific Squadron to look after American interests in that ocean, especially the whaling industry. From its early days, units of the squadron called on Pearl Harbor, a wide inlet near the Hawaiian capital of Honolulu on Oahu. The United States obtained exclusive rights from the Kingdom of Hawaii to use Pearl Harbor as a coaling and repair station in 1887. After the U.S. annexation of Hawaii (1898) and the squadron's elevation to the status of the Pacific Fleet (1907), American engineers began dredging Pearl Harbor's shallow estuary (entrance), enabling the lagoon to accommodate the navy's largest battleships.
>
> Although the military transformed Pearl Harbor into an important naval base, the Pacific Fleet remained headquartered in San Diego, California, until May 1940. The fleet moved to Pearl Harbor to counter the growing likelihood of war in the Pacific with Japan. However, U.S. leaders did not consider the possibility of a Japanese air attack on the facility. On the morning of December 7, 1941, most of the Pacific Fleet was at anchor in Pearl Harbor with the exception of the aircraft carriers, which were on maneuver. Twenty-one ships were lost or damaged during the attack, including eight battleships.
>
> Despite the destruction from Japanese bombs, operations at the port were rapidly restored, and most of the ships returned to service before the end of 1942. The naval installation remains a lynchpin for U.S. forces in the Pacific and operates today as Joint Base Pearl Harbor-Hickam.

Even at this late hour, many Japanese leaders hoped to avert war with the United States, starting with the emperor himself, who wondered about the prudence of such a move. Prince Konoye advocated war with the Soviet Union and tried desperately to find a diplomatic accord with the United States. There was talk throughout the summer of 1941 of a personal conference between Konoye and Roosevelt, but the United States insisted that a summit was impossible unless Japan halted "expansionist activities," a demand unacceptable to Japan's army command. The summer and fall of 1941 was a time of intrigue, conferences, and indecision among Japan's leadership. Weighing on their minds was the August 14 summit between Roosevelt and British Prime Minister Winston Churchill (1874–1965). The declaration resulting from that meeting, the Atlantic Charter, called for disarming aggressor nations and sovereignty for all occupied states. Some Japanese leaders read it as "tantamount to a declaration of war, for it obliged nations to accept the Anglo-American vision of a world order" (McClain 2002, 476). On September 6, civil and military officers gathered at the imperial palace in Tokyo to present their views to Hirohito. Konoe still spoke of final attempts to negotiate with the United States by promising to withdraw from Indo-China and halt further advances into China in exchange for restoring commercial relations. The emperor expressed his preference for peace by reading a poem extolling the brotherhood of humanity (Bix 2000, 414).

Despite anxiety over going to war, Japan's economy suffered from the embargo, and the army finalized plans to move against American, British, and Dutch colonies. The Philippines would be a springboard to the oil-rich Dutch East Indies (Indonesia). By taking Malaya and Burma, the Japanese hoped to cut Chiang's lifeline. The fall of Singapore would end British naval superiority in the Pacific. Hong Kong and Borneo would be seized; Guam and other U.S. islands in the western Pacific would be secured to help erect a picket fence of fortified islands to guard the empire. Meanwhile, Admiral Yamamoto was also ordered to prepare to attack Pearl Harbor. The war minister, General Tojo Hideki (1884–1948), insisted that nations must be willing to take risks, but even he had second thoughts as the hour approached (McClain 2002, 479). As those discussions continued, Konoe proclaimed the Great East Asia Co-Prosperity Sphere, a Japanese-dominated political-economic zone that would encompass East Asia and the Western Pacific. On October 16, after Konoye and his cabinet resigned, Tojo, named prime minister, finally received the Emperor's approval for war against the United States.

With fuel stocks running low, the navy was given until late November or early December to mount the attack. The date of December 7 was chosen in the hope that the fleet would be at anchor on a Sunday morning.

Admiral Yamamoto had tried to dissuade his superiors from pursuing war with the United States. Once the decision had been made, he focused on planning an assault to put American forces out of action long enough for Japan to consolidate its newly won empire. For the blow against Pearl Harbor, a fleet of aircraft had to be ferried within the 200-mile striking distance of Hawaii without being observed. Yamamoto's force of six aircraft carriers had to sail far from the shipping lanes, beginning in the Kuril Islands and cutting across the northern Pacific before plunging due south toward Hawaii.

The chief weapon for sinking warships, torpedoes, was useless in the 40-foot depth of Pearl Harbor. A torpedo dropped by air would sink to the bottom before it could get underway. Working frantically in time for the attack, Japanese technicians developed a stabilizing device that allowed torpedoes to operate in shallow water.

Despite the best planning, the operation was fraught with hazard. Should a stray foreign plane or fishing boat spot the Japanese fleet, the Americans would be alerted. Even if secrecy were maintained, there was no guaranty that the Pacific Fleet might not put to sea, leaving an empty port for Yamamoto to destroy. On the morning of December 6, Tokyo received word from its Hawaiian consulate that the fleet's battleships were at Pearl Harbor, but the three aircraft carriers were at sea. The admiralty decided to press ahead with the attack despite the missing carriers.

On December 7, the Pacific Fleet commander, Admiral Husband E. Kimmel (1882–1968), watched in stunned silence from the shore, and hundreds of tourists on Waikiki Beach thought they were witnessing a full dress naval drill. Despite the prospect of war in the Pacific, no one believed Hawaii could be struck by surprise. Within two hours, the second wave of Japanese planes had disappeared, leaving 2,402 dead Americans. Eight battleships and many smaller naval vessels had been sunk or badly damaged. Nearly 200 planes were destroyed. The Japanese lost only 29 of their aircraft plus several midget submarines. Yamamoto rejected sending a third wave of bombers to Hawaii, fearing that the missing American carriers might be able to locate his task force. If he had destroyed the dockyards and depots of Pearl Harbor, the Pacific Fleet might have been unable to operate from Hawaii for nearly a year. If the carriers had been sunk that morning, the United States would have been hard pressed to mount a rapid response.

In the United States, finger-pointing began within days. The commission of inquiry headed by U.S. Supreme Court Justice Owen J. Roberts (1875–1955) concluded in January 1942 that Admiral Kimmel and Hawaiian Department commander Lieutenant General Walter C. Short (1880–1949) were derelict in failing to take "appropriate measures of defense required by the imminence of hostilities." In fact, Kimmel and Short had prepared for an attack, but from the wrong direction, their measures aimed at Japanese saboteurs, not aviators. Washington had been reading Tokyo's coded diplomatic messages since late 1940 and knew that war was likely, yet the decoded signals included many mixed messages. Although an attack on the Philippines was anticipated, the U.S. commander, General Douglas MacArthur (1880–1964), did not expect it until spring.

One day after December 7, "a date that will live in infamy" as Roosevelt called it, the president appeared before Congress to ask for a declaration of war against Japan. The request was granted within hours. On December 11, Germany and Italy declared war on the United States, even though their treaty with Japan did not require them to do so. A day later, the United States returned the favor. America had been building its naval and air strength for over a year and had instituted the first peacetime draft in the country's history. Even before Pearl Harbor, the sleeping giant, the world's mightiest industrial power, had begun to stir. The Japanese attack served only to galvanize the nation.

DEPICTION AND HISTORICAL CONTEXT

Despite the pleasant climate, the army's Hawaiian Department was not a happy place for soldiers in the years before Pearl Harbor. *From Here to Eternity* suggests the toxic routine of apathy, alcohol, and arbitrary discipline characterizing the islands' garrisons. The islands were remote, connected by regular air service to the mainland only by the Pan-American China Clipper. Passage on the giant seaplanes was too expensive for enlisted men and most civilians. Soldiers and sailors felt isolated from mainland America and regarded Hawaii as a colonial outpost. They were often disrespected by Hawaiian civilians, who dismissed them as troublemakers loafing on the taxpayers' dollar. "Many servicemen hated the place. Some had not seen their families for almost two years." As shown in the film, they drank and played cards to kill the time. Violence was not uncommon; servicemen fought with gangs of local youths they called "gooks," and suicide rates at bases were abnormally high. A veteran of Schofield Barracks recalled the "pathetic sight" of soldiers lined up at bordellos; "with ten dollars a month in pay there was nothing for a private to do but take walks" (Clarke 1991, 140).

The military's presence on Oahu was inescapable. "A snapshot taken almost anywhere in Hawaii after 1900 would probably have included the figure of at least one soldier, sailor, marine, or defense construction worker" (Day 1955, 259). After its annexation by the United States (1898), Hawaii became America's bastion in the Central Pacific. The lynchpin was the naval station at Pearl Harbor, a natural inlet dredged of mud and coral to provide berths for battleships. Pearl Harbor was defended from attack by sea and land by a ring of forts, including the Hawaiian Department's headquarters at Fort Shafter. The largest Army base, Schofield Barracks, was established inland amid Oahu's pineapple fields. From *Here to Eternity*'s author James Jones recalled Schofield as "probably the most beautiful post the U.S. Army ever had" (Jones 1974, 242). During the 1920s, several army and navy airbases were constructed, including Wheeler Field adjacent to Schofield Barracks.

Along with the islands' pineapple and sugarcane plantations, "spending by the military and their dependents became vital to the economic well-being of the Territory." Prostitution was a major generator of revenue on Oahu. Territorial officials generally ignored the sex trade, and "military commanders preferred to allow prostitution in designated areas" to better control the spread of sexually transmitted diseases (Joestring 1972, 282).

The islands' racial tensions and animosity between segments of the population and the military was exemplified in the 1930s by the notorious "Massie Affair." Thalia Massie (1911–1963), the wife of a naval officer, left a party alone and turned up at home hours later, injured and claiming she was raped by "natives." The police arrested five "Honolulu hooligans" whose ethnicity included Hawaiian, Chinese, and Japanese. The evidence against them was so flimsy that the jury refused to bring a verdict in (Wright 1972, 81).

Rear Admiral Yates Stirling (1872–1948), the ranking naval officer in Hawaii, refused to accept the legal proceedings and demanded that the suspects be kept in jail "since their appearance on the streets of Honolulu might result in violence." Unease grew among officers, enlisted men, and their dependents, with many woman purchasing pistols for self-defense (Joestring 1972, 296). One of the defendants was kidnapped by Massie's husband and several sailors, who accidently killed him while trying to force a confession. The ensuing trial gained headlines across the United States, and although convicted of murder, their sentence was commuted by Hawaii's governor to one hour of detention (Wright 1972, 82).

The novel *From Here to Eternity* was more explicit, but the movie was confined within the censorship boundaries of the Hollywood Production Code. The screenplay barely suggests but never states the possibility that Lorene and her coworkers were selling sex to servicemen. *From Here to Eternity* was filmed at Schofield Barracks, which remained largely unchanged in the 12 years since Pearl Harbor. Street scenes were recreated accurately. The Honolulu of 1941 was a low-rise city of palm trees, shops with tin awnings, and homes with louvered windows. Dance halls and bars with jukeboxes and live bands lined the main streets and catered to GIs. Jones described a "swarming hive of bars, street vendors, tattoo parlors, shooting galleries, photo galleries, market shops, fruit and vegetable shops and hooker joints occupying the rooms upstairs" and called this half-mile area down close to Honolulu's docks as "the bottomless receptacle of our dreams and frustrations, and of our money" (Jones 1974, 242–243).

As seen in the newspapers read by Sergeant Warden, headlines in the months before Pearl Harbor were filled with rumors of war in Asia. American military and civilian leaders as well as editorial writers anticipated that Japan would expand its empire by attacking British and American possessions in Asia and the Pacific. The Philippines was regarded as a possible target, but Hawaii was deemed beyond reach. American policy and opinion makers underestimated the capacity of Japan's military.

In reality, as in the movie, life went on as usual in Hawaii in the days before the attack. An ocean liner docked in Honolulu, bringing tourists and no less than two college football teams to compete with the University of Hawaii. Hollywood cameramen were at work shooting backdrops for a movie set in Africa (Clarke 1991, 36). Honolulu was barely stirring on the morning of December 7 when Japanese dive bombers descended on the fleet and shore installations.

A more alert military might have been at battle stations before the first bombs fell. Over an hour before the attack began, a U.S. destroyer reported sinking a submarine trying to enter Pearl Harbor. Officers on land thought it was a false sighting, and Admiral Kimmel demanded "verification." Meanwhile, the army's new mobile radar unit on Oahu's northern coast picked up a large formation of planes 132 miles out, but their controllers at Fort Shafter decided it was a flight of B-17s due that day from California. The radar operator was told to "forget about it" (Symonds 2018, 204–205).

In later years, speculation circled around the "Magic" project, a secretive decoding operation maintained by military intelligence in Washington D.C. Isolationists charged that the United States deliberately ignored warnings and allowed the attack to occur in order to outrage American public opinion and pull the nation into war. Magic had broken Japan's diplomatic, but not its military, code. Suspicious messages from Tokyo to its embassy in Washington were intercepted, but there was no priority for what to decode and translate (Doenecke and Wilz 1991, 175). Two hours before the attack, a potentially alarming message reached the Chief of Naval Operations, who failed to call Kimmel but forwarded it instead to the Army Chief of Staff in Washington. It was too late by the time word reached Hawaii.

Snippets of actual footage shot at Pearl Harbor, showing the Pacific Fleet exploding into columns of fire and smoke are included in *From Here to Eternity*. The film is more focused on the damage to ground installations based on the fictionalized account of Jones, serving with the 27th Infantry Regiment at Schofield Barracks at the time of the attack. The movie falsely shows Schofield as one of the American bases targeted by Japanese planes, which overflew the barracks on the way to bombing Wheeler Field; the depiction otherwise conforms to events and might have been drawn from incidents at Kaneohe Naval Air Station. There, sailors broke into the armory and handed out pistols, rifles, and a .50 caliber machine gun. Positioning themselves on rooftops, the sailors fired on the second wave of low-flying Japanese planes. As in *From Here to Eternity*, they shot down two fighters (Clarke 1991, 215, 219–220).

Most of the movie's 1953 audience shared the experience of Prewitt and Lorene in learning of the attack while listening to the radio. The broadcasts heard in *From Here to Eternity* echo the high anxiety in Pearl Harbor's aftermath. Invasion was feared along with raids by parachutists and saboteurs. Hawaii was placed under martial law, and as in the movie, armed patrols scoured Oahu looking for suspicious activity. Although it could easily have happened in the confusion, no GIs were accidently killed. No incidents of sabotage occurred. However, nervous antiaircraft gunners at Pearl Harbor shot down four U.S. Navy planes, and at least six Hawaiian fishermen were killed when their boats were strafed by American aircraft that mistook the fishing boats for Japanese infiltrators.

Reflecting on the 50th anniversary of Pearl Harbor, one writer observed that none of the several cinematic depictions, including the highly detailed U.S.-Japanese coproduction *Tora! Tora! Tora!* (1970), gave any real glimpse of the carnage that occurred. The corpses of the dead were stacked up to the windowsills of the Hickam Field Army Hospital. "Forty garbage cans filled with amputated limbs were seen outside the Tripler Army Hospital" (Clarke 1991, 153). The water was blackened with a heavy coating of oil set ablaze by exploding ammunition stores. Sixty percent of American casualties on that day were from burns.

CONCLUSION

Although *From Here to Eternity* is the most beloved and popular movie about Pearl Harbor, scarcely 10 minutes of its two hours is set during the attack and its immediate aftermath. However, "the sudden collapse of urgent personal stories in the name of war is what is most impressive about this picture, and most true to the mood of 1941" (Thomson 2008, 314). For many audience members in 1953, Pearl Harbor was a defining and unforgettable incident in their lives regardless of where they were when news broke of the attack. Prewitt's trek from the comfort of Lorene's home to Schofield Barracks represented the way millions of ordinary people suspended their dreams, their hopes for the future, in the name of defending the nation in war. That Prewitt's trek was doomed only added to the pathos. Over 400,000 American service people lost their lives in the war that followed Pearl Harbor.

FURTHER READING

Barker, A. J. 1969. *Pearl Harbor*. New York: Ballantine Books.
Bix, Herbert P. 2000. *Hirohito and the Making of Modern Japan*. New York: HarperCollins.
Brogdon, William. 1953. "From Here to Eternity." *Variety*, July 29, 1953. https://variety.com/1953/film/reviews/from-here-to-eternity-2-1200417558/
Clarke, Thurston. 1991. *Pearl Harbor Ghosts: A Journey to Hawaii Then and Now*. New York: William Morrow.
Crowther, Bosley. 1953. "'From Here to Eternity' Bows at Capitol with Huge Cast, Five Starring Roles." *New York Times*, August 6, 1953. https://www.nytimes.com/1953/08/06/archives/the-screen-in-review-from-here-to-eternity-bows-at-capitol-with.html
Day, A. Grove. 1955. *Hawaii and Its People*. New York: Duell, Sloan and Pearce.
Doenecke, Justus D., and John E. Wilz. 1991. *From Isolation to War, 1931–1941*. Arlington Heights, IL: Harlan Davidson.
Ebert, Roger. 1995. "100 Great Movie Moments." RogerEbert.com, April 23, 1995. https://www.rogerebert.com/rogers-journal/100-great-movie-moments.
Jeansonne, Glen, with David Luhrssen. 2016. *Hoover: A Life*. New York: New American Library.
Joestring, Edward. 1972. *Hawaii: An Uncommon History*. New York: W. W. Norton.
Johnson, Paul. 1991. *Modern Times: From the Twenties to the Nineties*. New York: HarperCollins.
Jones, James. 1974. *Viet Journal*. New York: Delacorte Press.

Levy, Shawn. 1998. *Rat Pack Confidential: Frank, Dean, Sammy, Peter, Joey & the Last Great Showbiz Party*. New York: Doubleday.

McClain, James L. 2002. *Japan: A Modern History*. New York: W. W. Norton.

Symonds, Craig L. 2018. *World War II at Sea: A Global History*. New York: Oxford University Press.

Thomson, David. 2008. *Have You Seen . . . ? A Personal Introduction to 1,000 Films*. New York: Alfred A. Knopf.

Wright, Theon. 1972. *The Disenchanted Isles: The Story of the Second Revolution in Hawaii*. New York: Dial Press.

Yoshitake, Oka. 1992. *Konoe Fuminato: A Political Biography*. Lanham, MD: Madison Books.

Chapter 5

The Bridge on the River Kwai (1957)

Released on October 2, 1957, in Great Britain and on December 14, 1957, in the United States, *The Bridge on the River Kwai* is the most memorable cinematic depiction of the cruelty of Japanese prisoner of war (POW) camps in the Pacific and East Asia. Sam Spiegel (1901–1985), an American, produced the film, which Columbia Pictures released. An American, Spiegel assembled ideas, casts, and financing for pictures, often filmed overseas, and sold the finished product to Hollywood studios for distribution. Actress Katharine Hepburn (1907–2003) introduced Spiegel to the film's director, David Lean (1908–1991), little known outside his British homeland but already building an international reputation for directing prestige films. As a result of the success of *The Bridge on the River Kwai*, Lean became a go-to filmmaker for high-budgeted historical epics such as *Lawrence of Arabia* (1962) and *Doctor Zhivago* (1965).

A pair of Americans, Carl Foreman (1914–1984) and Michael Wilson (1914–1978), wrote the screenplay. Both were living in European exile, blacklisted in Hollywood for their refusal to expose members of the Communist Party. They adapted the story from the novel *Bridge over the River Kwai* (1952) by French author Pierre Boulle (1912–1994), who drew from his wartime experience in a prison camp. Lean rewrote much of their work, especially dialogue among the story's British prisoners of war (Santas 2012, 2).

Boulle's characters are retained but with a few significant alterations. Commander Shears, an escaped POW who returns to the camp as a member of an elite commando team, was British in the novel. After Spiegel requested the inclusion of a prominent American character for the sake of audience appeal in the United States, Lean transformed Shears into a Yank, played by popular Hollywood leading man William Holden (1918–1981). The Japanese POW camp commandant, Colonel Saito, was described by Boulle as a sadistic, drunken "grotesque figure" (Boulle 1964, 28–29). At Lean's insistence, Saito is a hard yet more sympathetic man as depicted by Sessue Hayakawa (1886–1973), a Japanese actor who had played Asian villains in Hollywood silent movies.

Set in early 1943 and focused on Japanese Camp 16 in Burma (Myanmar), *The Bridge on the River Kwai* is a battle of wits between Saito and his British counterpart, the senior Allied officer imprisoned in the camp, Colonel Nicholson, played by Britain's most popular film star at the time, Alec Guinness (1914–2000). Ironically, Saito and Nicholson are flip sides of the same recording, repeating the maxims inscribed on them by military discipline and dedication to what they regard as the particular virtues of their nations. Saito, whose code refuses to admit the possibility of an honorable surrender, despises his prisoners and uses them as slave labor to build a bridge on the jungle railroad line connecting Bangkok with Rangoon. Nicholson insists that the Geneva Convention on Prisoners of War (1929), the international agreement covering POWs, forbids the employment of captive officers as laborers.

Nicholson is determined to maintain discipline and esprit de corps among his troops. He leads his men into Camp 16 whistling and marching in snappy steps. If not for their ragged shoes and uniforms, they could have been at home on their regimental parade ground. Mounting a platform, Saito informs the newly arrived POWs that they will be tasked with constructing a segment of the strategically important railroad, including a bridge, and will be punished for any sign of idleness. Nicholson immediately brings up his point about the Geneva Convention, politely showing Saito his copy of the international agreement. Saito slaps Nicholson in the face with the pamphlet and orders the officers to get to work. They refuse. Saito brings up a machine gun detachment that appears ready to slaughter the prisoners, but the camp's British medical officer, Major Clipton (James Donald, 1917–1993), rushes in and demands, "Is this your soldier's code, murdering unarmed men?" Shamed by the accusation, Saito allows the officers to live but penalizes them with confinement to "punishment huts." The cramped, corrugated metal sheds grow hot as ovens in the tropical sun. Nicholson is kept in a separate hut, suffering in solitary confinement, but remains unbroken despite his agony.

Saito's problem is that the segment of the railroad he is responsible for building is falling behind schedule. He will be punished for failure. Clipton, perhaps the character in the story with the firmest grasp on reality, suggests that the British enlisted men would work harder, and refrain from deliberately sloppy work amounting to sabotage, if they were led by their own officers. He eventually sways Nicholson to the same view.

In a reversal of the roles of commander and subordinate, Saito places Nicholson in charge of the construction project and puts himself and his men at the British officer's disposal. Nicholson relishes not only the responsibility of command but sees the undertaking as an opportunity to rebuild the morale of his battalion, demonstrate British ingenuity and superiority to the Japanese "barbarians," and erect a monument as long lasting as the London Bridge. In the early scenes of *The Bridge on the River Kwai*, he seems a man of great moral courage, but by the end he is captive to delusions of grandeur.

The film's secondary plot concerns Shears. He is seen in early scenes offering wisecracking commentary on the situation in Camp 16. His easy manner in the face of danger and authority, his glib tongue and can-do optimism armored with a touch of cynicism, was a familiar American type in mid-20th-century popular culture. Determined not to die a prisoner, he escapes the camp with two fellow POWs; however, he is the only survivor. While recuperating in Ceylon, Shears is given the unwanted assignment of joining Force 316 because of his familiarity with their target, the bridge being built at Camp 16.

Force 316, commanded by Major Warden (Jack Hawkins, 1910–1973), also includes a Canadian, Lieutenant Joyce (Geoffrey Horne, 1933–). They parachute into the jungle of Thailand and, with the help of a Thai guide and a trio of women shouldering their arms and supplies, make their way to Camp 16. The commandos wire the bridge with plastic explosives and intend to detonate the structure just as a train, bearing a Japanese official, crosses the bridge.

Their mission is complicated by Nicholson, who spots their wires and leads Saito to the detonator. Suspense builds as the whistle of the approaching train grows louder. In the ensuing struggle, Saito, Shears, and Joyce are killed, and Nicholson, dying, stumbles onto the detonator, touching off the explosion and destroying the bridge he built just as the train is halfway across. Whether Nicholson's destruction of the bridge is accidental or the result of a sudden realization that he had become a collaborator with the enemy is left unclear. "Madness, madness," Clipton murmurs as he surveys the wreckage and the lost lives.

Although it was plagued by budget overruns, *The Bridge on the River Kwai* cost only $2,800,000, grossed $22 million worldwide, and was the top earning film in the United States and Canada in 1958 (Steinberg 1980, 23). Reviews by critics at the time of its release were generally positive. The entertainment industry trade paper *Variety* praised the film for its "mounting suspense," "memorable scenes," and "notable performances from the key characters." *Variety* cited Guinness's "unforgettable portrait of a typical British army officer," Hayakawa for rendering "an admixture of cruelty and correctness born of a lifetime of training," and Holden as "easy, credible and always likeable" (Kaplan 1957). The *New York Times* lauded the movie as "a towering entertainment of rich variety and revelation of the ways of men" as it explores the "discipline and conformity [that] are the obsession of the professional militarist." The critic added: "Here is a film we guarantee you'll not forget" (Crowther 1957).

His prophecy was proven correct. In the immediate future after release, *The Bridge on the River Kwai* earned seven Academy Awards, including Best Picture, Best Director, and Best Actor (Guinness), as well as Editing, Cinematography, and Music. *The Bridge on the River Kwai* also won for Best Screenplay, a prize awarded to Boulle even though he had no role in adapting his novel for the screen and did not speak English. He received the prize due to Foreman and Wilson being blacklisted at the time. In 1985, the academy posthumously awarded Foreman and Wilson with the Oscar they deserved, and after 1994, their names were added to home video releases (Phillips 2006, 252). Hayakawa received a nomination but did not win for Best Supporting Actor.

During the final decades of the 20th century, many film historians denigrated *The Bridge on the River Kwai* as "middle-brow" and stiffly directed (Thomson 2008, 125). However, recent years have seen a favorable reassessment (Santas 2012, xx), and film buffs and filmmakers never abandoned it. Steven Spielberg cited *The Bridge on the River Kwai* as an inspiration for *Indiana Jones and the Temple of Doom* (1984) (Spielberg 2003). It has been included in lists of Top 100 action movies of all time (Clark 2003) and as one of the most influential films ever made (Kenny 2004). Film critic Roger Ebert praised it for being "less interested in who wins than in how individual characters will behave" (Ebert 1999). The argument continues over whether to call it an American or a British film. In 1997, the Library of Congress added *The Bridge on the River Kwai* to the National Film Registry for its historical and cultural significance, and in 1999, the British Film Institute ranked it as the "11th Greatest British Film of the 20th Century."

HISTORICAL BACKGROUND

At the time *The Bridge on the River Kwai* was released, American audiences related the film to the widely circulated reports on the cruel treatment of prisoners by the Japanese army. The majority of American POWs had surrendered in the Philippines in the opening months of the war, and many were survivors of one of the most infamous episodes of the war in the Pacific, the Bataan Death March.

The Japanese assault on the Philippines, a commonwealth under the American flag, began within hours of Pearl Harbor. Despite months of rising apprehension over the coming of war, the commanding officer of the U.S. Army Forces in the Far East, General Douglas MacArthur (1880–1964), thought the Japanese attack would begin in April 1942 after the monsoon season ended (Underbrink 1971, x). Even when news of Pearl Harbor reached the islands, U.S. forces in the Philippines seemed surprised by the arrival of the Japanese. Some military personnel believed that Japan would bypass the islands on their campaign of conquest because the defenses were far too formidable to make a landing. Army Private Lester Tenney remembered, "We felt secure knowing that our air force would not be the victims of a surprise attack like those bombed on Pearl Harbor" (Tenney 1995, 1). However, within hours of the raid on Pearl Harbor, Japanese bombers filled the sky over Clark Field, 50 miles northwest of Manila, the capital of the Philippines. The B-17 bombers and P-40 fighters on the runways were reduced to twisted metal. The U.S. Navy was better prepared. The Asiatic Fleet left port before Japanese planes destroyed Cavite Navy Yard and survived to fight a losing battle at sea in the coming weeks.

On paper, the army forces of the Far East looked impressive. It numbered 120,000 men, but fewer than 20,000 were U.S. Army regulars. An additional 12,000 troops belonged to the Philippine Scouts, a well-drilled division that fought hard against the invaders. The remaining soldiers were Filipino army reservists, poorly trained and prepared and armed in some units with blanks instead of live cartridges. "The boldness of the attack amazed us," Smith said. Regarding U.S. military preparations, he added, "There appeared to be a general lack of organization and coordination all around us" in the U.S. military (Smith 1991, 6, 17).

The American forces faced more than 40,000 Japanese troops, who landed north of Manila on December 21, 1941. In a radio broadcast, MacArthur claimed, "My gallant divisions are holding ground and denying the foe the sacred soil of the Philippines. We have inflicted heavy casualties on his troops and nowhere is his bridgehead secure. Tomorrow we will drive him into the sea" (Ward and Burns 2007, 23).

In reality, the Japanese drove rapidly inland as a second landing force of 10,000 came ashore south of Manila. On December 24, MacArthur, his officers, and their families along with leading figures in the Philippines government, including President Manuel L. Quezon (1878–1944), fled Manila for the safety of Corregidor. The fortress island at the mouth of Manila Bay was honeycombed with tunnels and bunkers. Twenty-nine batteries of heavy artillery were embedded in the mountainside. Corregidor was called "the Rock" and "the Gibraltar of the Far East." It was regarded as impregnable (Smith 1991, 5).

Corregidor sat offshore near the tip of the Bataan Peninsula, a jungle-covered arm of land that was, along with Corregidor, essential to War Plan Orange. A long-standing contingency in place in the event of an attack on the Philippines, War Plan Orange called for a "fighting withdrawal" of ground forces to Bataan, covering the landward approach to Corregidor (Underbrink 1971, 19). The plan's premise was that Corregidor could withstand siege for as long as six months, denying Imperial Japanese Navy access to Manila Bay with its big guns while awaiting the arrival of reinforcements guarded by the Pacific Fleet. However, the attack on Pearl Harbor disabled the Pacific Fleet. No relief was in sight. By February, U.S. forces had already beaten back two major Japanese assaults on Bataan, but the Japanese had time and attrition on its side. Time was running out for the Americans and their Filipino allies.

With defeat in sight, MacArthur, Quezon, and key staff were ordered to evacuate Corregidor by PT boat on March 11, 1942. Quezon spent the remaining years of his life in the United States, where he headed a Philippines government in exile. MacArthur was posted to Australia as Supreme Commander of Allied forces in the Pacific. He dispatched a message to the Philippines, promising, "I shall return." He also ordered his troops to "fight to the last man." Faced with an enormity of suffering, his officers, in the end, had other ideas (Ward and Burns 2007, 38).

Even before their surrender, conditions were poor for the troops on Bataan. Wounds or disease incapacitated three of every four Bataan defenders. Medicine, ammunition, and food were in short supply. The men subsisted on short rations of rice and ate reptiles, wild pigs, water buffalos, and even their own horses and mules. By March 1942, rations were reduced to 800 calories per day. "At the end there was one can of salmon issued to thirty-five men and very little rice, so our situation was deteriorating and getting worse every day," recalled Corporal Glenn Frazier (Ward and Burns 2007, 38). Dengue fever and malaria became widespread. "We defenders of Bataan were killed or wounded at an alarming rate. The dispirited U.S. and Filipino troops were tired, sick, and starving. Continued resistance was virtually impossible," Tenney recalled (Tenney 1995, 31). On April 9, the commanding officer on Bataan, Major General Edward P. King (1884–1958), surrendered.

Conditions on Corregidor were considerably better. Fewer servicemen on the island contracted the tropical diseases that spread through the crowded camps in the Bataan jungle. When Major General Jonathan M. Wainwright IV (1883–1953) raised the white flag over Corregidor, the victorious Japanese found large stocks of canned food.

As a result of the one-month gap between the surrender of Bataan and Corregidor, the Japanese took control of U.S. POWs in two contingents. Seventy-six thousand U.S. and Filipino troops were taken on Bataan and 13,000 on Corregidor. The 25,000 Filipino civilians who fled to Bataan ahead of the Japanese advance added to the humanitarian disaster. The situation for Americans was seldom favorable, but the larger number of servicemen who surrendered on Bataan had it worst. Before surrendering, General King asked his Japanese counterpart, General Masaharu Homma

(1887–1946), if his men would be treated decently. The Japanese commander promised fair treatment. "We are not barbarians," he said (Ward and Burns 2007, 38).

In reality, the Japanese command gave no forethought to the fate of their windfall of prisoners on Bataan and began pushing them on foot up the peninsula as their own forces proceeded down toward the tip of the coast for the final move against Corregidor. Nearly 10,000 POWs perished during the Death March. Among the Japanese, "confusion reigned, and it seemed that no specific officer was in charge, which made the task of maintaining control almost impossible" (Tenney 1995, 44). The brutality that resulted from lack of planning was compounded by two factors. The Japanese army steeled its recruits with brutal discipline. Soldiers were forced to stand at attention for an entire day as punishment for infractions and were beaten for "disobeying orders" if they fell (Kinvig 1992, 10–11). Ill-treatment was no stranger to the Japanese soldier. In addition, the Japanese code of Bushido held surrender as shameful and called for death before dishonor. To many Japanese, enemy soldiers who capitulated were unworthy of respect or even human consideration.

In the early hours after the U.S. surrender on Bataan, some Japanese soldiers asked the POWs for cigarettes. Others simply took them (Tenney 1995, 43). The roads of the Death March had been ruined by tank and half-track treads and were pitted with holes and covered with broken gravel, which made walking difficult. Temperatures climbed to 100 degrees. POWs who fell from exhaustion were sometimes bayonetted by the Japanese or run over by trucks. Some Japanese soldiers shared their ration of rice and fish with the Americans, and some allowed them to fill their canteens from roadside wells. Others refused to let the POWs drink. Many prisoners were shot for no particular reason. Despite the difficulty in moving the columns forward, "the Japanese soldiers hollered and prodded us with their bayonets to walk faster" (Tenney 1995, 46).

The accounts by American survivors of the Bataan Death March seldom varied. "I saw men beaten with a rifle butt until there was no more life in them. I saw Filipino women (who tried to bring us food or water) cut," Frazier recalled. "I saw Filipinos and Americans beheaded just with one swipe of a saber" (Ward and Burns 2007, 41). Some GIs tried to read motivations in the behavior of their captors. "The Japanese were trying very hard to humiliate the Americans any way they could in front of the Filipinos, as if to prove Japanese superiority" (Tenney 1995, 60).

When they finally reached the top of the Bataan Peninsula, the POWs were herded onto cattle cars. As many as 100 men were packed shoulder to shoulder in each car and sent by rail on a three-hour journey. Some men died standing up. The survivors were forced to march an additional six miles on foot to Camp O'Donnell, formerly a base for Philippine reservists. More than 55,000 Filipinos and some 9,000 Americans were crowded into the facility, which "offered precious little comfort to the men who managed to reach it" (Ward and Burns 2007, 42–43). Nearly 22,000 POWs died from neglect.

The experiences of the men who surrendered on Corregidor a month after Bataan were similar yet distinct. Major John Wright Jr., an officer in the Coast Artillery, recalled that his watch was stolen by a Japanese soldier. However, a Japanese officer knocked the soldier down, returned the watch, and apologized. Other POWs were stripped almost entirely of their belongings. He also regretted the behavior of his own men. "The day after the surrender many men questioned the authority of any officer or enlisted man to enforce discipline," he complained. "There was an immediate collapse of discipline, respect, and the other elements of military training" (Wright 1988, 5, 7).

Many of the Corregidor POWs were kept for as many as 16 days on the beach without shelter until they were packed onto small boats and shipped to Manila. The boats were so crowded on deck "that many men were unable to find room to sit down." The Japanese "slapped faces, kicked shins, shoved groups of men until they fell down, then got together and laughed" (Wright 1988, 10). As they were marched down the streets of Manila, guards clubbed some men who fell. On the other hand, an elderly army officer who conducted himself with great dignity was helped to his feet and carried by his captors. The Corregidor prisoners were held at Manila's Bilibid Prison before being taken by train in cars with standing room only to Cabatuan, 90 miles north of Manila, a Philippines army base converted into a POW camp.

The capitulation of Bataan was the largest surrender in U.S. Army history. The Americans and Filipinos fought bravely with little chance of victory, yet their rearguard action gave the Allies time to shore up defenses in Australia, which became the forward base in the campaign to defeat Japan. In a process that began slowly within months of their surrender but accelerated as the war continued, many POWs were moved to labor camps in Formosa, Japan, Korea, Manchukuo, and Burma. The American commanding officers in the Philippines who arranged the surrender, General King and General Wainwright, were poorly treated in captivity. Both men expected to face a court martial after the war for disobeying MacArthur's orders to fight to the death. Instead, they were greeted as heroes in the United States and awarded the Medal of Honor. The Japanese commander responsible for the Bataan Death March, General Homma, was tried by an American tribunal for crimes against the rules of war and executed by the firing squad.

DEPICTION AND HISTORICAL CONTEXT

Had it been real, *The Bridge on the River Kwai*'s Camp 16 would have been rated among the best Japanese prisons for Allied POWs as a model facility whose inmates lived in relative comfort as long as they obeyed the rules. The film adaptation softened the cruelty and deprivation depicted in Pierre Boulle's novel. In his book, sick and starving prisoners endured "beating-up, butt-end blows, and even worse forms of brutality"; Boulle describes men "covered with ulcers and jungle sores. Some of them can hardly walk" (Boulle 1964, 4, 120). His description was closer to the truth than the movie.

In a History Channel documentary on *The Bridge on the River Kwai*, surviving POWs condemned the film as "Hollywood fiction" for "romanticizing" their experiences (History Channel 1999). However, the full horror of the prisoners would not have passed movie censorship in the 1950s, nor would it have found a large moviegoing audience. As one film historian put it, "It is not possible to starve actors to the point where they look as emaciated or sick as the prisoners of war were." He correctly added, "The filmmakers did attempt to render prison camp conditions as accurately as possible, being as loyal as they could to both the original source—the novel—and what history told" (Santas 2012, 11).

The original source for *The Bridge on the River Kwai* was a military thriller written by a veteran whose experiences became the basis for his fiction. Boulle was in the French army, stationed in Indo-China, when World War II began. An early convert to Charles De Gaulle's Free French, he deserted and joined an Allied commando team, Force 136, the inspiration for the novel and the film's Force 316. After landing in Indo-China on a mission, Vichy authorities captured Boulle and sentenced him to a prison camp. For his novel, he transposed his imprisonment experiences to a Japanese POW camp but had no firsthand contact with Japanese captivity.

The railroad project at the heart of *The Bridge on the River Kwai* was real. The Japanese laid some 400 miles of track through the jungle of Burma and Siam. Burma was a British colony that fell to Japan as part of the Pacific offensive that began on December 7, 1941, with the assault on Pearl Harbor. Siam was a different situation. The country's fascist regime, modeled after Benito Mussolini's Italy, was allied with Japan, and as the war began, it changed the country's name to Thailand to reflect the dominance of the land's ethnic majority group. However, the name change was seldom acknowledged by foreigners during the war years. Siam declared war on Great Britain and the United States in January 1942 and allowed Japanese troops to operate freely within its borders (Wyatt 1984, 252–260). The Siamese regime also permitted the construction of a railroad linking its capital, Bangkok, to Burma's capital, Rangoon, and extending from there to the Burmese border with India. The railroad seen in *The Bridge on the River Kwai* was a short segment of that line.

Japan hoped the railroad would secure Japan's control over Burma and ferry troops to the border of India for the planned invasion of the subcontinent. The Japanese forced 100,000 Allied POWs to work on the project; 14,000 perished during construction. Unseen in the film were the many thousands of Burmese and ethnic Chinese residents of Siam and Malaya "recruited" by the Japanese to cart supplies and lay track along with the POWs (Basche 1971, 93).

Boulle chose the site of his story randomly with no direct knowledge of conditions. He told his biographer, "I took an atlas and I looked for the river where they were building the Siam-Burma Railway. I didn't know the River Kwai before I wrote the book" (Becker 1996, 47). Boulle and director David Lean simplified the geography. There are two "river Kwais" in the real-life story. The Siam-Burma Railroad followed the course of the Kwae Noi (Little Kwai), and a bridge spanned the Kwae Yai (Big Kwai). That bridge was not destroyed by commandos as in the movie but by Royal Air Force B-24 Liberator bombers flying from India (Kinvig 1992, xii).

The plot of *The Bridge on the River Kwai* turns around the clash of values between the British POW commander, Colonel Nicholson, and the Japanese commandant, Colonel Saito. The sticking point was the Geneva Convention on the Treatment of Prisoners of War (1929), which Japan signed but never formally ratified. In 1942, the Japanese government promised to adhere to the treaty's principles, but the army ignored the spirit and only occasionally obeyed the letter of the pact. As seen in the film, POWs were sometimes given the packages sent to them by the International Red Cross, providing much needed food and personal items, but the Japanese released them only as an award for obedience (Smith 1991, 63).

The national composition of the POWs in Camp 16 is not unrealistic, yet, although the majority of prisoners building the rail line were of British or Commonwealth origin, many camps would have included a greater diversity of prisoners including Dutch and American POWs. The sole American in Camp 16, Shears identified himself as a crewman from the USS *Houston*, a heavy cruiser from the Asiatic Fleet. His story is realistic. The *Houston* was one of several Allied warships sunk in the Battle of the Sunda Strait (February 28, 1942). Nearly 400 of the *Houston*'s sailors swam to shore and were captured by the Japanese (Symonds 2018, 233–234).

Although the film's screenplay never alludes to the back story of its British POWs, nearly all of them would have surrendered with the capitulation of Malaya and Singapore (February 15, 1942). They endured nothing comparable to the Bataan Death March but maintained good order, "marching in strict step" to captivity according to Second Lieutenant Eric Lomax of the Royal Signal Corps (Lomax 1995, 71). His recollection sounds much like the opening scene of *The Bridge on the River Kwai*. Some soldiers may have sung or whistled the tune heard in the movie. "The Colonel Bogey March," originally a World War I Royal Army marching song, was revived in World War II with a new set of words mocking the leaders of Nazi Germany (Phillips 2006, 243). Given that they were fighting in the Asian theater against Japan, British troops may well have dispensed with the words and whistled the tune instead.

> **BATTLE OF SINGAPORE (FEBRUARY 8–15, 1942)**
>
> The British called Singapore the "Gibraltar of the East." The city at the tip of the Malayan Peninsula was Great Britain's largest naval base outside the home islands. Like Pearl Harbor for the United States, Singapore was key to British strategy in the Pacific and home port for a fleet of battleships supported by lesser warships.
>
> Heavy coastal artillery defended Singapore, firing armor piercing shells designed to sink warships; however, the artillery proved less useful against the waves of Japanese infantry that assaulted the bastion. Japanese decoys deceived the British commander, Lieutenant General Arthur Percival (1887–1966), who allocated his ground forces in the wrong sectors. Most of the aircraft at his disposal were obsolete and no match for Japanese flyers. Japanese planes sunk two of the Royal Navy's battleships on December 10, leaving the Malayan coastline vulnerable to amphibious attack. Once they landed, Japan's infantry advanced swiftly, often riding bicycles along jungle paths.
>
> Although Percival inflicted heavy casualties on the attackers, Japan largely isolated Singapore by air and sea, and the city's garrison ran low on ammunition and other supplies. Percival surrendered 80,000 British, Australian, and Indian troops, many of them ending up in forced labor camps, constructing projects similar to the rail line in *The Bridge on the River Kwai*. Singapore was one of Britain's greatest military defeats.

However, by the time British POWs reached Siam and Burma later in 1942, many had already been subjected to drastic punishments for refusing to obey Japanese orders. Several prisoners were publicly shot by the firing squad. When that failed to cow the POWs, 16,000 men were forced into Selarung Barracks near Changi, Malaya, a base meant to house only 800. Conditions were similar to Camp O'Donnell in the Philippines but were intended as a temporary situation, meant to force the POWs to sign a "non-escape form" pledging cooperation with Japan. British officers eventually ordered their men to sign, and afterward, prisoners were dispersed to less uncomfortable surroundings (Lomax 1995, 79–80).

Conditions varied for the POWs along the Siam-Burma Railroad. Lomax was first posted to a railroad repair yard in Ban Pong, Siam. He described the Japanese mechanics in charge as "humane men interested in getting a job done, and their workshops were not cruelly managed. I could respect them and they let me and my comrades alone" (Lomax 1995, 87).

The majority of prisoners worked in the jungle and had it much worse. *The Bridge on the River Kwai* does not depict the full severity faced by the POWs in laying track through difficult terrain, often hilly and choked by brush and bamboo. The prisoners labored without machinery, clearing thickets with saws and axes. "The pace of work was intense, the prisoners driven by Japanese guards under a hot sun on a patchy diet" as they laid steel rails in 24-foot lengths, "a massive thing for hungry men to lift and manoeuvre into position." Lomax added, "Rest periods were rare, and any slackening was met with abuse or violence" (Lomax 1995, 86). Earthen and rocky hills were hauled away by hand to make way for the track bed. "Hundreds of half-naked men were passing the earth in baskets" (Lomax 1995, 87).

The bamboo prisoner huts in *The Bridge on the River Kwai* are correctly built but convey no impression of how riddled they were with snakes, spiders, and insects. The film also avoids showing the toll charged by disease on the prisoners. Malaria, dengue fever, and dysentery were common. Latrine accommodations were crude. As in the film, the huts were grouped together inside camps encircled by barbed wire and guard towers. The jungle beyond the perimeter provided no easy escape routes.

Punishments meted out to Colonel Nicholson and his officers correspond to recorded events. "I had seen men forced to stand hour after hour in the full blaze of the sun for some infringement of camp discipline" (Lomax 1995, 94). The "ovens" or sweat boxes where Nicholson and his cohort are confined are also realistic. "The heat was suffocating after the sun came up and it seemed to suck the air out of the cage," Lomax wrote, adding that the torment was psychological as well as physical. "I could not even account for the normal interchange of night and day and my mind was confused, sometimes even to the point of oblivion" (Lomax 1995, 129–130, 131).

Perhaps Nicholson's mad zeal on behalf of his captors is the result of psychological breakdown under torture as much as the quirks of his own personality. His eagerness to do a good job for the enemy might be the one thing separating him from most Allied commanders in the camps. A British military historian dismissed Nicholson's portrayal, complaining that few prisoners "would have recognized their commanding officer in Alec Guinness's Colonel Nicholson" (Kinvig 1992, xii). However, that same historian cites the example of an Australian senior officer, Brigadier Arthur Varley (1893–1944), who "cooperated, as did all the other commanders in varying degrees, and by so doing gained considerable leverage" with the Japanese camp commandant (Kinvig 1992, 59). As a British POW wrote after the war, to survive, a prisoner could not avoid "collaborating with the Japanese" (Watt 1959).

Incongruously, amid the casual and negligent brutality of camp life, friendly exchanges occurred between captors and captives. Lomax recalled a Japanese officer who spoke to him in English about engineering and arranged for the POWs a subscription to the *Bangkok Chronicle*, a pro-Japanese English language newspaper (Lomax 1995, 99–100). He was not unlike Saito in his more solicitous and benign moods. The Japanese sometimes allowed prisoners to perform "vaudeville shows" for their own entertainment like the one shown in the movie (Smith 1991, 59).

The strong undercurrent of realism running through the film's production resulted in part from the efforts of screenwriter Michael Wilson, who served in the U.S. Marines in the South Pacific during the war. The film's military advisor, Major General L. E. M. Perowne, had commanded a British commando unit in the Far East during the war (Phillips 2006, 231, 235).

Many small details in the film are accurate. The bridge's design came from a sketch on faded rice paper of a bridge along the Burma railroad built by POWs during the war. The bridge seen in the film was not a model but was actually constructed and destroyed with explosives. The locomotive that toppled into the river was also real and not unlike the sort of trains the Japanese employed on the route (Phillips 2006, 235, 243). The ragged appearance of the prisoners reflected the reality of men who had been marched from place to place over many months of hard labor.

CONCLUSION

The Bridge on the River Kwai gives an accurate suggestion, but not a rendering in gruesome detail, of conditions in Japanese prisoner of war camps and touches on the importance of the Geneva Convention as a set of guidelines intended to govern the camps.

The Western Allies and Nazi Germany largely adhered to the Geneva Convention and generally sought to observe the rules of war for prisoners whose common humanity they acknowledged. Nazi mistreatment of Soviet prisoners was guided by a racist ideology that deemed them as members of lower races, and Soviet mistreatment of German POWs was fueled by hatred and revenge. Conditions for prisoners on the Eastern Front of the war in Europe were roughly comparable to the experience of Allied prisoners of the Japanese. Given the harshness of combat in the Pacific coupled with Japan's soldierly code, relatively few Japanese prisoners fell into Allied hands.

The only prisoners who suffered worse conditions were usually noncombatants, the European Jews deported by the Nazis to ghettos and death camps. The Japanese cared little if their Allied prisoners survived. By contrast, the Nazis were determined that their Jewish prisoners would not survive. Retribution from the Allies came swiftly. By the end of 1946, some 33 Japanese officers were executed by Allied tribunals for their inhumane treatment of POWs.

FURTHER READING

Basche, James. 1971. *Thailand: Land of Freedom.* New York: Caplinger.
Becker, Lucille. 1996. *Pierre Boulle.* New York: Twayne.
Boulle, Pierre. 1964. *The Bridge over the River Kwai.* New York: Time.
Clark, Jason. 2003. "100 Best Action Movies on DVD." *Premiere*, February 2003.

Crowther, Bosley. 1957. "'The Bridge on the River Kwai' Opens: Memorable War Film Stars Alec Guinness as Militarist Portrayed in Jungle Drama." *New York Times*, December 19, 1957. https://www.nytimes.com/1957/12/19/archives/screen-the-bride-on-the-river-kwai-opens-memorable-war-film-stars.html

Ebert, Roger. 1999. "The Bridge on the River Kwai." RogerEbert.com, April 18, 1999.

History Channel. 1999. *The True Story of The Bridge on the River Kwai*. Released on DVD 1995. https://www.amazon.com/Story-Bridge-River-History-Channel/dp/B000AABL12

Kaplan, Mike. 1957. "The Bridge on the River Kwai." *Variety*, November 19, 1957. https://variety.com/1957/film/reviews/the-bridge-on-the-river-kwai-2-1200418413/

Kenny, Glenn. 2004. "The 75 Most Influential Movies on DVD." *Premiere*, January 2004.

Kinvig, Clifford. 1992. *River Kwai Railway: The Story of the Burma-Siam Railroad*. London: Brassey's.

Lomax, Eric. 1995. *The Railway Man: A POW's Searing Account of War, Brutality and Forgiveness*. New York: W. W. Norton.

Phillips, Gene D. 2006. *Beyond the Epic: The Life and Films of David Lean*. Lexington: University Press of Kentucky.

Santas, Constantine. 2012. *The Epic Films of David Lean*. Lanham, MD: The Scarecrow Press.

Spielberg, Steven. 2003. *The Making of* Indiana Jones and the Temple of Doom. Documentary included in the DVD release of *Indiana Jones and the Temple of Doom*. Paramount, 2003.

Steinberg, Cobbett. 1980. *Film Facts*. New York: Facts on File.

Symonds, Craig L. 2018. *World War II at Sea: A Global History*. New York: Oxford University Press.

Tenney, Lester I. 1995. *My Hitch in Hell: The Bataan Death March*. Washington, D.C.: Brassey's.

Thomson, David. 2008. *"Have You Seen . . . ?": A Personal Introduction to 1,000 Films*. New York: Alfred A. Knopf.

Underbrink, Robert L. 1971. *Destination Corregidor*. Annapolis, MD: U.S. Naval Institute.

Ward, Geoffrey C., and Ken Burns. 2007. *The War: An Intimate History, 1941–1945*. New York: Alfred A. Knopf.

Watt, Ian. 1959. "Bridges over the Kwai." *Partisan Review*, Winter 1959.

Wright, John M., Jr. 1988. *Captured on Corregidor: Diary of an American P.O.W. in World War II*. Jefferson, NC: McFarland.

Wyatt, David K. 1984. *Thailand: A Modern History*. New Haven, CT: Yale University Press.

Chapter 6

Judgment at Nuremberg (1961)

Judgment at Nuremberg premiered on December 14, 1961, in West Berlin, near the places in the former Nazi German capital where plans were drawn for the atrocities described in the film. Released by United Artists, it opened in the United States on December 19. As a director, Stanley Kramer (1913–2001) was already known for a pair of movies on weighty subjects, *On the Beach* (1959), which dramatized nuclear war, and *Inherit the Wind* (1960), inspired by the 1925 "Scopes monkey trial" prosecution of a schoolteacher for teaching Darwinism. In *Judgment*, he took on the subject of the Nuremberg trials, which saw former Nazi officials on trial for atrocities committed before and during the war.

Kramer adapted the film from a 1959 production for the CBS-TV drama series *Playhouse 90*. The screenplay for the television program and film, written by an industry newcomer, Abby Mann (1927–2008), was inspired by one of several post–World War II trials of secondary German officials by U.S. tribunals in occupied Germany. Those hearings were subsequent to the proceedings against high-ranking Nazi leaders by the International Military Tribunal (1945–1946), and as a news reporter in the film complains, they received considerably less attention from the news media and public than the better-known trial of the most notorious Nazis.

Set in 1948, *Judgment at Nuremberg* is primarily a courtroom drama, with most of its more-than-three-hour running time devoted to testimony by victims of Nazism as well as legal and ethical debates between the prosecutor and the attorney representing the defendants. The actors playing the defense attorney, Hans Rolfe (Maximilian Schell, 1930–2014), and one of the defendants, the Nazi prosecutor Emil Hahn (Werner Klemperer, 1920–2000), reprised their roles from the *Playhouse 90* production.

Other leading roles were given to familiar Hollywood stars, as Kramer put it, in order to make the film more appealing to a larger audience. As an artist with a social conscience, Kramer was willing to push reluctant studios into examining the pressing issues of his time. "Do you think United Artists wanted to get involved in a film about war trials? They weren't interested at all in war guilt, people in ovens, or crooked judges," Kramer said, referring to Hollywood's reluctance to directly address the Holocaust. "So what I did was something of a compromise: I studded it with stars to get it made as a film that would reach out to a mass audience" (Spoto 1978, 228–229).

Spencer Tracy (1900–1967) plays the tribunal's chief judge, Dan Haywood, endowing his character with unassuming wisdom, unpretentious gravity, and a determination to maintain fair play throughout the trial. Kramer hired Laurence Olivier (1907–1989) as Dr. Ernst Janning, a distinguished German jurist accused of culpability with Nazi crimes, but at the last minute, the director was forced to replace him with leading man Burt Lancaster (1913–1994). "I thought he was the least believable person I had in this film," Kramer admitted, explaining that Lancaster was not persuasive as a German (Spoto 1978, 232). Richard Widmark (1914–2008) capitalized on his tough-guy persona and infused the U.S. prosecutor, Colonel Tad Lawson, with moral certitude and moral and vengeful fury. He met his match as a debater with the wily, intellectually resourceful attorney played by Schell. As a child, Schell had escaped Austria from the Nazis with his family. Investing their roles with palpable sadness and loss, Montgomery Clift (1920–1966) and Judy Garland (1922–1969) played German civilians tormented by Nazi policies.

Marlene Dietrich (1901–1992), a star of pre-Nazi German cinema who fled to Hollywood with Adolf Hitler's (1889–1945) rise to power, is the film's most prominent female character in her role as Frau Bertholt, the widow of a German general recently executed by the Americans for war crimes. William Shatner (1931–), five years before his famous role as *Star Trek*'s Captain Kirk, plays Judge Haywood's adjutant, Captain Harrison Byers.

The film's opening scenes define Judge Haywood's character and establish his "point of view through which we see and feel the events of the trial and outside the courtroom" (Spoto 1978, 232). He is curious about the Germans he encounters and makes a point of speaking with the husband and wife assigned as his servants and even with the former lady of the mansion where he has been posted, Frau Bertholt. Haywood is sympathetic to the losses sustained by the Germans; he listens closely but appears unconvinced by the servants' protestation that they "were not political" and Bertholt's declaration that "we did not know" about the mass killings.

Haywood is also patient but unmoved by the American politicians and military commanders, who urge him to wrap up the trial as soon as possible. Instead, he takes eight months, hearing testimony from victims of Nazi policies, including forced sterilization of the feeble-minded and persecution of the Jews, and deliberating with his two colleagues on the tribunal. Haywood is determined to understand the defendants and their motivations as well as the social context of their decisions and to assess their level of guilt as judges in a state that had committed grave crimes.

The four defendants in his courtroom represent a spectrum within the Nazi administration. Hahn is a fanatical believer in Nazism. Friedrich Hofstetter (played by Martin Brandt, 1903–1989) is a mild-mannered official who is content to go along with Nazi policies to get along. Werner Lampe (played by Torben Meyer, 1884–1975) appears confused and in cognitive decline. The focus of Haywood's interest is on the fourth defendant, Janning, a brooding figure who at first refuses to acknowledge the legitimacy of the tribunal hearing his case. Haywood recognizes Janning as a scholar with an international reputation among jurists and constitutional lawyers.

There is never any doubt in *Judgment at Nuremberg* that the defendants would be found guilty to one degree or another for facilitating Nazi policies. Hovering over the film is the question in Haywood's mind: How could a respectable man such as Janning, who once wrote so eloquently of justice and the rule of law, been a party to such crimes?

The dramatic climax of *Judgment at Nuremberg* arrives when Janning finally breaks his silence, ending his passive cooperation with the defense attorney's strategy that his clients were innocent because they carried out the laws of a legitimate government. "It is not easy to tell the truth, but if there is to be any salvation for Germany, we must admit it," Janning declares. He explains, "There was a fever in the land," democracy was torn apart, and Hitler identified the "devils among us." The country was in danger, and he acted from misguided patriotism. He admits his guilt.

After convicting all four defendants and sentencing each one to life imprisonment, Haywood visits Janning in his cell. "By all that is right in this world, your verdict was a just one," Janning tells Haywood. He then adds, about mass murder, "I never knew it would come to that." Haywood is unmoved, insisting, "It came to that the first time you sentenced a man to death you knew to be innocent."

Although West Berlin Mayor Willy Brandt (1913–1992), later Germany's chancellor, gave the welcoming speech at the film's premiere, Kramer claims that it was met with "a deafening silence" as the theater lights went up and failed to sell tickets in Germany (Spoto 1978, 229). In the United States, however, the film was a box-office success, grossing $6 million against a budget of $3 million (Balio 1987, 145).

Judgment at Nuremberg earned two Academy Awards, with Schell winning for Best Actor and Mann for Best Adapted Screenplay. It was nominated in nine other categories including Best Picture, Best Director, Best Actor (Tracy), Best Supporting Actor (Clift), and Best Supporting Actress (Garland).

The film received generally positive reviews upon release. The *New York Times* called it "a powerful persuasive film," a philosophical meditation on "how much responsibility and guilt the individual must bear for crimes committed or condoned by him on the order and in the interest of the state." The review praised the acting from a major and supporting cast with the exception of Lancaster, who "played weakly" (Crowther 1961). The *New Yorker* called the film "bold and, despite its great length, continuously exciting" (Gill 1961). The *Washington Post* declared it "extraordinary" for putting cinema to such "noble use" (Coe 1962).

The legacy of *Judgment at Nuremberg* is mixed. In 2008, the American Film Institute voted it as the 10th best courtroom drama, and in 2011, the Library of Congress added it to the National Film Registry as "historically significant." *Judgment at Nuremberg*, identified with the "liberal school of message movies" (Spoto 1978, 11), remains familiar to film buffs, yet Kramer's style of moviemaking has gone out of fashion. On *Judgment at Nuremberg*, film historian Dave Thomson wrote, "There are few films as depressing," and categorized it, along with Kramer's other message movies, as "middlebrow and overemphatic" (Thomson 2010, 534).

HISTORICAL BACKGROUND

For audiences at the time of its release, the title of *Judgment at Nuremberg* recalled a recent trial larger in significance than the one depicted in the film. Like the "Judges Trial" that inspired the film, Nuremberg was the site where the International Military Tribunal (IMT) held its hearings from November 20, 1945, through October 1, 1946. The IMT enlarged the scope of international law by sitting in judgment over high-ranking officials of Nazi Germany for their role in waging aggressive war and the atrocities committed in the name of their ideology and set the stage for the smaller, lesser-known Judges Trial depicted in the film.

Before Nuremberg, individuals and groups had no enforceable rights in the world arena. International law generally governed relations between states whose governments were constrained only by treaties. After World War I (1914–1918), the Permanent Court of International Justice was established at The Hague in the Netherlands, but its jurisdiction was limited to resolving disputes between states. Regardless of how outrageous, national governments continued to enjoy the right to murder or otherwise abuse their subjects within their sovereign territory.

However, the international media coverage of a particular set of incidents against civilians, the slaughter of over 1.2 million Armenian subjects of the Ottoman Empire by Ottoman Turks during World War I, gave rise to discussions on the role of international law in curbing such violence in the future. The phrase "crimes against humanity" was first used to describe the

Armenian massacres, and its legal implications were conceived as early as the 1920s by British jurist Hersch Lauterpacht (1897–1960) (Sands 2016, 113). In 1944, Lauterpacht's rival, refugee legal scholar Raphael Lemkin (1900–1959), coined the word "genocide" to describe the Armenian massacres and immediately applied it to the Nazi persecution of the Jews (Balakian 2003, 378). Lauterpacht and Lemkin provided the intellectual material on which the Nuremberg trials stood. Without their work, the IMT's verdicts could more easily have been dismissed as the punishments meted out by the winners of the war against the losers.

Lauterpacht and Lemkin probably never met but conducted their disagreements on the meaning of victimhood and the rights of man through intermediaries. Lauterpacht defined crimes against humanity as the large-scale killing of individuals, while Lemkin defined genocide as the deliberate destruction of particular religious or ethnic groups. Both crimes amounted to mass murder, yet the distinction was important because of their differing emphasis. The IMT's mission statement, the so-called "Nuremberg Charter," included genocide, but the proceedings focused more on crimes against humanity.

Emerging from similar backgrounds, Lauterpacht and Lemkin were Jews growing up in Eastern Europe with anti-Semitism and violent nationalism on the rise. Both attended law school in Poland at Lemberg University (now Lviv University). Lauterpacht immigrated to Great Britain in the 1920s and became a professor of international law at Cambridge University. Lemkin stayed on in Poland until he was forced to flee from the invading Nazis in 1939 and eventually found his way to the United States.

The leading American prosecutor at the Nuremberg trials, U.S. Supreme Court Justice Robert H. Jackson (1892–1954) read Lemkin's writings with interest, but nevertheless chose to sideline him in favor of Lauterpacht. Regarded as idiosyncratic and emotional, Lemkin was kept in the background and apparently never saw the inside of the Nuremberg courtroom where the IMT heard testimony, but Lauterpacht was at the prosecutorial table and played an active role throughout.

Regardless of their conflicting ideas and personalities, the concepts circulated by Lauterpacht and Lemkin during the war years influenced the evolution of Allied plans for the fate of Nazi leaders once victory was achieved. In January 1942, the Free French along with the Polish and other governments-in-exile from Nazi-occupied Europe issued the St. James Declaration, calling for using criminal law to punish perpetrators of atrocities; they would be "sought for, handed over to justice and judged." As a result of the declaration, the United Nations War Crimes Commission was established to collect information on atrocities with an eye toward gathering evidence (Sands 2016, 101–102). In October 1942, U.S. president Franklin D. Roosevelt (1882–1945) spoke against the "barbaric crimes" of the Nazis and promised that those responsible would face "courts of law" (Sands 2016, 179).

There was little precedent for any of this in international law and no immediate idea as to what sort of courts the defeated Nazis would face. The British held out against the idea of giving them a trial. Regarding the most infamous Nazis, Foreign Secretary Anthony Eden (1897–1977) argued that "the guilt of such individuals is so black that they fall outside and go beyond the scope of any judicial process" (Tusa and Tusa 1986, 62). However, the United States insisted on a legal process and convinced the other two nations among the Four Powers, the Soviet Union and France. Soviet leader Joseph Stalin (1878–1953) welcomed a trial but envisioned it along the lines of the show trials he staged to humiliate suspected dissidents. In the Soviet Union, prosecution on the dock inevitably led to a firing squad (Tusa and Tusa 1986, 63). Free French leader Charles De Gaulle (1890–1970) also announced support for a trial. The United States had outmaneuvered the reluctant British. There would be a trial, but it was not yet clear under whose laws and whose judges the trials would be conducted.

Regardless of the sort of legal process the British, Soviets, and French might have had in mind, the United States, emerging from the war as the world's superpower, was able to set the agenda. Given the title of U.S. Chief of Counsel, Robert Jackson, responsible only to President Harry S. Truman (1884–1972), stamped the proceedings with his own character. He was convinced that no one should be put before "anything that is called a court . . . under forms of judicial proceedings, if you are not willing to see him freed if not proved guilty" (Taylor 1955). Under Jackson's leadership, the Nuremberg trials would not become a lynching party but a sober exercise in justice that, at the same time, expanded the scope of international law by careful degrees.

The "Nuremberg Charter" signed by the Four Powers on August 8, 1945, represented not only political compromise between the Allies but also compromises between the Anglo-American legal system on one hand and on the other the Roman-law based Continental systems of France and the Soviet Union. The accused would be given the right of counsel; they would be indicted and tried in their own language. Defendants had the right to testify but could be subject to cross-examination. As in Continental Law, they would be provided with a full summary of all existing evidence against them. Jackson was satisfied that the blend of the two systems "gave rather more rights to the defendants than might have been available in either system separately" (Tusa and Tusa 1986, 85).

The Soviets wanted the trial to take place in Berlin, a city under Four Powers occupation, but Jackson insisted on Nuremberg in the U.S. occupied zone. The American military had declared Nuremberg 91 percent destroyed by air raids, and the city gave off a stench from thousands of bodies trapped beneath the rubble, yet a significant structure survived the relentless Allied bombing campaign. The fortress-like Palace of Justice, with an attached prison where defendants could be held, still stood.

"The building seemed simply to have shrugged off the blows and gone on dominating what was left of Nuremberg's skyline" (Persico 1994, 40).

Along with the surviving courthouse and jail, Nuremberg had symbolic significance. The city was the site of the annual Nazi Party rally, including the one notoriously documented by German director Leni Riefenstahl (1902–2003) in her film *Triumph of the Will* (1935). As a result of its special connection with Nazism, the city was the place where in a special session the Reichstag had passed the "Nuremberg Laws" (1935). The Reich Citizenship Law and the Law for the Protection of German Blood and German Honor "were unmistakably designed to fix the status of the Jews in the Third Reich" (Yahil 1990, 68). The new statutes restricted citizenship to persons "of German or related blood" and distinguished citizens from "subjects of the state" effectively barred from political rights; they also prohibited marriage or sexual relations between Germans and Jews and imposed other restrictions. Most of the succeeding anti-Semitic ordinances imposed by the Nazis were implemented under the authority of the Nuremberg Laws.

The International Military Tribunal that convened in Nuremberg consisted of eight judges, two from each of the Four Powers. Presiding over the court was Britain's Lord Justice Geoffrey Lawrence (1880–1971), a no-nonsense jurist whose job, as he saw it, "was simply to apply the law to the facts and to do so fairly and speedily" (Sands 2016, 285).

The IMT was given broad authority to investigate "crimes against peace," a newly coined term for waging aggressive war in violation of treaties; "war crimes," a more established legal category relating to violations of the rules of war; and "crimes against humanity." Genocide was mentioned in the Nuremberg Charter, as was Jackson's obsession to prove the Nazis were guilty of criminal "conspiracy." The charter made it clear that following orders was no defense for subordinates guilty of crimes. The panel of judges was granted a wide latitude to interpret its mandate and establish new precedents for international law.

It was not immediately clear which Germans would be put on the dock at Nuremberg. Several of the most prominent Nazis were unavailable for prosecution. Hitler, *Schutzstaffel* (SS) chief Heinrich Himmler (1900–1945), and Propaganda Minister Joseph Goebbels (1897–1945) had already taken their own lives. Various lists of possible defendants who survived Germany's defeat circulated among the Allies. Some were eliminated because their careers closely replicated other more prominent defendants. Some were added as a favor to the Soviets.

Finally, on August 29, 1945, 24 defendants were cited. Secondary as well as high-ranking officials were included as if to form a cross-section of the Nazi civil, military, and economic administration. One of the indicted, arms tycoon Gustav Krupp von Bohlen und Halbach (1870–1950) was senile and bedridden and was never brought to trial.

> **THE HOLOCAUST**
>
> Persecution of the Jews began under the Roman Empire for their refusal to comply with the empire's civic religion and accelerated with the rise of Christianity, which emerged from Judaism. In many parts of Europe, Jews were the only ethnic or religious minority and became objects of suspicion and hatred. By the 19th century, Jews made strides toward emancipation in many Western nations and, especially in Germany, considered themselves fully assimilated.
>
> Old prejudices took new form under the Nazis. Adolf Hitler believed in a struggle for world dominance between two races, the Aryan (Nordic) and the Jew. From the onset of his public life, Hitler pointed to the "necessity" of eliminating Jews from German society. Hitler's autobiographical manifesto, *Mein Kampf*, includes many implications that he might be prepared to go further than the discriminatory legislation, the Nuremberg Laws (1935), banning Jews from professional life and stripping them of civil rights.
>
> In 1941, with much of Europe under German occupation, Nazi leaders devised the "Final Solution to the Jewish Question" involving the mass deportation of Jews to killing fields and death camps. So obsessed were the Nazis with massacring Europe's Jews that even as defeat loomed they continued to devote work force and logistics to genocide.
>
> Altogether, some six million Jews perished in the massacres known in Hebrew as Shoah and, more generally, in the English-speaking world, the Holocaust.

The list of the indicted began with Nazi Party chief Martin Bormann (1900–1945), missing but tried in absentia. The defendants who stood trial included:

- Grand Admiral Karl Doenitz (1891–1980)
- Hans Frank (1900–1946), the governor general of Poland
- Wilhelm Frick (1877–1946), the principal author of the Nuremberg Laws
- Hans Fritzsche (1900–1953), a bureaucrat in the Propaganda Ministry
- Walther Funk (1890–1960), the president of the Reichsbank
- Hermann Göring (1893–1946), Luftwaffe (air force) commander and speaker of the Reichstag
- Rudolf Hess (1894–1987), former deputy führer
- Major General Alfred Jodl (1890–1947)
- Ernst Kaltenbrunner (1903–1946), an SS official responsible for the death camps
- Field Marshal Wilhelm Keitel (1882–1946)
- Constantine Freiherr von Neurath (1873–1956), a retired diplomat
- Franz von Papen (1879–1969), a prominent conservative politician sidelined by Hitler to the foreign service
- Grand Admiral Erich Raeder (1876–1960)

- Foreign Minister Joachim von Ribbentrop (1893–1946)
- Alfred Rosenberg (1893–1946), the Nazi's leading intellectual spokesperson
- Fritz Sauckel (1894–1946), responsible for the Nazis' slave labor system
- Hjalmar Schacht (1877–1970), former Reichsbank president
- Reich Youth Leader Baldur von Schirach (1907–1974)
- Arthur Seyss-Inquart (1892–1946), high commissioner for the occupied Netherlands
- Armaments Minister Albert Speer (1905–1981)
- Julius Streicher (1885–1946), publisher of the anti-Semitic scandal sheet *Der Stürmer*

One additional Nazi indicted at Nuremberg, Robert Ley (1890–1945), chief of the German Labor Front, did not survive until the end of the trial. He hanged himself in his cell. The U.S. commandant of the Nuremberg prison, Colonel Burton C. Andrus (1892–1977), a disciplinarian who strode through the cell blocks wearing a steel helmet and brandishing a riding crop, took additional measures to ensure that his captives would live to meet their executioner. Spotlights shone into every cell at night, and prisoners were not allowed to turn their faces away or cover their hands as they tried to sleep.

In addition to individuals, at Jackson's insistence, seven organizations were also indicted for conducting criminal conspiracies. They were the Reich cabinet, although it had not convened since 1937; the Nazi Party leadership corps; the SS; the Gestapo; the *Sicherheitsdienst* (SD), the intelligence agency of the SS; the *Sturmabteilung* (SA), the original Nazi brown-shirted stormtroopers, essential in the movement's early days but irrelevant since 1934; and the Oberkommando der Wehrmacht (Military High Command), which took its orders directly from Hitler but was hampered by rivalries among the Wehrmacht (army), Kriegsmarine (navy), and Luftwaffe.

The Nuremberg Charter's call for conspiracy charges against "criminal organizations" troubled several of the tribunal's judges. U.S. criminal law defined conspiracy much more broadly than the law in many other nations. In addition, the potential scope of conspiracy charges involved millions of potential defendants. In the end, three of the organizations were acquitted: the Reich cabinet, the SA, and the Oberkommando der Wehrmacht. The guilty verdict against the other four meant that anyone who was a member of those organizations after 1939, the start of the war, was automatically guilty of war crimes unless they had been drafted into one of those groups. Luftwaffe bomber squadron crews, grounded during the last months of the war, were converted into Waffen-SS combat units and became one example of individuals who could plead involuntary membership.

The consequence of membership in those criminal organizations was soon overridden by the "denazification courts" established by Allies but staffed by Germans to evaluate individual cases. "No member of a convicted organization was punished solely on the strength of the IMT verdicts," and to critics of Jackson, the proceedings against those organizations was "a pointless exercise" designed for newspaper headlines, not practical results (Persico 1994, 396).

The trials against prominent individuals were of greater significance. They were a disparate lot in personality and commitment to the regime they served. Göring, Hitler's designated successor until fired by the führer in the final weeks of the war, sought to become the leader of the prisoners through bluster, charm, and bullying. He was fatalistic when questioned by Captain Gustave Gilbert (1911–1977) and Major Douglas Kelley (1912–1958), the U.S. Army psychiatrists who regularly examined every prisoner. He told them, "I know that I am going to hang" but counted on history to vindicate him (Persico 1994, 91). Frank, awash in guilt, converted to Roman Catholicism and asked for the chaplain (Tusa and Tusa 1986, 235). Jodl and Keitel, though burdened by their own doubts over the master they served, were perplexed to be charged with obeying orders from Hitler, their supreme commander.

Hess sometimes claimed total amnesia for not only the Nazi period but also his entire adult life. Kelley diagnosed him as a "hysterical personality" but found him sane enough to stand trial (Tusa and Tusa 1986, 161–163). Streicher, so odious that the Nazi Party expelled him in 1940 as "unfit for human leadership," raved about conspiracies but was also found sane (Persico 1994, 99–100). On the other hand, Speer conducted himself with calm, purposeful dignity and expressed a measure of regret. The American guards, often abusive to their prisoners, addressed him respectfully as "Mr. Speer" (Persico 1994, 190).

The trial opened on November 20, 1945, with a statement from the IMT's president, Geoffrey Lawrence, urging decorum and reminding participants that their task was "of supreme importance to millions of people all over the globe" and to "discharge their duties without fear or favour, in accordance with the sacred principles of law and justice" (Tusa and Tusa 1986, 146). The galleries were crowded with press from around the world, including several distinguished writers. Novelist John Dos Passos covered the trial for *Life* magazine. Newsreel camera crews documented the proceedings in black and white.

For those present, the courtroom was a clash of colors. Seated on a dais before the flags of the Four Powers, the judges wore black robes except for the Soviets, who wore their uniforms. Jackson was dressed in morning coat and striped trousers, the traditional costume for an attorney addressing the U.S. Supreme Court. Many of his prosecutorial colleagues from the other powers were military men in uniform. The defense attorneys wore a variety of costumes; many were German law professors who turned up in black, blue, burgundy, and purple academic caps and gowns. Admiral Doenitz chose a German naval officer as his counsel, who came to court in full dress. The spit-and-polish Andrus designed special uniforms for his guards, consisting of white helmets and belts against olive tunics. White billy clubs dangled from their belts (Tusa and Tusa 1986, 146–147).

Least impressive in appearance were the defendants. Unlike suspects hauled before the infamous Nazi People's Court, who were made to look disheveled and disreputable, Andrus saw to it that each man was shaved every morning and dressed in suits or their military uniforms but with all insignia and medals removed. However, "the image everyone had of them was as the central characters of the Nazi newsreels," powerful figures commanding armies and audiences. "They now appeared as two rows of elderly, sallow men. They were all so much smaller than anyone had imagined" (Tusa and Tusa 1986, 148).

During the 11 months of deliberation, many days were devoted to the presentation of documents by the prosecution, and those documents, combined with the public record of the most infamous among the indicted, left little doubt that many would be convicted as charged. There was no difficulty in finding incriminating evidence among the enormous archives left by the fallen German regime. In their testimony, several defendants assumed a measure of responsibility for Nazi crimes while others were evasive. Field Marshall Keitel surprised the court by admitting that many of the orders he carried out went "against the inner voice of my conscience" (Persico 1994, 308). On the other hand, Ribbentrop made a poor impression when he denied that the invasion of foreign countries, including neutral nations, constituted aggression by Germany.

The most arresting testimony came from two defendants who took opposite approaches to the proceedings, the cynical Göring and the regretful Speer. Göring replied scornfully to the prosecutors, proudly admitting that he had worked to deliberately dismantle the German republic and replace it with a one-party dictatorship. When questioned about German aggression against the Soviet Union, Göring pointed to evidence that he was against the invasion of Russia. He made a fool out of Jackson by showing that the prosecutor did not understand some of the documents in front of him. "Göring appeared to be enjoying himself, a prizefighter who has yet to feel his opponent's glove" (Persico 1994, 277). However, the blows finally landed. The evidence was clear that Göring was party to many of the worst Nazi atrocities.

By contrast, Speer startled the court and the foreign media with a show of accepting responsibility and his criticism of Hitler. Historians have accused him of mounting an effective defense by contrasting himself with Hitler, emphasizing his role as a technocrat with a job to do and concentrating on his role in subverting Hitler's plans in the last months of the war. Speer disobeyed the führer's "scorched earth" orders to destroy everything in the Allies path. His moral stand has been called "either half-hearted or devious. His acceptance of responsibility was always hedged with saving clauses" (Tusa and Tusa 1986, 397).

This may be true, and yet, his rebuke of the Third Reich was strong enough to anger many of his co-defendants who murmured "treason," especially when Speer explained in great technical detail his plan to kill Hitler by injecting poison gas into the air-conditioning system of Hitler's Berlin bunker. While he sought to evade direct responsibility for the slave labor conditions in the armaments industry under his jurisdiction, Speer went further than his colleagues by calling the war "an inconceivable catastrophe," adding, "it is my unquestionable duty to assume my share of responsibility for the disaster of the German people" and "I, as an important member of the leadership of the Reich, share in the total responsibility" (Persico 1994, 353).

The Nuremberg trials included many moments that exposed the uneasy moral position of the Allies, especially the pious indignation of Soviet prosecutors accusing the Nazis of waging aggression given the Soviet invasion of Finland, Poland, and the Baltic republics. The Western prosecutors were also guilty in several cases of setting double standards. Until the German invasion of Poland on September 1, 1939, the Allies had ratified or acquiesced to Hitler's aggressive foreign policy. Allied charges that the German military engaged in "wanton destruction" were vulnerable in light of U.S. and British air raids on German and Japanese cities and the atomic bombs the United States dropped on Japan (Biddis 1995). Accused of violating international agreements by ordering his U-boats to sink merchant ships without warning, Admiral Doenitz's defense attorney secured an affidavit from Admiral Chester W. Nimitz (1885–1966), commander-in-chief of the U.S. Pacific Fleet, stating that American submarines conducted warfare against Japanese shipping exactly as the Germans had done against the Allies (Tusa and Tusa 1986, 360).

The arguments by the IMT's judges in their chambers were sometimes furious, not only over the guilt or levels of guilt of the men in the dock but also over points of law, especially the conspiracy charges and the criminality of organizations. Three defendants were found not guilty on all counts.

Franz von Papen, the conservative German chancellor who stepped aside and engineered Hitler's rise to power, thought that his nation's old elites could tame the Nazis, using them to mobilize the masses. He was acquitted because he served in only minor capacities after the Nazis pushed him aside. The American-born Hjalmar Schacht, the economist whose wizardry made Hitler's war possible, was acquitted because the judges were deadlocked; his case was helped by being imprisoned at Dachau during the last months of the Third Reich. Hans Fritzsche, described as a "propagandist not even on the outer rim of the inner circle," had no role in shaping or implementing policies and was acquitted (Persico 1994, 438).

Although none of the defendants convicted at Nuremberg had personally killed anyone, at least as civilians, all were implicated to some degree in the Nazi machinery of death and slave labor. Doenitz could argue that his naval tactics were identical to his American counterparts, but no U.S. Navy officer had concentration camp inmates working in his shipyards. He received the IMT's shortest sentence of 10 years of imprisonment. The conservative statesman Constantine von Neurath, who joined the Nazi Party only in 1937 and was on "sick leave" from all positions since 1943, received 15 years. Baldur von Schirach and Albert Speer were both sentenced to 20 years. Rudolf Hess, who flew to Scotland on a bizarre and unauthorized "peace mission" in 1941, was in British custody before many of the worst atrocities were committed. He received a life sentence.

In an exceptional case, Julius Streicher was convicted not for devising or administering policies but for "incitement to murder and extermination" through his newspaper, *Der Stürmer*. In 21st-century terms, he was sent to the gallows for hate speech. One convict cheated the hangman. Göring killed himself with a cyanide capsule despite the rigorous and regular searches (including rectal inspections) conducted by Andrus. "No explanation is very convincing," he said regarding how he obtained the poison (Tusa and Tusa 1986, 484).

The Nuremberg trial was controversial during its deliberations. The chief justice of the U.S. Supreme Court, Harlan Fiske Stone, called it "a high-class lynching" (Persico 1994, 324), and even sympathetic historians a half century later mention "that taint of 'victors' justice' which still leads us to moderate our admiration" (Biddis 1995). Even so, the trial was conducted in pursuit of justice with the rule of law as its guiding principle. Politics dictated the decisions of the Soviet judges, but they were often outvoted by their western colleagues.

The IMT was the model for the international war crimes trial held in Tokyo (1946) and "played a very positive role in publicizing the vicious origins, course, and consequences of Nazism, and thus in creating better prospects for democratic stability" in the German Federal Republic (West Germany), established by the western allies in 1949. Most Germans turned their backs on the Third Reich in light of the drumbeat of revelations at Nuremberg, and neo-Nazis were, at least until recently, barely visible even on the fringe of German politics (Biddis 1995).

The hope that Nuremberg would set precedents for responding to war and abuses of human rights was unmet for half a century despite war crimes and mass killings across much of the world. Finally, in response to the Balkan civil war that broke out after the Cold War ended, the United Nations established the Yugoslav War Crimes Tribunal in The Hague (1993). On November 8, 1994, the tribunal indicted its first defendant, a Bosnian Serb concentration camp commandant accused of murder, torture, and "illegal deportations" (ethnic cleansing). Serbian officials at first refused to acknowledge the court's authority, and the tribunal's mandate banned trials in absentia (Cohen 1994).

Despite the initial impasse, the Yugoslav Tribunal persisted, and with the eventual support of Serbian and other European agencies, it was able to bring 161 suspects to trial by the time it disbanded in 2017. The court convicted and sentenced 90 defendants, including Yugoslav president Slobodan Milosevic (1941–2006), who died in his prison cell before a verdict was reached. In a replay of Nuremberg, one convict, Croatian General Slobodan Praljak (1945–2017), took his own life with cyanide outside the courtroom. Building on the precedent of Nuremberg, the tribunal confirmed that politicians and senior military officers "will no longer escape with impunity but be held responsible for their actions, even in wartime" (Bowcott 2017).

DEPICTION AND HISTORICAL CONTEXT

The news media devoted many headlines to the IMT's Nuremberg hearings, and scholarship on the subject is voluminous. Much less was written at the time and afterward on the 12 "Subsequent Proceedings" conducted under U.S. Army auspices in Nuremberg from 1946 through 1947. Altogether 185 second-tier German officials were indicted and grouped as defendants according to their occupations. Trials were held for industrialists, military leaders, and SS officers. The "Doctors' Trial" attracted the most attention for its lurid testimony regarding experiments conducted on concentration camp inmates in the name of scientific research (Heberer and Matthaus 2008, 75, 78). The "Judges Trial" is remembered mainly for its depiction in *Judgment at Nuremberg*.

The film takes place in 1948 even though the trial actually ended a year earlier. This was done to link the proceedings to the Soviet blockade of Berlin and other notorious incidents in the Cold War. Despite taking artistic license with the chronology, the screenplay accurately echoes the attitude among American leaders, already expressed in 1947, that the hearings should be concluded because Germany needed to be rebuilt and cultivated as an ally against the Soviet threat. Remarks in the movie by a visiting U.S. Senator on Germany's key role politely render the "groundswell of hostility in Congress, where the focus had already shifted to the exigencies of the cold war" (Heberer and Matthaus 2008, 91).

Sixteen German jurists stood accused at the Judges Trial. By reducing their number to four in the film, the director made the dramatization more manageable; "the theme of the corruptibility of the legal system is thus thrown into greater relief" (Spoto 1978, 226). All of the defendants carried out the laws of their country, but what was their responsibility when given laws that violated any larger concept of justice? Likewise, each of the 16 defendants had his own counsel, but for simplicity, all four were represented in the film by one attorney.

Judgment at Nuremberg's defendants were fictional but charged with offenses similar to the indictments in the real Judges Trial. Many of the issues raised in the film's courtroom scenes reflect reality. Nazi German courts did order sterilization, and as the defense attorney points out, the U.S. Supreme Court upheld American sterilization laws. Jews accused of having sex with German women were charged under the Nuremberg Laws as shown in the film. In *Judgment at Nuremberg*, all four defendants were found guilty. In the real Judges Trial, several were acquitted, and the sentences of those who were convicted were eventually reduced.

The defendants, as all German judges under the Nazis, were forced to swear an oath to Hitler, and by calling it a "loyalty oath," the screenplay makes subtle reference to events in the United States during the 1950s, when many citizens were required to swear that they were not involved in communist or anti-American activities due to claims by Senator Joseph McCarthy (R-WI) that communists had infiltrated the military, U.S. government, and the arts.

Judgment at Nuremberg focuses on one defendant, Ernst Janning, a formidable legal mind who rose to authority within the Third Reich. One possible model for the character was the respected jurist Carl Schmitt (1888–1985). Like the fictional Janning, Schmitt enjoyed an international reputation for his writings on the philosophy of law and government. He never commented on the Nazis before they took power and was dismayed at first by Hitler's appointment as chancellor but joined the Nazi Party afterward (Gross 2007, 27).

Any inner reservations Schmitt entertained were quickly canceled by the realization that the Nazis represented a path to power and position, especially given the expulsion of Jews from the judiciary and academia and the resignation of a small number of judges who refused to serve the new regime. "Schmitt belonged to this group of guiding lights and commentators within Nazi legal policy and theory. But he also did *not* belong, since in his international renown and intellectual stature he towered over his Nazi colleagues" (Gross 2007, 23). Schmitt was named president of the Nazi attorneys association, editor of its newspaper, and coordinator of Nazi legal conferences.

Unlike Janning, Schmitt fell from power as rapidly as he rose. In December 1938, an editorial in the SS magazine *Das schwarze Korps* (*The Black Corps*) denounced him as a Roman Catholic and Hegelian philosopher, calling his embrace of Nazism opportunistic. Although protected from arrest by powerful friends in the regime, he withdrew from public life, retaining only his professorship at the University of Berlin.

Schmitt narrowly escaped indictment. He was arrested in Berlin by Soviet troops but was released by a communist official who admired his work. He was then arrested by U.S. troops but released after given a character reference by the daughter of a German resistance leader. In March 1947, he was arrested a second time by the United States and brought to the prison at Nuremberg's Palace of Justice. His interrogator, Robert M.W. Kempner (1899–1993), an American prosecutor for the IMT, had been a German Jew who knew Schmitt before fleeing the Nazis. Once again, he was released and "never agreed to undergo denazification" (Gross 2007, 200). Like Janning at his first court appearance, Schmitt did not accept the authority of the occupation tribunals, but unlike the fictional character, he never apologized.

Spencer Tracy's character, Judge Haywood, admits early in the film that he was no one's first choice to preside over the tribunal, adding that he came from "the backwoods of Maine." He accurately alludes to the difficulty the United States had in recruiting judges for the Subsequent Proceedings (Heberer and Matthaus 2008, 76). Not unlike the elderly Haywood, the real presiding judge in the "Judges Trial," Carrington T. Marshall (1869–1958), was a retired chief justice of the Ohio Supreme Court.

The courtroom in Nuremberg's Palace of Justice where the Judges Trial took place was recreated on a Hollywood sound stage. As in the film, the IBM International Translator System, developed just in time for the IMT hearings, was used in the Judges Trial. Interpreters worked rapidly from a control booth, allowing participants in the trial to hear deliberations through headsets in their own language (Tusa and Tusa 1986, 110). Sometimes the cross-examinations flew so quickly that translators fell behind. As shown in the film, a system of lights on tabletops was used with a yellow light meaning "please slow down" and a red meaning "please stop" (Gaskin 1990, 38).

The movie's depiction of Nuremberg closely resembles postwar photographs of the ruined city, down to such details as the armored personnel carriers standing guard outside the Palace of Justice. American and Allied participants and observers were, as in the film, comfortably accommodated in contrast to the desperate poverty endured by German civilians. "The conditions we lived in were palatial compared with those of the Germans," recalled a journalist. "We were living in a big castle, with all our food laid on and German cooks to cook it for us" (Gaskin 1990, 104).

CONCLUSION

The Germans, as in *Judgment at Nuremberg*, were sullen or in denial and eager for an opportunity to get on with their lives. "Today, Germans are almost completely disinterested in the Nuremberg trials," *Newsweek* reported, contrasting the Subsequent Proceedings with the IMT trial. "Those who do think about them find it hard to understand why Nazis should still be tried and punished at Nuremberg for the kind of crimes Russians are committing every day in the Eastern zone of Germany" (Thompson 1949).

Most Germans were to some degree compliant with the Nazi regime, if only to ensure their own careers or survival; no one was unaware of the persecution and deportation of Jews, although a few Germans understood the extent of the annihilation being conducted in concentration camps. Lack of interest in the Judges Trial and other Subsequent Proceedings reflected the need to put the past behind and build the country's future. West Germany's emotional and moral reckoning with the Nazi era became prevalent only in the 1960s after the country's booming economy afforded the leisure to ponder the past. In East Germany, the Communist regime simply declared that it had nothing to do with Nazism. The reckoning among East German survivors of the Nazi period would not occur until after the country's reunification (1990).

Although it counts as historical fiction, *Judgment at Nuremberg* is an accurate dramatization of a unique legal case putting judges and lawyers on trial for their role in an unjust regime.

FURTHER READING

Balakian, Peter. 2003. *The Burning Tigris: The Armenian Genocide and America's Response*. New York: HarperCollins.

Balio, Tino. 1987. *United Artists: The Company That Changed the Film Industry*. Madison: University of Wisconsin Press.

Biddis, Michael. 1995. "Victors' Justice? The Nuremberg Tribunal." *History Today*, May 1995. https://www.historytoday.com/archive/victors-justice-nuremberg-tribunal

Bowcott, Owen. 2017. "Yugoslavia Tribunal Closes, Leaving a Powerful Legacy of War Crimes Justice." *The Guardian*, December 20, 2017. https://www.theguardian.com/law/2017/dec/20/former-yugoslavia-war-crimes-tribunal-leaves-powerful-legacy-milosevic-karadzic-mladic

Coe, Richard L. 1962. "'Nuremberg' Is a Great Film." *Washington Post*, February 15, 1962.

Cohen, Roger. 1994. "Tribunal Brings First War Crimes Charges Since World War II against Serb." *New York Times*, November 8, 1994.

Crowther, Bosley. 1961. "'Judgment at Nuremberg': Palace Shows Stanley Kramer Production." *New York Times*, December 20, 1961. https://www.nytimes.com/1961/12/20/archives/the-screen-judgment-at-nurembergpalace-shows-stanley-kramer.html

Gaskin, Hilary. 1990. *Eyewitnesses at Nuremberg*. London: Arms and Armour.

Gill, Brendan. 1961. "The Current Cinema." *The New Yorker*, December 23, 1961. https://www.newyorker.com/magazine/1961/12/23/out-of-evil

Gross, Raphael. 2007. *Carl Schmitt and the Jews: The "Jewish Question," the Holocaust, and German Legal Theory*. Madison: University of Wisconsin Press.

Heberer, Patricia, and Jürgen Matthaus, eds. 2008. *Atrocities on Trial: Historical Perspectives on the Politics of Prosecuting War Crimes*. Lincoln: University of Nebraska Press.

Persico, Joseph E. 1994. *Nuremberg: Infamy on Trial*. New York: Viking.

Sands, Philippe. 2016. *East West Street: On the Origins of "Genocide" and "Crimes against Humanity."* New York: Alfred A. Knopf.

Spoto, Donald. 1978. *Stanley Kramer: Film Maker*. New York: G.P. Putnam's Son.

Taylor, Telford. 1955. "The Nuremberg Trial." *Columbia Law Review*. https://www.jstor.org/stable/1119814?seq=1

Thompson, John. 1949. "War Crimes: The Last Judgements." *Newsweek*, April 25, 1949.

Thomson, David. 2010. *The New Biographical Dictionary of Film*. New York: Alfred A. Knopf.

Tusa, Ann, and John Tusa. 1986. *The Nuremberg Trial*. New York: Atheneum.

Yahil, Leni. 1990. *The Holocaust: The Fate of European Jewry*. New York: Oxford University Press.

Chapter 7

Patton (1970)

Franklin J. Schaffner (1920–1989) directed the biographical film of General George S. Patton (1885–1945), *Patton*, which covered the general's exploits during the war, from North Africa to Europe. Producer Frank McCarthy (1912–1986) served as a brigadier general during World War II and knew Patton. The film debuted in major American cities in February 1970 and secondary markets in April.

20th Century Fox had long planned to make a film on the life of one of World War II's most familiar generals and purchased the rights to the biography *Patton: Ordeal and Triumph* (1963) by military historian Ladislas Farago (1906–1980). Because the studio pegged Francis Ford Coppola (1939–) as a war movie writer after his work on *Is Paris Burning?* (1966), Fox tapped him as *Patton*'s screenwriter. The studio brought in veteran Hollywood writer Edmund H. North (1911–1990) to revise Coppola's screenplay by strengthening the story's focus on key events (Sarantakes 2012, 42). The film also drew from *A Soldier's Story* (1951), the memoirs of General Omar N. Bradley (1883–1991).

Despite Fox's estimation of his interests, Coppola knew little about the military and was only vaguely aware of Patton. After immersing himself in books on the general, "I said, 'wait a minute, this guy was obviously nuts,'" Coppola recalled. "If they want to make a film glorifying him as a great American hero, it will be laughed at. And if I write a film that condemns him, it won't be made at all" (Schumacher 1999, 42). The result was a screenplay that introduced conflicting aspects of its subject's personality. Because of Coppola's ambiguity, *Patton* appealed to champions and opponents of the military, no small accomplishment at the time of its release in midst of massive protests against the Vietnam War (1955–1975).

Although filmed in a panoramic style meant to encompass entire battlefields, the enduring impression that remained came from Coppola's vividly written opening scene and the unforgettable performance in the title role by George C. Scott (1927–1999). A veteran character actor who became a star on the strength of his performance in the film, Scott poured over more than a dozen biographies on Patton in an effort to understand the man he was portraying (Sheward 2008, 178).

The film opens with Patton, wearing the full array of his medals and decorations, standing before a giant American flag. He gives a speech to an unseen audience of soldiers, establishing the scale of his grandiosity and self-confidence. The *New York Times* accurately called it an "overture that liberals can view as pure Camp, and Patton fans will interpret as pure inspiration" (Canby 1970). The opening speech summarizes Patton's attitude toward winning and war, and it seems as if spoken from the afterlife. He wears the four stars of a full general, a rank he did not achieve until April 1945 with victory at hand and only months to live.

The remainder of the film is a flashback chronicling his tour of duty through the end of World War II. Scene two begins in 1943 amid the wreckage of a decimated U.S. tank column. Bedouin are stripping the dead but flee at the arrival of General Bradley, played by Karl Malden (1912–2009), an actor whose résumé of well-meaning secondary characters was well known to moviegoers in 1970. The site was the Kasserine Pass in Tunisia, where the U.S. Army met the Germans for the first time in World War II and was crushed. Bradley declares that what he needs to win is the "best tank man we've got."

Patton, who had led the amphibious assault on French Morocco and is shown being decorated for his role by the country's sultan, is called to Bradley's II Corps headquarters. Patton arrives in a display of power, sirens blaring and wearing a pair of ivory-handled pistols. He finds the troops slovenly and undisciplined. "They don't look like soldiers. They don't act like soldiers," he declares. One of his aids pins the set of third stars to his uniform, identifying him as a lieutenant general, even though the U.S. Senate hasn't yet confirmed his promotion. Every gesture shows that Patton has taken command.

Throughout the film, Patton is shown visiting the sites of ancient battles and referring to strategies of past military leaders. He also has the good sense to read a book by his opponent, General Erwin Rommel (1891–1944), commander of the Afrika Korps dispatched by Hitler to rescue the faltering fortunes of his Italian ally in North Africa. Although outnumbered, Rommel's tactical genius gave the British a hard fight in the desert. Like Patton, tank warfare was his specialty. Patton looks forward to jousting with his counterpart but never has the opportunity to confront him head-on. Rommel, in poor health, returns to Germany and leaves the Afrika Korps to his subordinates. Patton has no trouble thwarting the Germans in his first encounter with the Afrika Korps.

Patton's success in North Africa leads to his role in the invasion of Sicily. Although his battle plans are overruled, he pursues his own agenda, determined to deprive his British rival, General Bernard Law Montgomery (1887–1976), of the honor of taking the island's key cities. Despite his military success, Patton's Sicilian campaign was a public relations disaster. The press reported his disparaging remarks against the British, and his ill-treatment of a shell-shocked enlisted man drew widespread condemnation. Patton berated the soldier as a "yellow belly" for claiming battle fatigue and slapped him several times.

As a result, his dream of commanding the Allied assault on Europe was denied. Patton was sent to Great Britain and put in charge of a decoy army with dummy divisions, false radio transmissions, and fake landing craft positioned to mislead the Germans on Allied intentions. Patton's make-believe army led the Germans to expect a landing at Pas de Calais. Instead, on D-Day (June 7, 1944), the Allies came ashore at Normandy.

With Allied forces pushing slowly into France against stiff resistance, Bradley sees the need for a skillful tank tactician and gives Patton command of the Third Army. Sometimes recklessly, Patton drives his armor toward Germany. When the final German counter-offensive threatens Allied progress in the Battle of the Bulge (1944), Patton's determination helps to hold the line.

With Germany defeated, Patton is given a role in the military occupation of the country, but his anti-Russian comments and comparison of the Nazi Party with Democrats and Republicans leads to his dismissal. He is shown walking toward an uncertain future in the final scene. Many moviegoers in 1970 knew that he never returned home but died of injuries in a car accident within two weeks of his removal.

The film generated great interest at the time of its release with much of the publicity focused on images of George C. Scott posed against the flag in the opening scene. The *New York Times*' critic Vincent Canby called the film "long (and from my point of view, appalling)," but added, "the subject matter and the style of the epic war movie are perfectly matched" and praised "the big, magnificently staged battle scenes (photographed in marvelous, clear, deep focus)" (Canby 1970). Like many critics at the time, the *Chicago Tribune*'s Gene Siskel focused on Scott, calling his performance "an acting tour de force" (Siskel 1970). The *Los Angeles Times*' Charles Champlin agreed, declaring, "George Scott gives one of the great and unforgettable screen characterizations" (Champlin 1970). The *New Yorker*'s Pauline Kael thought the film "strings us along and holds out on us. If we don't just want to have our prejudices greased, we'll find it confusing and unsatisfying, because we aren't given enough information to evaluate Patton's actions" (Kael 1970).

Despite some hesitancy among critics about the era's intensely anti-war and anti-military attitude, *Patton*, budgeted at $12 million, earned $61 million at box offices during its initial release (D'Este 2017). The film was nominated for 10 Academy Awards and won 7, including Best Picture, Best Director, Best Original Screenplay, and Best Actor. Scott refused to accept his Oscar, expressing disdain for the concept of acting competitions (Purtell 1993).

Patton's opening scene was employed for many years by the U.S. Army as a motivational clip for the troops and was used on the eve of Operation Desert Storm (1991), and the movie's martial theme melody was used in Armed Forces Network radio announcements (Sarantakes 2012, 180). The visual image of Scott's portrayal of Patton continues to define the public's impression of the general and remains stamped on the imagination. However, *Patton*'s overall reputation as a film has slipped. In America, *Esquire* magazine ranked it at only 15 in its "20 Best World War II Movies Ever Made," while Britain's *Time Out* magazine didn't see fit to include *Patton* in its "Best 50 World War II Movies." In film histories written in recent years, *Patton* merited only brief mentions as a stepping-stone in Francis Ford Coppola's career (Sklar 2002, 400; Cousins 2004, 337). Film historian David Thomson called it "mediocre and complacent" (Thomson 2012, 206). However, the film has not been forgotten. In 2003, the Library of Congress added *Patton* to the National Film Registry for its historical significance.

HISTORICAL BACKGROUND

From the first day when they appeared on the battlefield, lumbering across no-man's land on the Western Front (1916), the tank was formidable in appearance but vulnerable in reality. Especially early on, tanks were slow-moving targets. Even as the technology developed, tanks were plagued by mechanical problems and susceptible to landmines, air strikes, and even brave attacks by grenade-hurling infantry.

The introduction of the tank by British and French armies wasn't instrumental in World War I's outcome, but as a mobile bullet-proof gun platform, it provided a new kind of support for infantry struggling to advance against concentrated machine-gun fire.

Captain George S. Patton was a distinguished cavalry officer who had designed the U.S. Army's saber and wrote the manual for its use. He was dispatched to France in 1917 with the advance team of the American Expeditionary Force after the United States entered the war. Bored with his post at headquarters and with the cavalryman's traditional disdain for fighting on foot, Patton applied for a position in the army's newly formed Tank Corps. In stating his qualifications, he claimed that tanks would one day resemble cavalry in their operations and pointed to an incident in the recent U.S. "Punitive Expedition" in Mexico (1916–1917), where he became the first American officer to lead an attack using motor cars (Blumenson 1985, 96–97).

Promoted to major, Patton was put in charge of the first U.S. tank training school and given command of a tank battalion. He learned about tanks by observing the French and felt that light tanks "were rather like the mechanized equivalent of the mounted knight: mobile, armored, and deadly" (Axelrod 2006, 50).

Armed with French-made tanks, Patton displayed his ability and courage. He conducted dangerous reconnaissance near German lines to assess whether the ground was favorable for tanks. On their first day of combat, Patton's orders to his men were characteristic: "No tank is to be surrendered or abandoned to the enemy. If you are left alone in the midst of the enemy keep shooting" (Axelrod 2006, 53).

In September 1918, Patton's battalion took part in the massive Allied offensive at St. Mihiel. When he spotted tanks bogged down in muddy trenches, he walked two miles from his command post to help dig them out with shovels and continued on foot with his staff, leading his battalion as the tanks rolled forward (Axelrod 2006, 54). The battle was a great victory for the Allies, and although Patton lost nearly 50 tanks to enemy fire, engine failure, or impassible trenches, and another 30 ran out of fuel, his battalion performed splendidly under his hands-on leadership. When wounded in his second battle later that month, he instructed the orderlies to bring him to division headquarters, where he delivered his report, before taking him to the field hospital (Blumenson 1985, 114).

Although tanks were still unreliable and despite resistance from hidebound officers, forward-looking minds in the world's major armies were excited by the potential of armor as an antidote to the static warfare that had trapped Allied and German armies on the Western Front. Some of the most publicized advocates of armor were Britain's Major General J.F.C. Fuller (1878–1966) and Captain B.H. Liddell-Hart (1895–1970), whose writings were widely circulated.

Although forbidden to possess tanks by the Versailles Peace Treaty (1919), the German military avidly devoured the writings of Fuller and Liddell-Hart and collaborated in developing tank warfare with the Soviet Union. Both were pariahs in the family of nations and, despite their antagonistic ideologies, formed an uncomfortable marriage of convenience with Germany supplying technology and the Soviets providing proving grounds beyond the prying eyes of Western nations. German armament and automakers, including Daimler-Benz, eagerly drew up prototype tanks for the next war years before Hitler repudiated Versailles (1935). Germany's foremost proponent of panzers, as they called their tanks, Staff Officer Heinz Guderian (1888–1954), commanded the panzer army in World War II (Showalter 2009, 29–32).

Guderian helped conceive "blitzkrieg" warfare led by tanks supported by air cover, and Patton arrived at similar conclusions around the same time. In essays for military journals and speeches at the General Staff College, Patton stressed that the purpose of tanks was not to support infantry but to lead infantry to victory. Like cavalry in an earlier age, tanks would charge and break enemy lines, wreaking havoc that advancing infantry could exploit. However, Patton's plans remained on the shelf. The National Defense Act (1920) capped the army's strength and mandated that tanks be consigned to the infantry.

Patton rode out the interwar years as a cavalry officer, but the German blitzkrieg that overran Poland and Western Europe (1939–1940) gave him "a certain grim vindication" (Axelrod 2006, 75). In 1940, as the United States expanded its army and braced for the possibility of war, Chief of Staff George C. Marshall (1880–1959) authorized the establishment of two armored divisions. Patton was given command of an armored brigade and, in 1941, a full division.

Providing good copy for news reports by conducting heavily publicized military maneuvers with tanks in the lead, Patton became the public face of American-armored warfare in the year before Pearl Harbor. At the same time, a German rival emerged from obscurity. Although he had served as an infantry officer for most of his career, Rommel was given command of a panzer division in the blitzkrieg against France. For Rommel, "speed was the new mantra; rapidity of movement and thought was the key to modern battle" (Showalter 2009, 114–115).

Rommel's proficiency with armor proved vital in his next assignment. Hitler might have deemed the Afrika Korps as only a useful sideshow when it went into action in February 1942, but by June, Rommel had taken Libya from the British, sent them reeling back into Egypt, and threatened to cut the British Empire into half by seizing the Suez Canal. Rommel's panzer units "had little experience of desert conditions but possessed the considerable advantage of new equipment and a commander who was born a genius at this type of warfare" (Warner 2007, 87).

Bluffing and bewildering his opponents by rapid changes in direction, Rommel was promoted to field marshal by Hitler and dubbed the "Desert Fox" by the British. However, in October 1942, General Montgomery's Eighth Army stopped Rommel's advance at El Alamein. By the time Patton was given the lead role in defeating the Afrika Korps, Rommel was convalescing in Germany, and his forces had retreated to Tunisia. Germany proved increasingly unable to keep the Afrika Korps supplied with replacement tanks and crews, given Britain's command of the Mediterranean Sea and Hitler's preoccupation with subduing the Soviet Union.

With the possible exception of Patton, who looked to dueling knights in armor as a model for modern warfare, military strategists in the early years of the war gave little thought to pitting tanks against tanks. By the time the Afrika Korps swung into action against the British, the performance of tanks against each other became a consideration. As the Allies prepared to invade Europe, the U.S. M4 Sherman tank, manufactured in great number in

> ### ERWIN ROMMEL (1891–1944)
>
> Erwin Rommel was one of the only German officers of World War II recognized by the Allies not only as a capable tactician but also celebrated as a worthy opponent. A junior officer during World War I, Rommel steadily rose in the ranks of the postwar German army. Despite clashing with Nazi bureaucrats after Hitler came to power, Rommel's ascent continued. Hitler respected him based on his book on infantry tactics.
>
> When World War II began, Rommel's tactics of rapid maneuver gained him command of a panzer division during the fall of France. In 1941, he gained worldwide attention when given command of the Afrika Korps sent to Libya to buttress the Italians and threaten the Suez Canal. British journalists nicknamed him "the Desert Fox" in honor of his ability to evade pursuit and strike unexpectedly. He fought well but was unable to overcome Allied superiority in numbers and material, especially after America's entry into the war.
>
> Rommel became responsible for constructing the Atlantic Wall, the fortified shoreline barrier the Allies breached on D-Day (June 7, 1944). As Germany's fortunes rapidly declined, Rommel came to support the failed military coup against Hitler (July 20, 1944). Because of his status as a war hero, Hitler gave Rommel the option to quietly take his own life rather than face execution.
>
> Rommel's reputation for chivalry and opposition to Nazism remains controversial with historians continuing to seize on conflicting pieces of information to make their cases.

several variations, became standard in the American, British, Canadian, and Free French armies. Like all tanks, they were problematic and became the subject of many anecdotes. One story involved a defeated German officer explaining to his American captors the Sherman's vulnerability to his 88mm artillery. "The Americans kept sending tanks down the road. We kept knocking them out. We ran out of ammunition. You didn't run out of tanks." U.S. tank crews agreed with that assessment and dubbed the Shermans' "Zippos" for their proclivity to burst into flames when struck by a German shell (Showalter 2009, 334–335).

On the other hand, the Sherman tanks were fast and relatively reliable machines. As Patton had predicted 20 years earlier, speed was of the essence, and after the Normandy invasion, as Patton's tanks cut deep into France, U.S. infantry kept pace, riding in half-tracks and trucks rather than marching on foot. The Sherman's 75mm gun was inferior to the German 88, but its .50 caliber machine gun "chewed through earth and walls with devastating effect" (Showalter 2009, 341). With its mobility and speed, the Sherman tank proved itself as a worthy successor to horse cavalry of Patton's youth.

Patton's association with tank warfare was so pronounced that the U.S. Army named its primary postwar tank after him. The M48 Patton tank was America's primary battle tank from the 1950s through the 1990s and remains in service in many foreign countries. Patton was a pioneer of armored warfare from the first generation of tank strategists as well as combatants. Unlike most of his peers from those early days, he lived to fight in a war where tanks were decisive on some fronts.

DEPICTION AND HISTORICAL CONTEXT

Unlike most World War II movies produced in Hollywood, concerned with units of (usually) men and their diverse members, *Patton* focuses entirely on one man. The role of the secondary character, Omar Bradley, is to provide contrast. Bradley is represented as amiable and approachable in keeping with his identification as the "G.I. General," an image perpetrated during the war by syndicated cartoonist Ernie Pyle. Patrician and haughty, Patton's stern sense of a soldier's duty extends to the crease of his trousers and the shine on his boots and stands in high relief alongside the easygoing Bradley. Patton had been a proud member of that most elite branch of the U.S. Army, the cavalry, and wore his riding britches and carried his riding crop into the tank battles of World War II. The film never explains his biography or explores his personal life or the generations of offices his family nurtured beginning with the American Revolution. The screenplay and George C. Scott's portrayal gives viewers all they need to know about Patton's proudly bellicose sense of his place in the world.

Scott claimed to have read every available book on Patton and watched many hours of newsreel footage in a determined attempt to fully comprehend the spirit and manner of the man he portrayed. The only concession made was to ignore the reality of Patton's speaking voice, which was incongruously high pitched and less commanding in tone than Scott's.

Biographies of Patton written since the film's release only reconfirm how well Scott and Francis Ford Coppola did their homework. Even as a cadet at the Virginia Military Academy and West Point, Patton was "a stickler for protocol, regulations, impeccable uniforms, and the flawless practice of military courtesy, yet he nurtured within himself an unconventional boldness and an insatiable appetite for glory" (Axelrod 2006, 19).

Before the United States entered the war, Patton was determined to elevate the conscripts assigned to his armored division into professional soldiers of the highest caliber. He served as a role model and demanded nothing from his men that he wasn't willing to do himself. "He imposed strict discipline and strenuous standards and personally assured their attainment," teaching them not only how to march and shoot but also about the lore of military history (Blumenson 1985, 150). As shown in the movie, Patton loved to arrive at his new posts with police sirens wailing, behaving like a head of state in an armored motorcade.

Patton "impeccably represented the power of the United States at the Sultan's palace," honoring the dignity of local officials after seizing French Morocco from Vichy (November 1942). The pomp and circumstance pleased him, but he was eager to move on, defeat the Afrika Korps, and lead the planned invasion of Sicily (Blumenson 1985, 175). As a student of military history, he dreamed of following the footsteps of Hannibal, Scipio Africanus, and other great generals of the ancient Mediterranean world. A believer in reincarnation, Patton thought he had been one of Napoleon's generals and had fought the Turks in the 14th century (Axelrod 2006, 12). The scenes in *Patton* depicting him brooding over ancient ruins and speaking of having fought at those battlefields are not exaggerated.

Patton's actions upon taking command of the II Corps are reflected with pinpoint accuracy in the film. "He ordered everyone to wear clean, pressed uniforms, complete with neckties, leggings, and helmets. He established rigorous schedules and requirements for every activity no matter how mundane." The word in the army was that a "Patton man" could be recognized by the sharpness of his salute (Axelrod 2006, 96).

The invasion of Sicily was as contentious among the Allies as shown on screen. General Montgomery really did stride into a men's room, accosted an American adjutant, breathed on the mirror, and, tracing the outline of Sicily with his finger, drew his plan of attack. As in the film, Patton was outraged at the prospect of being overshadowed by Montgomery, confiding to his diary that his ability was greater than any Allied general and that he possessed a "greatness of soul based on a belief—an unshakable belief—in my destiny" (Axelrod 2006, 102–103). Once the troops were ashore, Patton moved quickly, almost as concerned with upstaging Montgomery as defeating the island's German and Italian defenders. Disregarding orders, he took Sicily's main cities, Messina and Palermo.

While visiting field hospitals in Sicily, Patton really did pin a Purple Heart on the chest of a dying soldier whose face was covered with an oxygen mask. The dialogue between Patton and a private in battle fatigue is also rendered accurately. When the soldier explains, "I can't stand the shelling anymore," the general flies into a rage, hurls insults, and repeatedly slaps the man with his gloves (Axelrod 2006, 115). Two incidents of this sort occurred, but the film condensed them into one. The Allied Supreme Commander, General Dwight D. Eisenhower (1890–1969), ordered the press to bury the story, but word leaked out. Reprimanded by Eisenhower, Patton made several speeches to his troops, given as one address in the film, apologizing while insisting that his behavior was intended to remind the men he slapped of "their obligations as men and soldiers" (Axelrod 2006, 118–119).

The scene in *Patton* set in Corsica, where the general gave a speech after the island's liberation from Vichy, encapsulates several points about Patton and his "post-slapping" career. Unlike most U.S. officers, he was fluent in

French and something of a Francophile. He spoke in a stream of profanity to his troops but was a pillar of dignity when representing America in a setting he found agreeable. After his conduct on Sicily, Eisenhower was wary of giving Patton a battlefield command. He was sent instead on a series of junkets around the Mediterranean, including visits to Algiers, Tunis, Cairo, Jerusalem, and Malta. Patton especially enjoyed visiting Napoleon's birthplace in Corsica.

One purpose of those trips was to deceive the Germans about Allied intentions (Blumenson 1985, 214). The film's periodic cutaways to German headquarters in Berlin accurately reveal the enemy's respect for Patton's martial skills. According to a German general captured after the war, Patton was "always the main topic of military discussion. Where is he? When will he attack?" Field Marshall Gerd von Rundstedt (1875–1953), Germany's commander in France at the time of the Normandy invasion, said, "Patton was your best" (Blumenson 1985, 296).

By some accounts, *Patton* strays into misrepresentation in its portrayal of Montgomery, played by Michael Bates (1920–1978), a British actor who had served as an officer in World War II. While treating Rommel (played by German actor Karl Michael Vogler, 1928–2009) sympathetically, Montgomery is cast as a preening peacock, arrogant and inept in the face of Patton's brilliant audacity. Reality was more complicated. Montgomery earned "a reputation for being a soldier's general, thanks to his regular contact with the units and men under his command" (Sarantakes 2012, 110). However, he was as tactless as Patton, and his 1958 memoir criticized the performance of generals in many armies, including Eisenhower.

Sensitive over lawsuits, 20th Century Fox changed the names of many Allied soldiers seen in the film but could not replace Montgomery, a hero in Great Britain, with a lightly fictionalized character. If angered by his portrayal, Montgomery could have sued in a British court, where libel was defined more broadly than in the United States. The possibility of legal action hung over the production like a dark cloud. After two years of discussions with lawyers, 20th Century Fox executive Darryl F. Zanuck (1902–1979) gambled that time was on the studio's side. Montgomery could be dead before his suit could reach judgment. In the end, Montgomery held his fire (Sarantakes 2012, 110–112).

Patton was filmed largely in Spain. The country's army, still equipped with World War II American tanks and command cars, became a willing pool of extras. Spanish troops in United States and German uniforms played entire battalions of soldiers on both sides after the producers convinced the country's military leaders that the screenplay was pro and not anti-military. The rugged, rocky Spanish terrain was an ideal stand-in for Tunisia and Sicily while the city of Pamplona was a believable backdrop for scenes set in France. The region around Segovia, cold enough for winter snow, was the setting for the filming of the Battle of the Bulge. The realism was enhanced by technical advisor Paul D. Harkins, a U.S. Army veteran who ensured that all vehicles bore correct markings and looked sufficiently gritty, as if they had survived a campaign in dusty country. The only involvement by the U.S. military concerned the loan of landing craft for an amphibious landing. As much as possible, director Franklin Schaffner choreographed the battle scenes as described in the official U.S. Army chronicle of the war (Sarantakes 2012, 113–116, 118–120).

At least one small mistake is visible. The Italian flag that decorated Messina when the city welcomed Patton as their liberator was adapted in 1946, three years after the event was depicted. In 1943, the Italian tricolor still bore the royal arms of the House of Savoy in its middle color bar. The era's 48-star American flag was correct throughout the film.

Well connected with the entertain industry, Bradley was hired by 20th Century Fox as *Patton*'s military advisor. Bradley's main objective was to maintain the "down-to-earth" reputation he cultivated during his wartime service. As a result, the film smooths over Patton's disdain for Bradley; in reality, they were never close friends. Bradley vetted the screenplay, and several of his minor changes were incorporated into the final version (Sarantakes 2012, 95–96).

Even with its nearly three-hour running time, *Patton* could not encompass the entirety of the general's wartime experience from 1943 through 1945 or his brief, controversial role in administering Occupied Germany. Many situations were condensed or combined for the sake of time and to maintain dramatic momentum. Characteristic of the method behind the screenplay was Coppola's construction of Patton's opening speech in front of the giant American flag, which never occurred, but words were taken from remarks the general made on various occasions. Although *Patton* is no longer fashionable among film adepts, it remains popular among military history buffs and for good reason. Few Hollywood war pictures adhered as closely to the facts as *Patton*.

FURTHER READING

Axelrod, Alan. 2006. *Patton: A Biography*. New York: Palgrave Macmillan.
Blumenson, Martin. 1985. *Patton: The Man behind the Legend, 1885–1945*. New York: William Morrow.
Canby, Vincent. 1970. "A Salute to a Rebel." *New York Times*, February 5, 1970. https://archive.nytimes.com/www.nytimes.com/packages/html/movies/bestpictures/patton-re.html?mcubz=1
Champlin, Charles. 1970. "'Patton' Features George C. Scott as 'Old Blood and Guts.'" *Los Angeles Times*, February 15, 1970.
Cousins, Mark. 2004. *The Story of Film*. New York: Thunder's Mouth Press.
D'Este, Carlo. 2017. "The Patton Film: From Real to Reel." HistoryNet, April 11, 2017. https://www.historynet.com/patton-film-real-reel.htm

Esquire. 2017. "The 20 Best World War II Movies Ever Made." June 13, 2017. https://www.esquire.com/entertainment/movies/g3476/best-world-war-2-movies-of-all-time/

Kael, Pauline. 1970. "The Man Who Loved War." *New Yorker*, January 31, 1970. https://www.newyorker.com/magazine/1970/01/31/1970-01-31-073-tny-cards-000295411

Purtell, Tim. 1993. "1971: George C. Scott Said No to Oscar." *Entertainment Weekly*, April 16, 1993. https://ew.com/article/1993/04/16/1971-george-c-patton-said-no-oscar/

Sarantakes, Nicholas Evan. 2012. *Making* Patton: *A Classic War Film's Epic Journey to the Silver Screen*. Lawrence: University of Kansas Press.

Schumacher, Michael. 1999. *Francis Ford Coppola: A Filmmaker's Life*. New York: Crown.

Sheward, David. 2008. *Rage and Glory: The Volatile Life and Career of George C. Scott*. New York: Applause.

Showalter, Dennis. 2009. *Hitler's Panzers: The Lightning Attacks That Revolutionized Warfare*. New York: Berkley Caliber.

Siskel, Gene. 1970. "Patton." *Chicago Tribune*, March 5, 1970.

Sklar, Robert. 2002. *Film: A World History*. New York: Abrams.

Thomson, David. 2012. *The Big Screen: The Story of the Movies*. New York: Farrar, Straus and Giroux.

Time Out. 2019. "The 50 Best World War II Movies." February 19, 2019. https://www.timeout.com/london/film/50-best-world-war-ii-movies

Warner, Philip. 2007. *World War Two: The Untold Story*. London: Cassell.

Chapter 8

Das Boot (1981)

The complicated history of *Das Boot* began with the 1973 autobiographical novel of the same name by Lothar-Günther Buchheim (1918–2007), which by 1981 had been translated into 14 languages and had sold two million copies around the world. American investors purchased the movie rights in the mid-1970s and hoped to lure familiar stars such as Robert Redford (1936–) and Paul Newman (1925–2008) into the picture. *Das Boot* finally debuted in Germany on September 17, 1981, and found international distribution early the following year.

For that project, the U.S. production company Pressman Film hired John Sturges (1910–1992), director of the popular World War II movie *The Great Escape* (1963), and screenwriter Ronald M. Cohn (1939–1998). The film was intended for tax purposes as a German-U.S. coproduction, but after the German partners rejected the script for being riddled with Teutonic stereotypes, Sturges became unavailable, and the project went dormant before the rights were sold to German distributer Neue Constantin (Kramer 2017). The film's eventual writer and director, Wolfgang Petersen (1941–), had been a television and film director with a reputation in his West German homeland for tackling controversial subject matter.

When first released in the United States by Columbia Pictures, *Das Boot* was screened in two versions, one dubbed in English for wider release and another with English subtitles for the art house circuit. Later, it was released in different edits of varying lengths for home video and shown in a three-hour version as a German TV mini-series before resurfacing theatrically in 1997 in a 210-minute director's cut, which was more than half an hour longer than the version first seen in 1981.

Das Boot opens in La Rochelle, an Atlantic port in German-occupied France, in the autumn of 1941. Drunken sailors stagger onto the road to the U-boat base, blocking the car carrying Lieutenant Werner, played by Herbert Grönemeyer (1956–). The officers he meets in a La Rochelle cabaret are similarly drunken and rowdy. Lieutenant Werner is a submarine novice, a war correspondent assigned to accompany the crew of *U-96* on their next mission. He is expected to write a stirring report of heroism. He will see heroism at close hand soon enough, but his eyes will also be opened to the horrors of submarine warfare and the dissatisfaction with the Nazis among the fighting men.

One of the U-boat flotilla's commanders, Captain Thomsen (played by Otto Sander, 1941–2013), is being honored at the cabaret for receiving Germany's highest decoration, the Knight's Cross. Instead of making the requisite remarks about Germany's destiny, he begins to mock Adolf Hitler; perceiving the room's stunned silence, he quickly shifts to a scurrilous attack on Britain's Winston Churchill (1874–1965). Before leaving the cabaret, Werner is as drunk as his new companions and begins to suspect that the binge drinking is driven by the men's need to black out the trauma of their missions.

Werner finds lack of political enthusiasm once *U-96* sets off with a brass band playing from the dockside. That submarine's captain, affectionately called "Der Alte" (The Old Man) by the crew and played by Jürgen Prochnow (1941–), grumbles about the war. Only one officer is a dedicated Nazi, and he is mocked by his colleagues for being a true believer.

The film grants little time to politics, and the U-boat's crew is more concerned with lovers and family left behind than with ideology. When Der Alte shouts "Alarm!" and "Get into diving positions!" *U-96* rapidly descends to a depth of 160 meters (524 feet) where the water pressure causes the hull to creak. It's only a drill, but during their three-week patrol in the North Atlantic, they will be forced to repeat their exercise under battlefield conditions.

After receiving a coded radiogram, Der Alte orders *U-96* toward the reported position of a convoy bound for Britain. This exemplifies the "wolf pack" tactic in which several U-boats converge on a convoy and launch torpedoes at targets as they come into range. *U-96* cruises on the surface of the stormy Atlantic for many miles to gain greater speed. Visibility is poor, but through the mist and spray, Der Alte, standing on the conning tower, suddenly spots a British destroyer bearing down on them. *U-96* dives quickly, and the anxious crew waits as the sound of the destroyer's propellers pass overhead. More terrifying is the sound of exploding depth charges that rock the submarine. To escape the explosions, Der Alte orders *U-96* to descend deeper than it was designed to go. They wait for the destroyer to depart.

Rising to the surface, *U-96* heads toward the convoy and sights columns of ships on the horizon. The submarine fires torpedoes and dives. The crew hears the moan of sinking freighters, their bulkheads breaking, and they know that British escort ships are coming for revenge even before they hear the ominous ping-ping of Asdic. A British version of sonar developed as early as in the 1920s, Asdic is a device that sends out repeated electronic impulses (pings), timing and measuring the echo to locate submerged submarines. A direct hit by a depth charge would have shattered the *U-96*, but even the near misses are destructive, causing a small explosion and fires that have to be put out immediately. As the ping-pinging continues, *U-96* descends deeper into the ocean, tightening the water pressure's grip on the hull and causing bolts to pop and water to gush into the boat. Chief Mechanic Johann (played by Erwin Leder, 1951–), a veteran of nine patrols, suffers a breakdown from the stress and has to be restrained.

The crew repairs the damage and waits for the destroyers to depart, their direction and distance traced through the submarine's hydrophone, a listening device that detects propellers at a great distance. The *U-96* surfaces. Der Alte decides to "finish off" a burning tanker with a torpedo but discovers, to his regret, that sailors were still alive aboard the ship. They jump and swim toward the U-boat for help, but the submarine withdraws under standing orders against rescuing enemy sailors. Johann reemerges, apologizing to Der Alte for his behavior under fire. "My nerves cracked somehow," he says. Der Alte threatens him with a court martial but relents. Good U-boats mechanics are scarce.

ASDIC

During World War I, German U-boats threatened to bring Great Britain to its knees by enforcing a blockade on the British Isles. U-boats sank thousands of ships carrying many tons of cargo to Britain. When the war began, unless U-boats surfaced, there was no way to detect their presence except by scanning the sea for periscopes.

The Allies scrambled to develop detection technology starting with the hydrophone, enabling surface ships to listen for the sound of submarines under water. As the war continued, Britain invented a more sophisticated system called ASDIC, which sent sound waves into the ocean to detect submarines. The British tested prototypes in 1918, but it was too late for introduction into the war against U-boats. The Royal Navy began installing ASDIC in warships intended for anti-submarine warfare beginning in 1922.

With the start of World War II, Germany repeated its strategy for victory by maintaining an undersea blockade of their enemy. The longer range of newer U-boats posed a greater threat to the Western Hemisphere. As early as 1940, as part of its bid for an alliance with the United States, the British shared ASDIC technology with the U.S. Navy. At the same time, American engineers developed their own underwater detection system called sonar.

Running low on fuel, Der Alte intends to return his sub to base, but a radiogram orders *U-96* to restock its supplies at the Spanish port of Vigo and proceed into the Mediterranean Sea. The crew is angry. They hoped to be on land for Christmas. Der Alte is worried because passage into the Mediterranean means running the British gauntlet at Gibraltar, where only nine miles of heavily patrolled channel separates the British stronghold from North Africa.

His plan to slip past the British is foiled when *U-96* is spotted and comes under attack. The submarine is badly damaged and sinks to the bottom but miraculously lands softly on sand instead of being crushed against hard rock. Water pours in from all sides and oxygen runs low, yet the crew's herculean efforts enable the badly damaged submarine to rise and make its way to La Rochelle.

In an ironic conclusion, the *U-96* arrives in port, greeted by a brass band, just in time for a British air raid. The port facilities go up in flames, many crew members are killed while running for shelter in the bomb-proof U-boat pens, and Der Alte dies after watching his submarine sink from a direct bomb hit.

Das Boot was among the most expensive German films produced up to that time and one of the most profitable. Made on a budget of $18.5 million, it grossed $84.9 million worldwide. The author of the novel on which it was based, whose screenplay had been rejected, complained loudly, claiming Petersen had subverted his antiwar message. However, in Germany, the United States, and elsewhere, audiences responded enthusiastically to a sympathetic and realistic portrayal of men in combat under extreme duress.

American reviewers were generally favorable. The *New York Times* praised the film for "the quiet compassion and precise detail with which its story has been told" and Petersen for presenting episodes familiar from an earlier generation of submarine warfare movies such as *Run Silent, Run Deep* (1958) "more graphically than Hollywood might" and for ending "this already-embittered movie on an unusually grim note, sending home its anti-war message in no uncertain terms" (Maslin 1982).

Although *Das Boot* won no Oscars, it received an unusual level of recognition for a foreign language film at the 1983 Academy Awards by earning six nominations, including Best Director. For Petersen, *Das Boot* was a springboard to a career in Hollywood, where he enjoyed mixed success.

If judged by the response to the 1997 release of the longer director's cut, critical assessment of *Das Boot* only grew more positive with time. According to the *Washington Post*, the director's cut "propels itself through your consciousness with ever greater power" than the edited version that appeared in American theaters 15 years earlier (Howe 1997). Roger Ebert agreed, calling the director's cut "not a minor readjustment but a substantially longer film" and praising the "long sequences here—especially when the boat is sinking out of control—when we feel trapped in the same time and space as the desperate crew" (Ebert 1997).

Das Boot ranked 41 in a recent list of the "45 Best War Movies of All Times" (Lynch 2018) and was included in the British Film Institute's "10 Great Battleship and War-at-Sea Films" (Parkinson 2018).

HISTORICAL BACKGROUND

The first successful use of submarines in warfare occurred during the American Civil War (1861–1865) when the Confederate navy pitted primitive submersible craft against U.S. warships. By 1900, the U.S. Navy launched the first fully practical submarine, propelled not by steam but a gasoline engine while on surface and an electric motor when submerged. Periscopes enabled submarines to see their targets while lurking just below the waterline. The newly invented self-propelled torpedo became the vessels' primary weapon.

With the onset of World War I (1914–1918), all the major powers possessed submarines, yet only Germany explored their full potential. Their strategy was impelled by geography. Great Britain commanded the approaches to northwest Europe and was able to bottle up Germany's surface fleet and impose a nearly impenetrable naval blockade. Germany struck back with its fleet of *Unterseebooten* (U-boats), which sank British warships and preyed on shipping bound for the British Isles. In the early months of the war, U-boats sometimes surfaced after spotting merchant ships and granted their crews the opportunity to lower lifeboats. Given the vulnerability of surfaced submarines to deck guns mounted on merchant ships, the practice was abandoned in favor of stealth attack by torpedo.

Germany declared a war zone in the waters around Great Britain and placed advertisements in U.S. newspapers warning travelers that ships bound for Britain would be torpedoed. However, travel continued, and international outcry followed the sinking of the British ocean liner *Lusitania* off the Irish coast by a U-boat on May 7, 1915. With over 100 American passengers dead, the attack prompted a shift in public attitude toward intervening in the war. Hoping to maintain American neutrality, Germany restrained its U-boat attacks in the face of criticism.

However, with hunger and shortages increasing under the iron chokehold of the British blockade, German leaders saw no choice but to counter with an undersea blockade of Great Britain. In February 1917, Germany issued a declaration of "unrestricted submarine warfare," including attacks on ships sailing from neutral nations toward Britain. The move precipitated America's declaration of war against Germany. In April 1917, U-boats sank 430 Allied or neutral merchant ships and "came within a whisker of bringing Britain to its knees" (Bishop 2006, 8). The introduction of a convoy system guarded by escorting warships and the deployment of the U.S. Navy turned the tide against the U-boats.

Mindful of Germany's success with submarines, the Treaty of Versailles (1919) adamantly forbid Germany from possessing U-boats. Germany surrendered all surviving submarines to the Allies and scrapped submarines under construction. The treaty overlooked the documentary records and engineering specifications of the U-boat fleet, which the much reduced German navy kept for future use. Although prohibited from constructing submarines, Germany "actively marketed her expertise in this field," selling designs to Japan and establishing a front company in the Netherlands. The ostensibly Dutch company built submarines for Turkey and Finland and provided experts to train their crews (Williamson 2002, 3–4).

In 1933, Germany established an Anti-Submarine Defense School as a cover while preparing to relaunch the U-boat fleet. New designs were developed. With Hitler's renunciation of the Versailles Treaty (1933) and the subsequent Anglo-German Naval Agreement (1935), the subterfuge was removed, and Germany began an ambitious program of U-boat construction.

By the time World War II began (September 1, 1939), Germany possessed a flotilla of modern U-boats capable of voyaging deep into the Atlantic. They went into action immediately. On September 2, *U-30* sighted the British liner *Athenia* a few hundred miles off the Irish coast. Because she sailed with lights off and on a zigzag course, the U-boat's commander assumed the liner was a military transport or naval auxiliary. He fired torpedoes and sank the *Athenia*, causing over 100 deaths including 28 American passengers.

The attack was a violation of international law. Germany was among the signers of a 1936 protocol governing submarine warfare. The treaty insisted that submarines must surface before opening fire on merchant ships, send a boarding party to examine the cargo manifests, and allow passengers and crew to escape on lifeboats. Dreaming of luring Great Britain to the peace table, Hitler was furious over the sinking of the *Athenia* and denied responsibility. In the months ahead as it became clear that Britain was unlikely to seek compromise with Germany, Hitler lifted all restrictions on submarine warfare (Symonds 2018, 8, 10).

Naval targets were always fair game. In October 1939, *U-47* embarked on a mission to penetrate the Royal Navy's stronghold at Scapa Flow, an anchorage in the Orkney Islands off the northern tip of Scotland. The British thought the channel leading into Scapa Flow was impregnable. The channel to the anchorage was guarded by coastal artillery and screened by minefields, wire mesh nets to trap submarines, and the sunken hulks of ships that narrowed the passage. Surfacing at night, *U-47* threaded through the obstacle course and into the anchorage. Despite the failure of several torpedoes to explode or find their target, *U-47* managed to sink the battleship *Royal Oak*, killing 800 crewmen. Confident that no submarine could enter Scapa Flow, the British thought they were under air attack and never detected the *U-47* as it slipped into the open sea (Symonds 2018, 13–16). The *U-47* went on to sink a total of 31 ships before being sunk with all hands by a British destroyer in March 1941 (Williamson 2002, 22).

The commander of the U-boat force, Admiral Karl Dönitz (1891–1980), devised the "tonnage strategy" (*Tonnengeschlacht*) for starving Britain into surrender. The plan was based on the assumption that U-boats "could sink Allied ships faster than they could be replaced by new construction" (Symonds 2018, 104). He was never able to fully implement the scheme. Dönitz struggled for resources against fellow admirals in Germany's surface fleet and against the Berlin high command's insistence on dispersing U-boats to the Mediterranean and Arctic seas. The U.S. entry into the war made the tonnage strategy untenable. American industry could produce freighters faster than Germany could sink them. German industry produced more than enough U-boats to replace units sunk by the enemy but was hard pressed to drastically increase the overall size of the U-boat fleet.

During the war's early months, U-boats were hampered, like the *U-47* at Scapa Flow, by dysfunctional torpedoes. In May 1941, German engineers examined a captured British submarine and found that its torpedo triggers were "both simpler and more reliable than their own." The Germans quickly copied the British design, increasing the deadliness of their boats (Symonds 2018, 105).

Remembering the effectiveness of convoys in the final year of World War I, Britain established a convoy system as World War II began. Usually they consisted of 20–40 merchant ships traveling in widely separated columns to avoid giving U-boats a concentrated target and to avert collisions in rough seas. A 40-ship convoy filled a stretch of ocean five miles across and three miles long as it crossed the Atlantic (Hague 2000, 26–28).

Even when the best precautions were in place, convoys continued to be attacked, and even when a torpedoed ship sank slowly enough for crew and passengers to follow evacuation plans, lifeboats often provided poor sanctuary for survivors. A *Life* magazine photographer who scrambled onto a lifeboat after her ship was struck by a torpedo provided American readers with a vivid account. "The sea, which from above had looked so calm, rose up against us wave after wave and began beating us back against the side of the ship. Our crew strained at the oars." The boat was so crowded that the rowers had difficulty manning the oars; the ocean washed into the boat whose occupants continuously bailed out water; many survivors were seasick (Bourke-White 1943).

Convoys were escorted haphazardly at first, sometimes by merchant ships rigged up with deck guns. Later, most convoys were accompanied by a bodyguard of destroyers and smaller warships called corvettes, many of the latter in service with the Royal Canadian Navy on the long journey from Halifax, Nova Scotia, to Liverpool and Glasgow. Desperately short of warships, Churchill begged U.S. president Franklin D. Roosevelt (1882–1945) for 50 obsolescent World War I-vintage destroyers "mothballed" for years in Atlantic ports. In September 1940, Roosevelt traded them with Britain for leases on British bases in the Caribbean.

Although U.S. neutrality laws and isolationist sentiment among the American public hampered his desire to aid Great Britain, Roosevelt declared a "security zone" reaching 200 miles into the Atlantic from the U.S. East Coast. Although the security zone's stated purpose was to prepare the defense of the Americas should the European war spill over into the western hemisphere, the destroyers of the U.S. "Neutrality Patrols" searched the zone for U-boats and broadcast their location to the British. American warships shadowed British convoys to the mid-Atlantic, which allowed the Royal Navy to concentrate its thinly stretched forces in the "Western Approaches" to the British Isles. Meanwhile, alarmed by the fall of France, Congress appropriated money to dramatically increase the U.S. Navy's size.

Roosevelt and Hitler played a dangerous game of chicken in the North Atlantic. According to Interior Secretary Harold Ickes (1874–1952), Roosevelt was "waiting for the Germans to create an incident" (Ickes 1954, 523), while Hitler, preoccupied with subjugating Eastern Europe, ordered his U-boats to attack convoys but give America no excuse to enter the war.

Despite caution on both sides, incidents at sea began to occur. On September 4, 1941, the U.S. destroyer *Greer* and *U-652* exchanged fire near Iceland. On October 10, the destroyer *Kearny*, escorting a British convoy, was struck but not sunk by a torpedo. The 11 sailors who died were the first American military casualties in the Battle of the Atlantic, as historians have called the nearly five-year struggle for control of the ocean. On October 30, *U-552* sank the destroyer *Reuben James* while on convoy duty. America and Germany remained wary combatants as they circled each other in the Atlantic until Pearl Harbor (December 7, 1941), when the Japanese attack thrust the United States into war against the Axis on all fronts.

As Japan advanced in the Pacific, Hitler finally authorized Dönitz to unleash his U-boats against the U.S. Eastern Seaboard. Calling his plan Operation Drumbeat (*Paukenschlag*), Dönitz sent fifteen U-boats to the shores of Canada and the United States in January 1942. They sat quietly on the bottom of the Continental Shelf by day and surfaced at night, finding tankers and freighters sailing with lights on or silhouetted against the bright lights of coastal cities. In the first two weeks of Operation Drumbeat, the Germans sank 41 Allied ships, many in sight of the shoreline. Peter Cremer (1911–1992), commander of *U-333*, recalled that "through the night glasses we could distinguish equally the big hotels and the cheap dives, and read the flickering neon signs" (Cremer 1982, 69).

American newspapers were filled with alarming headlines such as "U-boat Torpedoes Tanker Off Long Island" and "War is Brought Nearer to U.S. in Sea Attack." Although the U.S. government tried to minimize news of the sinkings, word got out. Katherine Phillips (1923–), a teenager in Mobile, Alabama, recalled finding debris from sunken ships, "the life preservers and the canned goods washed up on our beaches" (Ward and Burns 2007, 22). Operation Drumbeat continued unabated into spring 1942 and spread into the Gulf of Mexico. In an especially daring thrust, a U-boat sank a freighter in the mouth of the Mississippi River (Symonds 2018, 257). The threat to America's coastal waterways diminished that summer after Dönitz was ordered to redirect his efforts closer to the British Isles and to Allied convoys ferrying supplies to the Soviet Union.

As in previous wars, commanders in belligerent nations communicated with their units by code, and their enemies invested great effort in breaking the ciphers. The German military used the most sophisticated encoding device known at the time, the typewriter keyboard-operated Enigma machine. By striking a key, the operator generated an electrical impulse that passed through three metal rotors. With each rotor's 26 settings, coupled with other mechanical and electrical variables, each keystroke could produce 160 quintillion outcomes. Messages sent by Enigma could only be reassembled into a coherent message by another Enigma machine whose operator knew the settings, which changed daily (Kahn 1991, 195–196).

The analysts at Britain's Government Code and Cypher School at Bletchley Park near London began work on cracking Enigma even before the war began when they were alerted to the machine's existence by a Polish mathematician. In May 1940, Britain seized an Enigma machine from a German ship and retrieved a code book from a sinking U-boat. Led by mathematician Alan Turing (1912–1954), the Bletchley team constructed an electromagnetic computer to mimic and process Enigma messages.

Even so, decoding remained difficult. By the summer of 1941, Bletchley Park could decipher messages within 36 hours of interception, which often resulted in altering the routes of convoys to avoid wolf pack attacks, yet the "breaking of the Enigma code did not produce a complete reversal of fortune" (Symonds 2018, 250). In February 1942, the German navy upgraded the Enigma machine, baffling Bletchley Park for many months. Losses to U-boats jumped significantly before British codebreakers could catch up. At the same time, Germany monitored British naval signals, using decoded messages to dispatch wolf packs to ambush convoys.

As in World War I, the United States' entrance into the war, bringing the full force of the country's industrial might and population into the fight, blunted the U-boat campaign. By late 1943, U.S. aircraft carriers were escorting some convoys, and radar-equipped, long-range B-24 Liberator bombers proved lethal to submarines riding on the surface.

Dönitz ordered his U-boats to remain submerged during daylight to avoid air attack, resulting in fewer Allied ships being sunk. Also, by the end of 1943, the Royal Navy changed its code system, frustrating German intelligence. "There were just too many escorts, and too many aircraft buzzing around the waters of the Atlantic for the U-boats to achieve victory" (Hoyt 1988, 198).

The Allied invasion of France forced U-boats to abandon bases on the French Atlantic coast. U-boat losses mounted, and the toll on Allied shipping fell. By 1945, Germany had introduced a new generation of U-boats—faster, armed with homing torpedoes, able to travel 90 days without refueling, and equipped with snorkels that brought fresh air into submerged vessels. Despite the superior technology, Allied air attacks on factories, railroads, shipyards, assembly points, and ports grew more destructive. Germany was unable to build or deploy enough of the super U-boats to alter or even slow the course of the war.

DEPICTION AND HISTORICAL CONTEXT

The author of the novel that was the source for *Das Boot* described his story as "a novel but not a work of fiction." Buchheim's account was a lightly fictionalized memoir of his experience as a war correspondent assigned to a U-boat to report on their patrol in the Atlantic. Buchheim changed the names of the personnel, his submarine, and its home base. The real *U-96*, more successful than its fictional namesake, was in service from September 1940 to March 3, 1945, when British fighter bombers sank the vessel at Wilhelmshaven, Germany, rather than La Rochelle, France (Gröning 1966, 386).

Petersen's screenplay follows the book, condensing its 600 pages into three hours; like the novel, the movie opens with drunken revelry during shore leave and follows the crew of *U-96* on their mission. Petersen's modifications and editing resulted from the necessities of cinema for dramatizing the story within a time frame acceptable in movie theaters. He shifted Saint-Nazaire, the U-boat base in Buchheim's novel, to La Rochelle where World War II U-boat pens still stood intact. The novel was told from the correspondent's point of view, but the movie broadens the perspective and reduces him to one character among many.

Das Boot maintains a high degree of historical accuracy, beginning with the statement in the opening title that 40,000 sailors went to sea in U-boats during World War II and 30,000 died. The numbers are true (Williamson 2002, 22). The wild night on the shore with officers and enlisted men enjoying their reveling separately reflects the arrangement in the French ports, where U-boat officers occupied first-class hotels and sailors slept in second-rate hostels. Regardless of rank, their "need to relieve the stress was immediate and powerful" (Hoyt 1988, 70). Most U-boats didn't carry war correspondents into combat, but the purpose of their occasional presence was understood by all. "The Nazi propaganda machine was going full blast, and the names of the most successful captains were becoming household words in Hitler's Europe" (Hoyt 1988, 87).

Like Thomsen with his Knight's Cross in the opening scene, successful submarine commanders were lionized in the German media as "U-boat aces." The most acclaimed, *U-99*'s captain, Otto Kretschmer (1912–1998), sank 11 enemy ships on his first patrol. He eventually destroyed 56 Allied ships, sending 313,000 tons to the ocean floor, before a British destroyer sank *U-99* in March 1941. Unlike most of his colleagues, trapped in sinking U-boats, Kretschmer survived as a prisoner of war and became an admiral in the postwar navy of the German Federal Republic (West Germany) (Williamson 2002, 23).

The departure and homecoming of *U-96* is correctly rendered. The crew would have stood at attention on deck as a brass band played and dignitaries watched their departure from the shore. When not at sea, the submarines slipped into U-boat pens, constructed of reinforced concrete to prevent damage from air raids. As seen at the film's climax, British fighter bombers shattered harbor facilities, but their bombs were unable to penetrate the U-boat pens (Hoyt 1988, 69–70). Today, the La Rochelle U-boat pens remain intact and are sometimes used by the modern French navy.

Most U-boats were 220 feet long, carried a crew of 44 sailors and 14 torpedoes and had a range of up to 7,400 miles. Diesel engines enabled U-boats to sail on the surface at a brisk 17 knots. Powered by a 124-cell battery, electric motors could carry submerged U-boats for 80 miles at a top speed of 7.6 knots. *Das Boot* accurately displays the details of the U-boat's design and engineering down to the blue-and-white checked patterns of the bunks' sheets.

The vessel was no wider than a galley kitchen. Smoked meats, sausages, and sacks of produce hung along the corridor, and as enough accommodations for everyone were lacking, enlisted men took turns on the bunks. Every inch of space was accounted for. No portrait of Hitler was visible; in his place was a photograph of Dönitz, beloved to U-boat crews for his personal interest in their welfare. U-boat officers and sailors drank alcohol while on patrol as shown in several scenes. The film makes the close atmosphere vivid, and the dialogue alludes to the smell of socks and foulness of the air after the boat is submerged for long stretches.

Early on, Der Alte remarks that his crew consists largely of "baby faced kids" and calls their mission a "children's crusade." He reflects on the reality that seasoned submariners, lost in combat in growing number, were replaced by green sailors and officers. Before the war began, U-boat crews received 12 months of training. By 1941, their apprenticeship was reduced to three months (Hoyt 1988, 88).

The most dramatic scenes accurately visualize the situation of a U-boat under attack. British warships sometimes emerged suddenly from night and fog, bearing down on U-boats and forcing the submarines to crash-dive. U-boats were also subject to depth charges dropped by aircraft or naval ships, seen in several scenes as the British propellers and Asdic whir and ping overhead. As shown, the British dropped a "pattern of depth charges," scattered over a U-boat's suspected position and set to detonate at different depths. To escape destruction, U-boats descended to fathoms "far deeper than any engineer had promised the vessels would survive" (Hoyt 1988, 39).

At such depths, the heavy pressure of the water threatened to crush the hull like an eggshell; valves popped, water gushed in, and repairs were made rapidly with no time for indecision. U-boat captains, like Der Alte, ordered their men to rush aft or forward to compensate for the weight of the rushing water threatening to pitch the submarine out of balance (Hoyt 1988, 41).

In *Das Boot*'s most talked about scene, "the episode that was endlessly discussed when the film came out in 1981" (Ebert 1997), *U-96* surfaces to view the burning tanker it had torpedoed hours earlier. Der Alte chooses to dispatch the ship with a torpedo, but this was not the usual procedure. Torpedoes were too valuable to waste, and U-boats normally "finished off" a sinking enemy ship with a shot from their deck guns (Williamson 2002, 36).

However, the scene assumes moral rather than logistical significance with the realization, after the torpedo was fired, that some of the tanker's crew remain onboard and are forced to jump and swim toward *U-96*. The situation is realistic on two levels. Convoys under U-boat attack often kept moving and made no attempt to rescue sailors from torpedoed ships; Der Alte's refusal to pick up the desperate swimmers complies with Dönitz's order to not risk attack by rescuing enemy sailors. Early in the war, some U-boat commanders disobeyed Dönitz and brought enemy crewmen onboard after sinking their ships, but by 1941, as danger from Allied ships and planes increased, all vestiges of chivalry disappeared (Hoyt 1988, 39, 45–47).

The order to proceed through the Strait of Gibraltar coincides with the reality of Germany deployments. At the end of November 1941, Dönitz reluctantly obeyed orders from Berlin and sent six U-boats to the Mediterranean Sea; in December, he sent 10 more. "He was, he told his associates grimly, being told to send his boys into a trap" (Hoyt 1988, 119). The shallow, confined waters of the Mediterranean were not ideal for Dönitz's U-boat tactics, and passage through the Strait of Gibraltar was difficult. However, the screenplay exaggerates the challenge by implying it was virtually impossible to pass British patrols of Gibraltar when, in reality, many U-boats were able to make the passage.

Like *U-96*, German submarines called on the port of Vigo in Spain, where a German cargo ship provided fuel and supplies. The comment by that ship's commander that the Spanish "have no great love for us" is odd. Although officially neutral, Spain sent the Blue Division of over 20,000 troops to fight alongside Axis forces in the Soviet Union and dispatched thousands of volunteers to work in German factories.

Das Boot depicts a truth about warfare seldom shown as clearly or frankly in movies. Men in combat veered from boredom to desperation and from routine duty to mortal danger, often with no warning. *Das Boot*'s international success testifies to the power of its screenplay and cast to overcome resistance to the idea of sympathizing with World War II German combatants. The men of *U-96* fought less for political conviction than for their own survival. Der Alte had a job to perform, and he was determined to do it well.

FURTHER READING

Bishop, Chris. 2006. *Kriegsmarine U-Boats, 1939–45*. London. Amber Books.
Bourke-White, Margaret. 1943. "Women in Lifeboats." *Life*, February 22, 1943. From *Reporting World War II, Part One: American Journalism, 1938–1944*. 1995. New York: Library of America, 456.
Cremer, Peter. 1982. *U-Boat Commander: A Periscope View of the Battle of the Atlantic*. Annapolis, MD: U.S. Naval Institute.
Ebert, Roger. 1997. "Das Boot." RogerEbert.com, April 4, 1997. https://www.rogerebert.com/reviews/das-boot-1997
Gröning, Erich. 1966. *Die deutschen Kriegsschiffe, 1815–1945*. Munich: J. F. Lehmanns Verlag.
Hague, Arnold. 2000. *The Allied Convoy System, 1939–1945*. Annapolis, MD: U.S. Naval Institute.
Howe, Desson. 1997. "Director's 'Das Boot': A Cut above the Original." *Washington Post*, April 4, 1997. https://www.washingtonpost.com/wp-srv/style/longterm/movies/review97/dasboothowe.htm
Hoyt, Edwin P. 1988. *The Death of the U-Boats*. New York: McGraw-Hill.
Ickes, Harold. 1954. *The Secret Diaries of Harold Ickes*. Vol. 3. New York: Simon and Schuster.
Kahn, David. 1991. *Seizing the Enigma: The Race to Break the German U-Boat Codes, 1939–1943*. Boston, MA: Houghton Mifflin.
Kramer, Peter. 2017. "*Das Boot*: Probably the Biggest German Blockbuster of All Time: How Did This Epic Bestseller Come to be Turned into a Movie?" purmovies.co.uk, October 8, 2017. https://www.puremovies.co.uk/columns/das-boot-probably-the-biggest-german-blockbuster-of-all-time/
Lynch, John. 2018. "The 45 Best War Movies of All Times, According to Critics." businessinsider.com, September 4, 2018. https://www.businessinsider.com/best-war-movies-all-time-critics-2018-8
Maslin, Janet. 1982. "'Das Boot,' The Fortunes of a U-boat." *New York Times*, February 10, 1982. https://www.nytimes.com/1982/02/10/movies/das-boot-the-fortunes-of-a-u-boat.html
Parkinson, David. 2018. "10 Great Battleship and War-at-Sea Films." bfi.org.uk, August 10, 2018. https://www.bfi.org.uk/news-opinion/news-bfi/lists/10-great-battle-sea-films
Symonds, Craig L. 2018. *World War II at Sea: A Global History*. New York: Oxford University Press.
Ward, Geoffrey C., and Ken Burns. 2007. *The War: An Intimate History, 1941–1945*. New York: Alfred A. Knopf.
Williamson, Gordon. 2002. *Kriegsmarine U-Boats, 1939–45*. London: Osprey Publishing.

Chapter 9

Saving Private Ryan (1998)

Directed by Steven Spielberg (1946–) and written by Robert Rodat (1953–), *Saving Private Ryan* released on July 24, 1998. Spielberg, Mark Gordon (1956–), Ian Bryce (1956–), and Gary Levinsohn (1959–) co-produced the film, which Spielberg's DreamWorks Pictures released in North America and Paramount Pictures distributed internationally. The idea for *Saving Private Ryan* came to Rodat while reading the best seller *D-Day: June 6, 1944: The Climactic Battle of World War II* (1994) by historian Stephen Ambrose (1936–2002). Rodat was struck by a reference to a pair of brothers who died storming the beaches at Normandy in the same week when a third brother died in Burma. The fourth brother, a paratrooper with the 101st Airborne Division, was evacuated from the front line in Normandy to spare the family more tragedy (Ambrose 1994, 316–317).

Gordon liked Rodat's idea for composing fiction around that nugget of fact and arranged for Paramount to commission a screenplay from the writer. The script made the rounds and eventually gained Spielberg's attention. Like many of Spielberg's films, *Saving Private Ryan* concerns ordinary people coping with extraordinary events. World War II is a consistent thread through the director's career. Spielberg first came to attention, as a teenage winner of an Arizona statewide amateur filmmaker's prize, for a 40-minute movie set in World War II. As a schoolboy, his favorite film was *The Bridge on the River Kwai* (McBride 1997, 12, 392). In a 1988 interview, Spielberg said he owned a copy of every available World War II documentary (Forsberg 2000, 128–129). "I love that period. My father filled my head with war stories," he said. "I have identified with that period of innocence and tremendous jeopardy all my life" (McBride 1997, 64).

Before *Saving Private Ryan*, he had already depicted World War II in the fact-derived *Empire of the Sun* (1987) and *Schindler's List* (1993), as well as the heroic fantasy of *Raiders of the Lost Ark* (1981). The only false note was his film *1941* (1979), a slapstick farce about American anxiety in the days after Pearl Harbor, described by film historian Molly Haskell as Spielberg's "delayed descent into a variant of counterculture anarchy" (Haskell 2017, 80). Spielberg remained largely immune to skepticism about the U.S. military and foreign policy prevalent in Hollywood through the 1970s, and with the greater conservatism of the Ronald Reagan era, it became harder in any event to find a mass audience for films that questioned the integrity of America's intentions in foreign wars.

Bookending the film are scenes in the present day of an elderly World War II veteran (played by Harrison Young, 1930–2005) visiting the Normandy American Cemetery in Colleville-sur-Mer, Normandy. He is overcome with emotion and wonders about the meaning of his life and the sacrifices that were made during the war to save him. The action shifts quickly to the D-Day invasion of Normandy and the bloody carnage on the shore. The audience is unaware until the film's conclusion that the elderly man was not on the beach that day. However, the character introduced in the landing scene, Captain John H. Miller (played by Tom Hanks, 1956–), was instrumental in saving his life. After the bridgehead at Normandy is secured, Miller is ordered to lead a squad behind enemy lines to rescue a stranded paratrooper, Private James Ryan (played by Matt Damon, 1970–).

Like the fourth brother in the account of D-Day that inspired the screenplay, Ryan's three brothers have been killed in action. In *Saving Private Ryan*, the Army Chief of Staff, General George C. Marshall (1880–1959), issues the order to retrieve Ryan from danger in his forward position. Miller is given the task and chooses seven men from his Ranger company.

As in many earlier World War II movies, the members of Miller's squad represent different aspects of American life. Sergeant Mike Horvath (Tom Sizemore, 1961–) is the tough army "lifer." The familiar role of the streetwise Italian enlisted man is filled by Private Adrian Caparzo (Vin Diesel, 1967–). Private Stanley Mellish (Adam Goldberg, 1976–) is a Jewish American for whom the war is a grudge match. Private Daniel Jackson (Barry Pepper, 1970–) is the religious Southerner. Medic Irwin Wade (Giovanni Ribisi, 1974–) is compassionate. Private Richard Reiben (Edward Burns, 1968–) is the skeptical Brooklynite. The language interpreter, Corporal Timothy Upham (Jeremy Davies, 1969–), is the intellectual. Religions, regions, ethnicities, and temperaments are mixed in the crucible of a combat unit. No African Americans were included because the U.S. Army was segregated; no black combat units were engaged at the places where *Saving Private Ryan* was set.

Miller's odyssey is fraught with danger and misdirection. They proceed to the town of Neuville, where a contingent from Ryan's 101st Airborne

Division is under fire from German defenders. Caparzo is killed by a sniper. Miller discovers he has found the wrong Private Ryan and is told that the Ryan he seeks is defending a key bridge nearby in Ramelle.

At Ramelle, Miller's squad finds Ryan hunkered down with his comrades. Although saddened by the news that his brothers have died, Ryan refuses to abandon his comrades. Unwilling to return empty-handed, Miller orders his squad to stand with the paratroopers and face down an assault by SS panzers. While inflicting heavy casualties on the Germans, Jackson, Mellish, Horvath, and Miller are killed; their deaths while holding back the enemy permit Ryan to return to American lines.

Saving Private Ryan received mostly favorable reviews upon release. The *New York Times* cited it as a "soberly magnificent new war film" that "restored passion and meaning" to the war movie genre (Maslin 1998). *Entertainment Weekly* called it "a movie of staggering virtuosity and raw lyric power, a masterpiece of terror, chaos, blood, and courage" (Gleiberman 1998). Comparing it to the classic *All Quiet on the Western Front* (1930), Roger Ebert wrote that Spielberg and Rodat "made a philosophical film about war almost entirely in terms of action" that "says things about war that are as complex and difficult as any essayist could possibly express, and does it with broad, strong images, with violence, with profanity, with action, with camaraderie" (Ebert 1998).

Saving Private Ryan was a blockbuster hit, costing $65 million to make, earning $479 million worldwide, and dominating conversations going into the 1999 Academy Awards. Nominated for 11 Oscars, *Saving Private Ryan* won for Best Director and, on the strength of the opening sequence, earned Oscars in technical categories for cinematography, sound, sound effects editing, and film editing. It also won at the Golden Globes for Best Motion Picture and Best Director.

Mirroring the sentiments of Tom Brokaw's best seller, *The Greatest Generation* (1998), *Saving Private Ryan* embodied and reinforced a prouder, more confident national mood by honoring veterans of the last war universally embraced by Americans. It was "seen as an antidote to the Vietnam-induced gloom and cynicism in movies like *Apocalypse Now*. America was ready to celebrate the brave soldiers in a just war" (Haskell 2017, 166). The film was put to political uses. Conservative columnist George Will called its popularity a "measure of the depth of the nation's yearning for honor as it tastes the bitter dregs of Clinton's presidency" (Will 1998). In the aftermath of *Saving Private Ryan*'s success, Spielberg and Hanks regrouped to produce a World War II series for HBO, *Band of Brothers* (2001).

Saving Private Ryan's acclaim and influence have endured and is acknowledged by film historians as groundbreaking for its use of new technology in crafting D-Day's immersive combat scene. According to David Thomson, "In those first twenty minutes Steven Spielberg established new standards for the din and chaos of combat, for the terrible, deafening blast and explosion of it all" (Thomson 2008, 755). The American Film Institute included *Saving Private Ryan* in several of its movie rankings, rating it as the 71st greatest American movie, the 45th most thrilling film, the 10th most inspiring film, and the eighth best epic. In 2014, the Library of Congress added *Saving Private Ryan* to the National Film Registry for its historical significance.

HISTORICAL CONTEXT

Describing the logistical feat performed by the Allies on D-Day, Stephen Ambrose, in the book that inspired *Saving Private Ryan*, wrote, "It was as if the cities of Green Bay, Racine, and Kenosha, Wisconsin, were picked up and moved—every man, woman and child, every automobile and truck—to the east side of Lake Michigan, in one night" (Ambrose 1994, 25).

The statistics are staggering. In one night and day, American, Canadian, and British naval units transported 175,000 soldiers and 50,000 vehicles, from motorcycles to tanks, across the 60–100 miles of the English Channel and hurled that mass of men and equipment at heavily defended shores. Over 5,300 ships and boats crowded the Channel and 11,000 aircraft performed missions overhead. For many of the Allied soldiers, the most difficult amphibious assault in history was their first taste of combat.

Looming over D-Day was a disaster from the previous war, Gallipoli (1915), the largest failed landing to date. The World War I Allied assault on Turkey was a spectacular failure, costing the lives of 250,000 soldiers from Australia, France, Great Britain, India, and New Zealand. The Gallipoli invasion was devised by Winston Churchill (1874–1965), then Britain's First Lord of the Admiralty, whose strategic ambitions outstretched the technology of the time. Now serving as prime minister, Churchill was wary of the Normandy plans. "I was not convinced that this was the only way of winning the war, and I knew that it would be a very heavy and hazardous adventure," he said, adding that the "fearful price" in human life from World War I "was graven in my mind" (Balkoski 2004, 7).

Churchill was always in favor of prioritizing the Mediterranean campaign to secure control over not only Italy but also Yugoslavia and Greece. However, the United States and the Soviet Union pushed for invading France. In the end, the United States had its way, spurred by General Marshall, who saw an invasion of German-occupied France as the fastest way to the heart of Germany and victory.

World War II was the first major conflict in which amphibious warfare was crucial. The Allied counter-offensive against Japan in the Pacific involved a series of landings against heavily defended islands. The prelude of the European theater began in North Africa with Operation Torch (November 1942), the invasion of Vichy French Morocco under Major General George S. Patton (1885–1945). The major threat to Patton came from

French warships and German U-boats because the coastline was unfortified. As U.S. Major General Lucian Truscott (1895–1965) said, the Moroccan landings were "a hit-or-miss affair that would have spelled disaster" against an entrenched enemy (Morrison 1947, 123).

In Operation Torch, soldiers waded ashore from car ferries, whale boats, and any craft capable of coming close to the beach. Afterward, the United States and Great Britain developed an array of purpose-built landing craft designed for amphibious warfare. They were slow and ungainly but solved the problem of landing everything from tanks to foot soldiers. The largest model, the LSTs (Landing Ship Tanks), could accommodate as many as 20 tanks or 32 trucks in its hold, plus 30 jeeps or artillery pieces on deck. The flat-bottomed craft could push against the sand and open their hinged prows to allow troops and vehicles to dash onto the shore. Other vessels were only large enough to carry three or four tanks; smaller craft held no more than a platoon of infantry. It was almost always a rough ride for the men on board. "The crews probably would have found it more comfortable sailing on the Santa Maria," wrote a journalist who rode a landing craft across the English Chanel on the first wave at D-Day (Liebling 1944).

The Allies also developed an amphibious truck, the DUKWs (called "Ducks" by servicemen). The six-ton vehicles were launched several miles offshore from LSTs and proceeded at six knots to the beach and onto land. "Collectively these new vessels were a game changer" that "redefined the character of amphibious warfare" (Symonds 2018, 430).

Patton was involved in the war's next amphibious assault, Operation Husky, the Anglo-American invasion of Sicily (July 1943). The naval force that assembled for Husky dwarfed any previous armada. Some 2,600 ships plus hundreds of landing craft brought 160,000 men, 15,000 tanks and other vehicles plus artillery and supplies to shore (Symonds 2018, 424). Following the defeat of Sicily's German and Italian defenders, the Allies landed on the Italian mainland at Anzio (January 1944), where they "achieved complete surprise and the initial landings were virtually unopposed" (Symonds 2018, 504). In the aftermath, the main logistical problem involved transporting the LSTs from the Mediterranean to Great Britain in time for the planned invasion of France.

For the Germans, the invasion of France was no surprise. However, Adolf Hitler was convinced it would occur at Pas de Calais across from England on the Strait of Dover, a channel so narrow that the French coast was visible from the British side. The Allies decided instead on Normandy, across the wider and notoriously choppy English Channel. The shore there was less strongly defended by the Germans but was fronted by sheer cliffs and presented other obstacles. At high tide, the waves lapped against the seawalls. At low tide, soldiers leaping from landing craft would have to cross 600 yards of open beach to reach those seawalls. "It was an invasion planner's nightmare" (Balkoski 2004, 11).

The Allies gave code names to the five Norman beaches where its forces came ashore. British and Canadian units landed on Gold, Juno, and Sword beaches. The Americans chose Utah and Omaha beaches. General Dwight D. Eisenhower (1890–1969) commanded the invasion plan, called Operation Overlord. Britain's General Bernard Law Montgomery (1887–1976) served under him as senior ground forces commander and Admiral Sir Bertram Ramsay (1883–1945) presided over the naval operation. Below Montgomery in the chain of command was General Omar Bradley (1893–1981), in charge of the attack on Utah and Omaha beaches, and under him was Major General Leonard T. Gerow (1888–1972), directly responsible for the assault on Omaha Beach, depicted in *Saving Private Ryan*.

Eisenhower reinforced Hitler's supposition of a landing at Calais by establishing the mirage of an army at Dover under General Patton while the real invasion force assembled elsewhere. The Allies rehearsed the invasion for months on Slapton Sands west of Dartmouth. The terrain of the beach and the countryside beyond, with green fields crisscrossed by hedges, was similar to Normandy. Entire divisions were loaded onto ships and landed on Slapton Sands. Engineers laid steel traps, barbed wire, and live mines in anticipation of the combat conditions the men would face on D-Day (Symonds 2018, 520–521). At the same time, British and American airborne troops

DWIGHT D. EISENHOWER (1890–1969)

"Plans are useless but planning is absolutely essential," said Dwight D. Eisenhower. He liked to cultivate the reputation as a simple soldier but proved to be a shrewd commander and politician in peace as well as war.

Eisenhower was a career soldier who held a variety of posts before World War II, including adjutant to Douglas MacArthur. On December 12, 1941, he was appointed to the army's War Plans Division and began charting the Allied invasion of Europe. He drew plans to unify all U.S. forces in Europe under a single command, and in June 1942, he was named the commanding general of American Forces in the European Theater of Operations. He planned the invasions of North Africa, Sicily, and Italy and, finally, the D-Day invasion of Normandy. In December 1944, he was named General of the Army, the army's highest rank.

After victory, Eisenhower supervised the drawdown of the U.S. military and, in 1950, became NATO's Supreme Commander. He accepted the Republican nomination in 1952 and served as president for two terms. During his administration, Eisenhower maneuvered carefully, ending the Korean War with an armistice, refusing to commit U.S. forces to Vietnam and working to curb Soviet expansion while avoiding war. On the domestic front, he quietly undermined the fervid anti-Communist Senator Joe McCarthy and moved slowly but deliberately on civil rights. To enforce the U.S. Supreme Court's school desegregation ruling, he dispatched one of his crack units from D-Day, the 101st Airborne Division, to protect black students in Little Rock, Arkansas.

rehearsed their role, which was to land in Normandy ahead of the amphibious attack and secure the bridges and other approaches to the beaches, preventing the arrival of German reinforcements.

When D-Day finally came, more than 175,000 soldiers and 5,300 ships crossed the English Channel to Normandy. The soldiers were loaded on board ships several days before the invasion began, as a blanket of secrecy fell across the English coast. The fleet was even larger than the one assembled for the invasion of Sicily. Naval units included every sort of vessel from battleships to barges. An additional 2,000 landing craft ferried the troops to shore (Ward and Burns 2007, 195–196).

The invasion was scheduled for June 5, but forecasts of bad weather, which could have lashed ships together and swamped the flat-bottomed landing craft, caused Eisenhower to postpone. With meteorologists predicting a slight improvement, and the difficulty of maintaining secrecy as the invasion fleet prepared to sail, Eisenhower set the final date for D-Day as June 6 and hoped for the best.

On June 6, the British and Canadians took their beaches with relative ease, and U.S. forces seized Utah Beach with only 197 casualties. Among the first to be onshore at Utah was the fifth cousin of the sitting president and the son of a former president, Brigadier General Theodore Roosevelt Jr. (1887–1944). Armed with only a pistol and a walking stick, he emulated his father by leading the charge. Roosevelt died a month later in France from a heart attack but achieved victory on D-Day. "By late morning, Roosevelt's most serious problem was directing traffic as American tanks roared off the beach and onto the four causeways airborne troops had captured just hours before" (Ward and Burns 2007, 196).

Omaha Beach, where *Saving Private Ryan*'s flashback begins, was another story entirely. The first wave ran from the ramps of the landing craft through three feet of water "with tracer bullets flying around them and only a nearly level, coverless beach immediately in front of them and with a beach pillbox and more of the enemy on a cliff inshore blazing away with everything they had," wrote *The New Yorker*'s war correspondent, huddled in the rear of the tiny craft with the U.S. Coast Guard crew manning the boat. "We decided that hardly any of our men could have survived" (Liebling 1944).

Once the bridgehead had been established, a second wave of troops clambered down the portsides of the ocean-going troop ships on "scramble nets" and with the help of sailors struggled onto the landing craft. A few men lost their grip and fell to their death in the cumbersome procedure. "It often took as much time to unload the soldiers from a big ship as it did for the ship itself to get from Britain to the Normandy coast" (Liebling 1944).

Pulitzer Award-winning syndicated columnist Ernie Pyle (1900–1945) arrived the morning after D-Day after "the fighting had moved a couple miles inland." He was struck by the shells of burned-out tanks and vehicles, the capsized hulks of landing craft, and the profusion of personal effects scattered across Omaha Beach, "a gigantic and pitiful litter of wreckage along miles of shoreline" with "the bodies of soldiers lying in rows covered with blankets." Despite the hard fight to take Omaha, he encountered "intense, grim determination of work-weary men to get this chaotic beach organized and get all the vital supplies and the reinforcements moving more rapidly" (Pyle 1944). The wounded were evacuated by landing craft serving as "water ambulances" to a hospital ship riding offshore and lifted from those ambulances to the hospital's deck on stretchers (Gelhorn 1944).

The Allies enjoyed command of the air, and fighter bombers flew low against German targets with no resistance save from antiaircraft ground batteries. However, progress on the ground since D-Day "had come painfully and at great cost" with progress measured in yards (Ward and Burns 2007, 226). The Allies secured a 60-mile wide stretch of shore but were able to penetrate no deeper than 20 miles inland in most places within the first weeks. The terrain hindered the advance. Normandy was carved into countless small fields surrounded by earthen ramparts, tall centuries-old hedges, and drainage ditches. It was ideal territory for ambush and proved nearly insurmountable for tanks until a GI devised a set of steel prongs, mounted on the front of tanks, able to cut through the hedges.

By late July, the Allies had suffered 122,000 casualties since D-Day. German losses were similar. Determined to break the stalemate, General Omar N. Bradley (1893–1981) ordered Operation Cobra (July 25–31), an intensive carpet bombing by thousands of aircraft and an artillery barrage of a narrow band of German strongholds blocking the way out of Normandy and the road to Paris. The bombardment crushed German forces and caused friendly fire casualties, including the death of Lieutenant General Leslie J. McNair (1883–1944), commander of U.S. Ground Forces and the highest-ranking American casualty of the war. The countryside and cities of Normandy were destroyed, but by August, the Allies had broken free of the D-Day bridgehead and were on their way toward liberating the French capital of Paris.

DEPICTION AND HISTORICAL CONTEXT

With the Omaha Beach landing sequence, Steven Spielberg was determined to surpass previous war movies by staging combat as realistically and vividly from the perspective of the men in the middle of the fight. He scattered 1,000 fake corpses on a beach in Ireland chosen for its resemblance to the Norman coast and employed real amputees as extras (Haskell 2017, 163). Recreating the uncertainty of actual combat documentary filmmakers, Spielberg encouraged his camera crew to respond to unexpected developments and improvise. Spielberg even recreated, as much as possible, the deafening sounds of exploding shells. In the movie, Captain Miller briefly loses his hearing under shell fire, and the soundtrack goes dead.

The Omaha scene opens with Miller's platoon packed into a tiny flat-bottomed landing craft rocking perilously on the choppy waters off the beach. Their anxiety and discomfort are palpable. Soldiers vomit from sea sickness and fear as they draw closer to the shore. The sharp metallic ping of German bullets is heard as machine guns splatter the sides of the craft. Many Americans fall dead into the surf. The withering fire continues as the troops try to move up the beach. One GI picks up his severed arm from the ground and staggers away. Blood reddens the water, and the cries of the wounded fills the air.

The Second Ranger Battalion, Miller's unit, was among the first contingents at Omaha Beach on the morning of June 6. Spielberg's depiction of their high level of performance under deadly fire and their ingenuity is no exaggeration. The Rangers were trained "for special combat missions according to the extraordinarily rigorous model of the legendary British commandos," and as elite troops, "the Rangers rightfully considered themselves the U.S. Army's best" (Balkoski 2004, 30).

Captain Miller, like his real-life counterparts, appears surprised at the difficulty his men faced. Allied planners believed that bombing runs over German positions coupled with a barrage from the big naval guns would cripple the enemy's defenses at Omaha and any shell-shocked survivors would quickly be overcome. Reality proved more complicated than the plans.

Saving Private Ryan truthfully conveys the confusion and the sense among the GIs that nothing was going according to plan. Miller was forced to ask Horvath if he knew where they were. "The thing that struck me was the complete chaos on the beach. Dead men seemed to be everywhere," said Captain Edgar Arnold, commander of Company B, Second Ranger Battalion (Balkoski 2004, 30). Many landing craft skippers, confused by brush fires set by exploding Allied naval shells and desperately avoiding offshore mines, set their troops ashore in the wrong places, which is when, as seen in the film, Horvath responds to Miller, "Right where we're supposed to be, but no one else is."

Cloud cover on the morning of June 6 obscured targets from the air; "far more Norman cattle were killed than enemy soldiers" from bombs that fell inland (Ward and Burns 2007, 200). Also, the U.S. Eighth Air Force, responsible for softening German fortifications, took great care to avoid friendly fire, given that the landing forces were only 400 yards offshore when the bombing was timed to begin (Balkoski 2004, 87). Moreover, the German installations were cunningly disguised on the cliffs and difficult to spot from any distance.

Even when Allied fire struck their targets, the German positions proved to be able to withstand the impact. The pillboxes were mammoth structures with sloping cement walls six feet thick. "Generally only a direct hit from a heavy naval shell could hope to penetrate the concrete" (Balkoski 2004, 45).

The German defenses along the coast of Normandy were only one sector of the formidable "Atlantic Wall," a line of concrete bunkers stretching across the northern shore of Nazi-occupied Europe, whose artillery batteries were defended by machine gun emplacements, barbed wire, minefields, and steel traps designed to rip the hulls of incoming landing craft. The Atlantic Wall was constructed under the direction of Field Marshall Erwin Rommel (1891–1944), who believed that the war would be "won or lost on the beaches" (Ward and Burns 2007, 189). Omaha was the deepest of the Norman beaches, and its high cliffs were the most heavily fortified. Rommel built well on Omaha, situating fortified gun emplacements to rain invaders with overlapping fields of fire from the dreaded 88mm guns, acknowledged as the war's best artillery piece. The batteries were protected by anti-tank ditches, infantry trenches, and concealed machine gun nests (Ward and Burns 2007, 196).

As Miller mentions, the Allies were expecting Omaha to be defended only by elements of the 716th Bodenständig (Static) Division, an inferior force poorly armed and recruited in part from conquered lands in Eastern Europe. Through bad luck, the 716th was reinforced on D-Day by the battle-hardened 352nd Infantry Division, which "by coincidence had been conducting anti-invasion exercises when the American landing commenced and had promptly been swept into the battle" (Balkoski 2004, 47–48).

The Rangers were expecting close support as they advanced up the shore from amphibious tanks, but the technology failed. Most of the tanks sank, carrying their crews with them. *Saving Private Ryan* captures the hard going faced by the first wave of GIs. In the film, German machine gunners fire on Allied soldiers out in the open on the beach. "Burdened by equipment and waterlogged uniforms, the Rangers found it hard to move swiftly across the soft sand and the Germans cut many more of them down" (Balkoski 2004, 116).

Many small details in the Omaha scene come from real life. There really was a Roman Catholic chaplain on the beach, comforting the dying and praying for the dead (Balkoski 2004, 176). The advancing troops had no choice but to huddle behind the steel obstacles, planted by the Germans on the shore, for the slight shelter they afforded from incoming machine-gun rounds. As in the movie, the Rangers made audacious assaults up the bluffs, disabling pillboxes by hurling grenades through the apertures and clearing obstacles with explosive charges placed at the end of long tubes called Bangalore torpedoes.

Throughout *Saving Private Ryan*, Miller "embodies the Frank Capra vision of the American soldier" as "a schoolteacher who becomes a warrior of necessity not bloodlust, who wants only to finish the job and get back home to his wife" (Doherty 1999, 308–309). Like real Ranger commanders, Miller never leads from behind. "Officers did everything the enlisted men did," recalled First Lieutenant Charles Parker, who led Company A, Fifth Ranger Battalion, on D-Day (Balkoski 2004, 30).

The GIs who survived the June 6 landing on Omaha Beach spent the first hours after the fighting ceased in confusion and desperation as implied in *Saving Private Ryan*. "To them, the landing looked like a catastrophe," recalled Andy Rooney, a correspondent for the army's *Stars and Stripes* newspaper assigned to report on the invasion. "Each knew a friend shot through the throat, shot through the knee. Each knew the names of five hanging dead on the barbed wire twenty yards off shore." He added that "in Allied headquarters in England, the war directors, remote from the details of tragedy, were exultant" (Rooney 2000, 157). They had good reason. Despite the hard fighting at Omaha and the difficulties faced by U.S. paratroopers, by nightfall the Allies punctured a 45-mile breach into the Atlantic Wall and landed 150,000 troops in France. More men and supplies poured in by the hour.

The situation of Private Ryan and his comrades, scattered across the Norman landscape and trying desperately to regroup into fighting units, is also accurate. Operation Overlord began with a night drop of paratroopers behind the beaches late on June 5. Members of the U.S. 82nd and 101st Airborne divisions, totaling 13,000 paratroopers and 3,900 glider troops, along with the British Sixth Airborne Division, were tasked with seizing bridges and roads to prevent the Germans from rushing reinforcements to the Atlantic Wall.

British paratroopers achieved their objectives by dawn on June 6, destroying targets and seizing bridges. Their American colleagues were less fortunate. German antiaircraft batteries downed many C-47 transport planes; paratroopers "fell helplessly into the sea or drowned in fields and river valleys flooded by the Germans" to create obstacles for the anticipated Allied assault. "Still others were dropped so low their parachutes had no chance to open; they hit the ground, one man remembered, with 'a sound like ripe pumpkins being thrown down against the ground'" (Ward and Burns 2007, 194).

The gliders from 101st Airborne, towed over to France by transport planes and set loose near their landing sites, were large enough to contain vehicles and light artillery. More than half of the 1,200 gliders missed their target zones in the darkness; many crashed instead of landing softly; others were impaled on the forest of 12-foot spikes planted by Rommel to thwart airborne troops. The scene in *Saving Private Ryan* when Miller's squad comes across a field of broken gliders is entirely accurate. As one of the survivors tells Miller, piloting the heavily loaded glider was "like trying to fly a freight train." As mentioned in the movie, the 101st Airborne Division's assistant division commander, Brigadier General Don Forrester Pratt (1892–1944), died when his glider slid across a wet grassy field and into a row of poplar trees. He was the highest ranking U.S. casualty on the D-Day. During the first days of the invasion, the U.S. lost 2,499 airborne troops (Ward and Burns 2007, 195). Paratroopers from the 101st were scattered across an area 15 by 25 miles, many of them lost and unable to communicate with their commanders in the first days of the assault.

Some elements of Ryan's struggle were fictionalized or enhanced for dramatic effect. The paratroopers fought many small engagements, but there was no battle of Ramelle. Several real-life engagements provided inspiration for the film's final combat scenes, including a battered contingent of the 82nd Airborne holding out against repeated German attacks at the crossroads town of Sainte-Mere-Eglise and, nearby, the four-day fight for a stone causeway over the Merderet River at La Fiere, pitting glider infantry against German tanks. At that point, U.S. forces in Normandy held back units of Germany's regular army. The Second SS Panzer Division "Das Reich," whose advance is thwarted by the film's protagonists, did not engage in combat in Normandy until July. Spielberg chose the "Das Reich" Division for its reputation as part of the well-drilled and murderous Waffen-SS, the Nazi Party's private army.

For the most part, the conversations between GIs are plausible and include period military slang such as "fubar," a term of frustration indicating a situation beyond repair. Occasional anachronisms creep into the dialogue. Miller's remark that the war "had taken a turn to surreal" would not have been understood by the average GI in World War II.

Although the U.S. Army did remove a soldier from the front line in Normandy, who had lost three brothers in action, the scenario of *Saving Private Ryan* is unlikely. Risking an entire squad by sending them into a combat zone to save one man would be recklessly sentimental in wartime. However, as a plot device, Miller's odyssey affords an opportunity to explore the moral calculus of war. Like many war movies and the literature that preceded film by thousands of years, *Saving Private Ryan* asks eternal questions about what a soldier should die for, what constitutes a noble sacrifice, and what counts only as a waste of life. Despite the film's tendency toward sentimentality, Spielberg refuses to give the audience an easy answer.

FURTHER READING

Ambrose, Stephen E. 1994. *D-Day: June 6, 1944: The Climactic Battle of World War II*. New York: Simon & Schuster.

Balkoski, Joseph. 2004. *Omaha Beach: D-Day, June 6, 1944*. Mechanicsburg, PA: Stackpole Books.

Doherty, Thomas. 1999. *Projections of War: Hollywood, American Culture, and World War II*. New York: Columbia University Press.

Ebert, Roger. 1998. "Saving Private Ryan." *Chicago Sun-Times*, July 24, 1998. https://www.rogerebert.com/reviews/saving-private-ryan-1998

Eller, Claudia. 1998. "Producing Partners Step Aside for Spielberg with Saving Grace." *Los Angeles Times*, July 24, 1998. https://www.latimes.com/archives/la-xpm-1998-jul-24-fi-6604-story.html

Forsberg, Myra. 2000. "Spielberg at Forty: The Man and the Child." In *Steven Spielberg: Interviews*, edited by Friedman, Lester D., and Notbohm, Brent. Jackson: University of Mississippi Press.

Gelhorn, Martha. 1944. "The First Hospital Ship." *Colliers*, August 5, 1944. From *Reporting World War II, Part Two: American Journalism, 1944–1946*. 1995. New York: Library of America, 151.

Gleiberman, Owen. 1998. "Saving Private Ryan." *Entertainment Weekly*, July 24, 1998. https://ew.com/article/1998/07/24/saving-private-ryan-4/

Haskell, Molly. 2017. *Steven Spielberg: A Life in Films*. New Haven, CT: Yale University Press.

Liebling, A. J. 1944. "Cross-Channel Trip." *The New Yorker*, July 1, 1944. From *Reporting World War II, Part Two: American Journalism, 1944–1946*. 1995. New York: Library of America, 105.

Maslin, Janet. 1998. "Panoramic and Personal Visions of War's Anguish." *New York Times*, July 24, 1998. https://www.nytimes.com/1998/07/24/movies/film-review-panoramic-and-personal-visions-of-war-s-anguish.html

McBride, Joseph. 1997. *Steven Spielberg: A Biography*. New York: Simon & Schuster.

Morrison, Samuel Eliot. 1947. *Operations in North African Waters*. Boston, MA: Little, Brown.

Pyle, Ernie. 1944. "Scripps-Howard Wire Dispatch." June 12. In *Reporting World War II: American Journalism, 1944–1946* (1995). New York: Library of America, 142..

Rooney, Andy. 2000. *My War*. New York: PublicAffairs.

Symonds, Greg L. 2018. *World War II at Sea: A Global History*. New York: Oxford University Press.

Thomson, David. 2008. *"Have You Seen . . . ?": A Personal Introduction to 1,000 Films*. New York: Alfred A. Knopf.

Ward, Geoffrey C., and Ken Burns. 2007. *The War: An Intimate History, 1941–1945*. New York: Alfred A. Knopf.

Will, George F. 1998. "A Summons to Gratitude." *Newsweek*, August 17, 1998.

Chapter 10

Enemy at the Gates (2001)

French filmmaker Jean-Jacques Annaud (1943–) drew his inspiration for *Enemy at the Gates* from a work on nonfiction, *Enemy at the Gates: The Battle for Stalingrad* (1973), by William Craig (1929–1997), an American novelist and history writer. Annaud, who won an Oscar for the short film, *Black and White in Color* (1976), but is best known for *Quest for Fire* (1981), directed and cowrote the film with his longtime collaborator Alain Godard (1946–). Annaud produced *Enemy at the Gates* with British-born Hollywood producer John D. Schofield (1933–). Paramount Pictures released the film in the United States on March 16, 2001. Pathé Distribution released the film in France and Constantin Film distributed it in Germany.

Like the book, the film focuses on a Soviet soldier in the Battle of Stalingrad (1942–1943), Vasily Zaitsev (1915–1991), a sniper in a rifle regiment. Played by British actor Jude Law (1972–), Zaitsev learned to hunt as a boy. His outstanding marksmanship saves the life of Commissar Danilov (played by Joseph Fiennes, 1970–). Conferring with Stalin's personal representative in Stalingrad, Nikita Khrushchev (1894–1971) (played by Bob Hoskins, 1942–2014), Danilov convinces the Soviet leader to play up the story of Zaitsev's heroism and skill, making him a hero in the cause of defeating the Nazis. *Enemy at the Gates* becomes a duel in the ruins of Stalingrad between Zaitsev and his German counterpart, the sniper Erwin König (Ed Harris, 1950–).

Traveling between German and Soviet lines is a Russian boy, Sasha (Gabriel Marshall-Thomson, 1986–). Sasha provides König with information in exchange for food but proves a patriot in the end by helping Zaitsev locate the German sniper. The film climaxes in a personal victory for Zaitsev when he shoots König. Along the way, a love triangle forms when

Zaitsev and Danilov fall in love with Tania Chernova (1920–) (played by Rachel Weisz, 1970–), a member of the Soviet militia whose language skills make her valuable as an interpreter.

Enemy at the Gates enjoyed only modest success at box offices. Budgeted at $68 million, it failed to break even in its U.S. release but earned a total of $97 million worldwide. Audience members booed the film at the Berlin International Film Festival, and it received no nominations for major awards (Dreier 2001).

Film critics gave *Enemy at the Gates* mixed reviews at best. The entertainment industry trade paper *Variety* said the film "takes a great setting, some resonant themes, a turning point in 20th-century history—and bleeds them of all power with bad dialogue and uninspired direction" (Elley 2001). *Entertainment Weekly* called *Enemy at the Gates* "Saving Private Ryan for Dummies" and the work of "a showman with an eye towards the international market" (Schwarzbaum 2001).

The *Chicago Sun-Times*' Roger Ebert was more forgiving, but criticized the unrealistic inclusion of a love triangle, writing, "The film might have been better and leaner if it had told the story of the two soldiers and left out the soppy stuff. Even so, it's remarkable, a war story told as a chess game where the loser not only dies, but goes by necessity to an unmarked grave" (Ebert 2001).

The film failed to rank in any significant listing of "Best World War II" in the United States or Great Britain and is sometimes disparaged in contrast to a grittier, more realistic film with the same setting by German director Joseph Vilsmaier, *Stalingrad* (1993). Although it's notable as the only major English-language film about the Soviet sector of World War II ever since a spate of wartime propaganda flicks from Hollywood, *Enemy at the Gates* attracted little notice from film historians. David Thomson dismissed it as "a laborious, hollow recreation of war-torn Stalingrad to support a trite, old-fashioned story" (Thomson 2010, 26).

HISTORICAL CONTEXT

The fighting that began with Germany's invasion of the Soviet Union on June 22, 1941, has been called "the greatest and longest land battle which mankind has ever fought" (Clark 1965, ix). By the time Berlin fell to the Soviet army on May 2, 1945, World War II's Eastern Front claimed the lives of more than thirteen-and-a-half million Russian combatants and three-and-a-quarter million Germans. Additional casualties were suffered by forces from Axis and other nations marching with the Germans into Russia. Millions of civilians from many nations died due to the consequences of the war in Eastern Europe, including air raids and starvation (Bullock 1992, 973). Added to the death toll were the victims of the Holocaust perpetrated by the Nazis in occupied Eastern Europe.

No one who took Adolf Hitler (1889–1945) at his word, especially his autobiographical manifesto, *Mein Kampf* (1925), should have been surprised by his assault on the Soviets. In the struggle between the Aryan "master race" and the Jewish "subhumans" that obsessed Hitler, the destruction of "Jewish Bolshevism" was given priority. For Hitler, war in the east was a titanic struggle of ideologies, a brutal race war, and a field of conquest. Defeating the Western powers was not a priority. Hitler insisted that Germany must "turn our gaze toward the land in the east" and never forget that "the international Jew who completely dominates Russia today" is the enemy (Hitler 1943, 654, 661).

Given the well-known antipathy between the two nations, a startling development occurred just days before the outbreak of World War II in the sudden alliance between Nazi Germany and Soviet Russia, the so-called "Non-Aggression Pact." On August 22, 1939, Hitler's foreign minister, Joachim von Ribbentrop (1893–1946), flew to Moscow to negotiate the deal. The bold diplomatic gamble almost ended when Soviet antiaircraft batteries, unaware that a German visitor was expected, fired on Ribbentrop's plane (Kotkin 2017, 663). The German diplomat signed the pact with his counterpart, the Soviet foreign commissar, Vyacheslav Molotov (1890–1986). The agreement included secret protocols that divided Eastern Europe into spheres of influence. The two nations split Poland; the Germans generously granted the Soviets permission to overrun much of Eastern Europe, knowing full well their own plans to dominate those lands once the time was right. The empire-building scheme was not publicized and was only disclosed when secret German archives were uncovered after the war. In 1939, the public only knew that the world's most implacable foes toasted each other and pledged friendship.

The Non-Aggression Pact shook the world and led many Communists to doubt their faith in Soviet leadership. As many foreign leaders feared when the pact was announced, it opened the door to war. With its Eastern Front secured against the possibility of Soviet interference, Germany invaded Poland on September 1, triggering declarations of war from France and Britain. On September 17, as planned, the Soviets struck Poland, seizing the country's eastern districts. During the first two years of the war, Germany and the Soviet Union enjoyed a flourishing trade relationship, with German finished goods exchanged for Soviet raw materials, until the hour of the Nazis attack on June 22, 1941.

German planning for the Soviet invasion began after the fall of France. In the summer of 1940, Hitler told the chief of staff of the military high command, Colonel General Alfred Jodl (1890–1946), that he intended to rid the world of Soviet Bolshevism "once and for all" with a surprise attack as early as possible in 1941 (Toland 1976, 624). Some of his generals worried about a two-front war, but flush with victory in Western Europe, they imagined the British might remain confined to their home islands or even pounded into a peace accord by the Luftwaffe.

On paper, the Soviet Union appeared vulnerable to a German blitzkrieg. The country's industrial and political centers were concentrated within 500 miles of its European border. The long frontier was divided into half by the Pripet Marshes, whose dense swamps and thick woods were an obstacle for invaders but a hindrance for defenders forced to split their zones of operation if an enemy attacked from north and south of the marshes. The Soviets boasted of fortifications dubbed the Stalin Line in imitation of France's impenetrable Maginot Line, but unlike the French, they were unable to stretch a line of fortresses across their long frontier. Instead, the Stalin Line amounted to a set of fortified cities such as Minsk and Odessa, widely separated on the vast landscape of Russia, Belorussia, and Ukraine. The Soviets weakened their ability to respond to invasion through the Great Purge (1936–1938) that decimated the military's command structure. The purge claimed hundreds of high-ranking officers including the hero of the Civil War, Marshal Mikhail Tukhachevsky (1893–1937). Under torture, he "confessed" to being a German spy and plotting a coup with other officers. Victims of Stalin's insatiable paranoia, most of the judges in the court martial that sentenced the officers to firing squads were themselves arrested and executed (Montefiore 2004, 219–227).

Stalin's international intelligence network had greater insight than Stalin had wisdom, and his spies bombarded the dictator with warnings of German intentions. They even identified the exact date of the attack, June 22, 1941. Stalin remained convinced it was disinformation, perhaps spread by the British to lure him into the war (Montefiore 2004, 352–356).

At dawn on June 22, the date Napoleon's Grand Army marched into Russia 129 years earlier, 6,000 German artillery pieces opened fire on Soviet positions as tanks rolled across the border. "We are being fired on; what shall we do?" the hapless forward commanders radioed headquarters. They were told not to provoke the Germans. Moscow at first refused to acknowledge that the Non-Aggression Pact was being trampled upon (Clark 1965, 44). As the Soviet generals dithered, Stalin remained in denial over Hitler's betrayal. In an emergency meeting at the Kremlin, he insisted that the invasion was led by rogue German generals seeking to provoke an unwanted war (Montefiore 2004, 365).

Regardless of Stalin's delusions, over three million soldiers crossed the frontier at Hitler's orders. German forces were accompanied by divisions of Croats, Finns, Romanians, Hungarians, Italians, and Spaniards. The mammoth army crashed through Soviet lines as the Luftwaffe took command of the air, bombing air bases and tank parks and strafing roads. On the first day of the invasion, the bulk of the Soviet air force was destroyed.

Spearheading the invasion were panzers, with motorcycles, armored cars, and infantry in half-tracks streaming behind, followed by troops on foot. Within five days, German forces pushed hundreds of miles deep into enemy territory, but spread across the vast terrain were pockets of undefeated

Soviet troops, many of them forming the nucleus of the partisan bands that harassed the Germans throughout the war and eventually grew into a second front of operations behind Nazi lines.

Even in the invasion's early months, the Germans, apparently victorious and moving forward, faced "a certain haunting disquiet; the endless, aimless succession of counterattacks, the eagerness to trade ten Russian lives for one German, the vastness of the territory, and its bleak horizon" (Clark 1965, 55). Momentum began to slow as supply lines lengthened and the autumn rains turned dirt roads into rivers of mud.

In Leningrad, the Soviet Union's second city, millions of civilians worked in shifts, day and night, building a defensive perimeter of earthworks and antitank ditches. The public was stirred to action by pronouncements from ranking official and propagandist Andrei Zhdanov (1896–1948): "The enemy is at the gates of Leningrad! Grave danger hangs over the city. The success of the Red Army depends on the heroic, valiant stand of each soldier, commander and worker" (Clark 1965, 117–118).

The people of Leningrad fought for their lives, even if they were unaware that no surrender was possible. Hitler wanted them dead. According to the directive "concerning the future existence of the City of Leningrad," circulated among military officers, "The Fuehrer has decided to erase the city of Petersburg [Leningrad] from the face of the earth. We propose to closely blockade the city and erase it from the earth by means of artillery fire of all caliber and continuous bombardment from the air" (Glantz 2002, 85–86).

Backed by the massive guns of the Soviet Baltic Fleet, and provisioned by factories that continued to manufacture tanks as well as munitions, Leningrad held out for 872 days, starved and besieged, until 1944. The city's inhabitants burned books and furniture for warmth in winter and were fortunate to receive a meager ration in the breadlines. Anyone caught stealing bread was summarily shot by security patrols (McAuley 2019, 14–15). "People dropped dead in the streets, in their beds, whole families." Nearly half of the city's 2.2 million residents died (Montefiore 2004, 388). Some four million Soviet service members were killed, wounded, or captured in fighting on the Leningrad sector. Their sacrifice succeeded in grinding down a significant component of the German army.

Stalin was determined that Leningrad, the former imperial capital renamed for the Soviet Union's founder, would stand even as other major cities fell. One week into the invasion, the Germans seized the capital of Belorussia, Minsk, taking 319,000 prisoners. In August, Kiev, Ukraine's capital, fell. Among the millions of Soviet POWs was an artillery officer, Yakov Djugashvili (1907–1943), Stalin's eldest son. His captivity was an embarrassment for the dictator, who refused to trade his son for the German commander captured at Stalingrad, Friederich Paulus (1890–1957).

In the early months, the greatest Soviet success occurred away from the battlefield when 1,500 factories from the country's western end were

> **JOSEPH STALIN (1878–1953)**
>
> Unlike his rivals, Benito Mussolini and Adolf Hitler, Joseph Stalin was not a man who worked audiences into frenzies of adulation. A revolutionary long before the Bolsheviks seized power in Russia (1917), Stalin was comfortable in the shadows and amassed power within the Communist Party through controlling its bureaucracy. As General Secretary in 1929, he assumed the leading role in the Soviet Union and ruthlessly killed or imprisoned all opponents real and potential. A true believer in the Leninist branch of Marxism, Stalin was willing to send millions to their death in the interest of building his version of utopia.
>
> Stalin admired Germany for its modern industry and innovation but feared it as a nation with designs on expanding eastward. Almost inevitably, he came in conflict with Hitler, the self-appointed "destroyer of Marxism" and ardent believer of Germany's destiny to rule Europe. In the end, the terrain and fortitude of the Soviet people, fortified by the terror of Stalin's regime, defeated Hitler.
>
> While never abandoning the vision of a future Communist world, Stalin focused on imposing Communist regimes in Eastern Europe after World War II as a buffer against western aggression. His imposition of Soviet tyranny sparked the Cold War with the United States as his principal adversary. By the time of his death, his policies resulted in the death of 20 million Soviet citizens.

evacuated to safe havens beyond the Urals in Central Asia and Siberia. Some 10 million laborers and their families moved eastward with the factories. Conditions were severe, but within four months, some plants were producing at full capacity (Heller and Nekrich 1986, 376–377). The Soviet industrial output of tanks, planes, and small arms sustained the nation's war effort, supplemented by U.S. supplies shipped by convoy to Russia's subarctic ports.

After emerging from mental confusion in the first week of the invasion, Stalin shrewdly tapped a deep well of traditional sentiment for Russia. He played every emotional key he could reach, calling the conflict the Great Patriotic War and invoking memories of Napoleon's defeat in 1812. On July 3, when Stalin finally broke his silence with a speech on radio, he spoke to his countrymen not only as "comrades," the Bolshevik greeting, but as "brothers and sisters," the way an Eastern Orthodox priest addressed his congregation.

As a teenager, Stalin had been expelled from the seminary in his homeland, Georgia, and in his time of catastrophe "the ex-seminarist had decided to involve the aid of the God he had rejected" (Radzinsky 1996, 472). *Pravda* publicized his meeting with the head of the Russian Orthodox Church. Priests were released from prison camps. Stalin also called on the wonder-working icon, Our Lady of Kazan, credited by Russians for victory against European invaders in previous centuries. Our Lady of Kazan was paraded in a procession around Leningrad before being ceremoniously displayed in Moscow and sent from there to the city named for the Soviet dictator, Stalingrad (Radzinsky 1996, 473). As a pair of Soviet-era historians put it, "In this difficult hour the best and noblest instincts were aroused among the people: the spirit of self-sacrifice, the feeling of responsibility for the country, and a sense of patriotic duty" (Heller and Nekrich 1986, 374). Resistance to Hitler's onslaught was also stiffened by fear of Stalin. "Exact numbers may never be known with complete certainty, but the total of deaths caused by the whole range of Soviet regime's terrors can hardly be lower than some fifteen million" (Conquest 2007, xvi).

As early as in October, doubt was cast on Hitler's boast to Field Marshal Gerd von Runstedt (1875–1953) about Soviet weakness. "You have only to kick in the door and the whole rotten structure will come crashing down" (Clark 1965, 43). On October 27, Germany's Propaganda Minister Josef Goebbels (1897–1945) was forced to announce that "weather conditions have entailed a temporary halt in the advance" (Clark 1965, 167).

Although Stalin assumed supreme command of the military and he distrusted his generals, he handed the defense of Moscow to one of his most capable commanders, Marshal Grigori Zhukov (1896–1974), who had recently smashed a Japanese assault along the Mongolian-Manchurian border. Zhukov brought his troops from the Far East command to the front lines, some 700,000 men wearing warm quilted uniforms, hooded and in white to match the onset of winter. They charged at the Germans in November, riding shaggy Siberian ponies or the sides of the formidable T 34 tank, whose sloping armor made it invulnerable to all but the heaviest guns.

By early December, temperatures dropped to 40 degrees below zero and continued to fall as dumbfounded German troops staggered back from the Soviet advance. Confident of a quick and easy victory, the Germans had brought no winter clothing and tried to keep warm by layering uniforms and stuffing newspapers between layers for insulation. German automatic weapons froze. Oil hardened in gas tanks. Axles refused to turn. In German field kitchens, butter was cut with saws (Clark 1965, 173–174).

Moscow was saved, but Leningrad remained besieged, and the German retreat signaled no change in direction for Hitler. Stalin ordered an ill-conceived offensive in the opening months of 1942, gaining little aside from more casualties on both sides. Stalin's interference resulted in additional Soviet defeats in spring. By June, the fortress city of Sevastopol, home port of the Black Sea Fleet, fell to advancing German armies.

Many citizens of the Baltic states of Estonia, Lithuania, and Latvia, seized by Stalin in 1940, welcomed the Germans. Nazi rule in those states was relatively benign; according to the regime's racial theories, the Baltic peoples were superior to their Slavic neighbors. Losing millions of people during a famine in the 1930s whose conditions were blamed on Stalin, many Ukrainians greeted the Germans as liberators. There were also Russians who would gladly trade Stalin for Hitler, but Nazi racism stood in the way. Hitler issued clear instructions for the fate of the Soviet Union: "While German goals and methods must be concealed from the world at large, all the necessary measures—shooting, exiling, etc.—we *shall* take and we *can* anyway. The order of the day is first: conquer second: rule third: exploit" (Clark 1965, 60).

All portions of the Soviet Union that fell to the Germans were theoretically placed under the authority of the Nazi Party's philosopher, Alfred Rosenberg (1893–1946). Rosenberg pragmatically hoped to reach an accord with Ukrainians and other Soviet minority groups. However, his authority as Minister for the Occupied Eastern Territories was undermined at every turn by minions loyal to his enemy in Hitler's circle, Party Chancellery Chief Martin Bormann (1900–1945); by agents of Hermann Göring (1893–1946) representing his economic fiefdom; and most of all by the SS. The SS sought to kill every Jew in the Occupied Territories, but their efforts were sometimes thwarted by other Nazis with an economic interest in their survival. Confusion and uncertainty reigned.

With the attack on Stalingrad, the German armies reached their breaking point. Located at a strategic turn of the Volga River, Stalingrad was a busy provincial factory town, roughly comparable in 1941 to such heartland American industrial hubs as Cincinnati or Milwaukee. Its importance to Stalin was sentimental. He was victorious there during the Russian Civil War and had renamed the city of Tsaritsyn in his honor. For Hitler, Stalingrad was a way station toward his strategic objective of seizing the oil fields of Azerbaijan or at least severing them from Moscow. Once Hitler thought he had Stalingrad in his grasp, holding the city that bore his rival's name "had become a matter of prestige" guided by emotions rather than strategy (Longerich 2019, 840).

The assault on Stalingrad began on August 19, 1942, when Paulus's Sixth Army advanced "with surprising speed and economy" to the banks of the Volga and began a near encirclement of the city (Hanson 2017, 319). August 23–24 saw one of Luftwaffe's heaviest airstrikes of the war, as heavy bombers in a series of sorties dropped thousands of tons of explosives and incendiaries onto Stalingrad, consuming the wooden houses of the workers' districts and leaving most of the city in ruins. One day later, the Communist Regional Party Committee issued a proclamation to survivors reflecting Stalin's determination: "We shall never surrender the city of our birth to the depredations of the German invader. Each single one of us must apply himself to the task of defending our beloved town, our homes, and our families. Let us barricade every street; transform every district, every block, every house, into an impenetrable fortress" (Clark 1965, 218).

Surprised by the tenacity of the resistance, the German advance devolved into a battle for every building, railway embankment, and pile of rubble. The diaries and letters of German soldiers complained of the "madness" and "insane stubbornness" of their opponents. The Soviets were described as "devils" and "barbarians"; one writer claimed they were "not men, but some kind of cast-iron creatures; they never get tired and are not afraid of fire" (Clark 1965, 222). Despite enjoying superior numbers of men and tanks, as well as full command of the air, the Battle of Stalingrad began badly for the Germans. Panzer crews were reluctant to go down narrow streets where they were vulnerable to grenades dropped from the upper stories of the ruined buildings overhead. Paulus expended a good deal of his manpower and material in assaults on stoutly constructed grain elevators and fortified factories, losing men at every step against the determined defenders. The Soviets fought in small groups with machine guns, submachine guns, and antitank weapons and laid killing zones with mines. By the end of October, the Germans took most of the city's strong points, but by then, the "Sixth Army was spent," its men exhausted and riddled with anxiety (Clark 1965, 239).

Come November "the besiegers of Stalingrad soon became the besieged (Hanson 2017, 320). With winter setting in, the Soviets overwhelmed the flanks of the Sixth Army, held by poorly armed and motivated Romanian divisions, and encircled Stalingrad. Cut off by land, the Germans hung on to portions of the city, receiving inadequate supplies by air while subjected to withering Soviet bombardment as well as the cruel Russian winter. In Nazi propaganda, Stalingrad was described as a "fortress" on the frontier of Germany's expanding empire. The description bore no relation to reality on the ground, where German troops struggled to maintain defensive perimeters in the rubble. As Soviet soldiers probed into the city, many Germans raised their hands in surrender. They were increasingly subject to rats, lice, and typhus as well as extreme cold and malnourishment (Craig 1973, 363–365).

In the final hours, as Soviet tanks tightened the noose around Paulus's headquarters in the basement of the Univermag department store, Hitler promoted the beleaguered general to the rank of field marshal. "Knowing that no German field marshal had ever surrendered, Hitler hoped that Paulus would take the hint and commit suicide" (Craig 1973, 377). Instead, Paulus shocked his superiors in Berlin by surrendering on February 2, 1943, to Lieutenant Fyodor Yelchenko, a young officer whose tank happened to be closest to the department store at the moment of capitulation.

Between 90,000 and 100,000 Germans were taken prisoner that day. All but 6,000 perished, many within the first weeks from sickness and others during captivity in the years to come. The survivors finally returned home in September 1955 (Hanson 2017, 322).

Germany's crushing defeat at Stalingrad didn't mark the end of Hitler's campaign to subdue the Soviets. Ignoring the advice of his generals, Hitler launched Operation Citadel, an attack against Soviet positions around Kursk in a region the size of New Jersey. The battle began on July 4, 1943, and culminated on July 12 in a clash of tanks involving hundreds of vehicles from both sides. By day's end, the Germans were obliterated. Kursk was

> **TEHRAN CONFERENCE (NOVEMBER 28, 1943–
> DECEMBER 1, 1943)**
>
> Held in Iran's capital, the Tehran Conference was the first strategic summit meeting between the three major Allied leaders: Joseph Stalin, Winston Churchill, and Franklin D. Roosevelt. The site was chosen to accommodate Stalin. The dictator feared flying and was unwilling to travel far. Roosevelt made the difficult journey despite his declining health. Churchill was the only avid flyer among the trio.
>
> The "Big Three," as the press called the leaders, agreed on the necessity of an invasion in the coming year in France, a move Churchill opposed, to relieve the Soviet army of the burden of holding back the German military on the European continent. For his part, Stalin agreed to launch an offensive to divert German strength from defending the French coastline and to allow U.S. bombers to operate from bases in Ukraine. The little known "shuttle-bombing" operation, involving American aircraft based in Britain overflying Germany and landing in the Soviet Union for refueling and reloading the bomb bays, achieved little except to anticipate Cold War tensions. U.S. forces in Ukraine were spied on and accused of promoting subversion.

the final turning point of the war on the Eastern Front. "Any lingering doubts about where the strategic initiative now lay were over too, as Soviet offensives became bolder, and largely dictated the pace of events" (Burleigh 2000, 511).

Although outnumbered and ill supplied, German troops, stretched across a thousand-mile front from the Baltic to the Caucasus, continued to fight hard and gave up territory to the advancing Soviets reluctantly. Hitler was fighting for time as well as space. He reasoned that the Soviet Union's improbable alliance between the United States and Great Britain could not endure. Hitler was proven correct but not before his defeat and death.

With Operation Bagration (June 22, 1944, to August 19, 1944), over two million Soviet troops, many of them riding on American-supplied trucks, pushed toward Poland, inflicting a massive defeat on the German army. The road to Warsaw was opened, as was the border of East Prussia, "the heartland of traditional German militarism" (Hanson 2017, 290). By early 1945, Germany's Eastern European satellites had either fallen to the Soviets or switched sides as Stalin prepared for the final spring offensive into Germany.

The last months of the Eastern Front were bloody as Germans troops, fearing death less than capture by their enemies and gambling on the possibility of surrendering to the Americans or British, held on as best as they could. The "retreating German armies vainly sought to create their own Leningrad or Stalingrad that might exhaust the Red Army amid the rubble and lead to better terms of surrender" (Hanson 2017, 309). One million

Soviet and Axis troops were killed or wounded in fighting at Budapest, Breslau, and Berlin. Refusing to retreat from his bunker beneath the rubble of Berlin's government district, Hitler chose suicide over surrender.

DEPICTION AND HISTORICAL CONTEXT

The historical problems of *Enemy at the Gates* begin with the map of Europe filling the screen to illustrate the extent of Nazi conquests on the eve of Stalingrad. The style emulates Hollywood during World War II, except that Hollywood directors of the era knew where to draw the lines. The map in *Enemy at the Gates* shows the black ink of Nazism spreading across Switzerland and Turkey, countries that remained outside the Axis's grip.

Enemy at the Gates drew its name, characters, and plot elements out of William Craig's well-researched yet not flawless nonfiction account. Craig devoted only 12 of his more than 400 pages to the exploits of Vasily Zaitsev, a sniper celebrated in the Soviet press for killing nearly 40 Germans in 10 days. As shown in the film's prelude, he learned to shoot as a boy in the forests of the Ural Mountains (Craig 1973, 121). Tania Chernova received several paragraphs in the book. She was college educated as in the film but in medicine, not German literature (Craig 1973, 106). Chernova's combat role was not especially unusual. One million women served in the Soviet army during the war. "They mastered all specialties, including the most 'masculine' ones" (Alexievich 2017, xii).

The scene when Zaitsev and Chernova arrived near the Stalingrad front was only half accurate. In many Russian battle zones, troops were hauled close to the front, packed tightly into boxcars, as shown in the film. However, there were no tracks leading to the Volga River's east bank. In reality, troops reached the Volga on foot or in trucks (Nieuwint 2015.

The film adds many subplots to the book but subtracts many details. Among the latter was the sniper-training program run by Zaitsev. Chernova was one of his students. They became lovers. However, Danilov received only a passing mention in Craig's book with no reference to a love triangle. In Craig's narrative, Danilov was shot by the German master marksman, called Konings in the book (Craig 1973, 122, 129).

The duel between Zaitsev and Konings is one of the book's problematic aspects. Recent researchers found no one with that name fitting Konings' description serving in the German army during World War II (Nieuwint 2015). A different version of the duel between Soviet and Nazi marksmen surfaced a decade before Craig's book in the memoir of General Vasili Chuikov (1900–1982), who became the Soviet commander in Stalingrad after the first weeks of the German assault in September.

In Chuikov's account, the German was the head of the sniper's school at Zossen but was an SS officer, Standartenführer Heinz Thorwald. Similar to the book and the movie, Chuikov recalled that "we had to find him, study his habits and methods, and patiently await the right moment for one, and only one, well-aimed shot." Thorwald, like Konings and Konig, "altered his position frequently" and was finally brought down, not in the open, as in the film's melodramatic climax, but when he made himself briefly visible from behind the sheet metal that formed his final sniper's nest (Chuikov 1963, 142–143).

Unlike the film, Stalin's envoy, Khrushchev, dismissed Chuikov's predecessor but did not demand his suicide. Khrushchev is accurately shown as a man of "tireless energy and resource" (Clark 1965, 130). In speaking with subordinates, Khrushchev, in life as on film, referred to Stalin as "the Boss" (*Vodzh* in Russian).

The boy running between German and Soviet lines, called Sacha Fillipov in Craig's book, was more or less accurately rendered on screen. He was a frail-looking 15-year old when the Germans arrived in the suburb of Dar Gova, where he lived with his parents and younger brother. Trained as a cobbler in trade school, he offered his services to the Germans. "Amused at the thought of someone so young and delicate having such a skill, the Germans promised him work soling army boots" (Craig 1973, 97). He also contacted Soviet army intelligence and arranged to spy on German headquarters in Dar Gova. He stole documents and reported on troop movements. The book does not link Sacha to Zaitsev or Konings, but as in the film, the Germans eventually discovered his deception and hanged the boy, leaving his body to swing in full view (Craig 1973, 170).

The visually striking scene depicting Zaitsev's passage across the Volga to Stalingrad owes its cinematography to the example of Steven Spielberg's *Saving Private Ryan* (1998) but its content to descriptions in Craig's book and elsewhere. Fresh soldiers were brought to the city, escorted by naval gunboats with antiaircraft batteries, on ferries, barges, and fishing boats crewed by civilian Volga boatmen, "all of them skilled and demonstrably brave" (Erickson 1984, 411). German artillery fire chopped many of the boats into pieces. Soviet General Alexander Ilyich Rodimtsev (1905–1977) watched as one boat "was suddenly engulfed in smoke and then an ear-splitting explosion spread out from it for a hundred yards. When fountains of water fell back into the river, the boat and its sixty-five occupants had vanished" (Craig 1973, 94). Swooping like black birds of prey, German Stuka dive bombers, generating their distinctively terrifying shrill noise as they descended, dove to 100-foot altitudes to bomb and strafe the riverboats.

Although they are wearing the wrong colored hats in the film, the uniformed security troops of the NKVD, Stalin's secret police, were on hand to prevent retreat. From the onset of the German invasion, NKVD "rear security detachments" with machine guns stood ready to "check panic" and "prevent unauthorized withdrawal" (Clark 1965, 55). They were reportedly on hand in Stalingrad, shooting "deserters" and lining the rails of the

Volga boats to prevent fearful soldiers from jumping overboard as the Stukas descended at them (Craig 1973, 104–105).

Some movie scenes are staged for dramatic effect. Squadrons of German Ju 88 bombers did overfly Stalingrad on bombing runs that destroyed parts of the city, but their pilots would not have flown at the low altitude depicted in the film. Their aircraft would have been damaged by their own bombs exploding beneath them at such close range. The screenplay is also careless in identifying military units that took part in the Battle of Stalingrad (Nieuwint 2015).

However, despite several errors and a great deal of fictionalization, *Enemy at the Gates* gets some facts and characterizations straight. More importantly, it catches the peculiar nature of the Battle of Stalingrad, where each engagement "evolved itself into a combat between individuals" and soldiers could hear their enemy "breathing in the next room while they reloaded; hand-to-hand duels were finished in the dark twilight of smoke and brick dust" (Clark 1965, 220).

FURTHER READING

Alexievich, Svetlana. 2017. *Unwomanly Face of War: An Oral History of Women in World War II*. New York: Random House.
Bullock, Alan. 1992. *Hitler and Stalin: Parallel Lives*. New York: Alfred A. Knopf.
Burleigh, Michael. 2000. *The Third Reich: A New History*. New York: Hill and Wang.
Chuikov, Vasili. 1963. *The Beginning of the Road*. London: McGibbon & Kee.
Clark, Alan. 1965. *Barbarossa: The Russian-German Conflict, 1941–1945*. New York: William Morrow.
Conquest, Robert. 2007. *The Great Terror: A Reassessment, 40th Anniversary Edition*. New York: Oxford University Press.
Craig, William. 1973. *Enemy at the Gates: The Battle for Stalingrad*. New York: Reader's Digest Press/E.P. Dutton.
Dreier, Harriet. 2001. "Buhrufe statt Prominenz." *Der Spiegel*, March 8, 2001. https://www.spiegel.de/consent-a-?targetUrl=https%3A%2F%2Fwww.spiegel.de%2Fkultur%2Fkino%2Fberlinale-eroeffnung-buhrufe-statt-prominenz-a-116477.html&ref=https%3A%2F%2Fen.wikipedia.org%2F
Ebert, Roger. 2001. "Enemy at the Gates." *Chicago Sun-Times*, March 16, 2001. https://www.rogerebert.com/reviews/enemy-at-the-gates-2001
Elley, Derek. 2001. "Enemy at the Gates." *Variety*, February 6, 2001. https://variety.com/2001/film/reviews/enemy-at-the-gates-1200466918/
Erickson, John. 1984. *The Road to Stalingrad: Stalin's War with Germany*. Boulder, CO: Westview Press.
Glantz, David M. 2002. *The Battle for Leningrad: 1941–1944*. Lawrence: University Press of Kansas.
Hanson, Victor Davis. 2017. *The Second World Wars: How the First Global Conflict Was Fought and Won*. New York: Basic Books.

Heller, Mikhail, and Aleksandr M. Nekrich. 1986. *Utopia in Power: The History of the Soviet Union from 1917 to the Present.* New York: Summit Books.

Hitler, Adolf. 1943. *Mein Kampf.* Boston, MA: Houghton Mifflin.

Kotkin, Stephen. 2017. *Stalin Waiting for Hitler, 1929–1941.* New York: Penguin Press.

Longerich, Peter. 2019. *Hitler: A Biography.* New York: Oxford University Press.

McAuley, Mary. 2019. *Remembering Leningrad: The Story of a Generation.* Madison: University of Wisconsin Press.

Montefiore, Simon Sebag. 2004. *Stalin: The Court of the Red Tsar.* New York: Alfred A. Knopf.

Nieuwint, Joris. 2015. "The Many Movie Mistakes of Enemy at the Gates." War History Online, September 25, 2015. https://www.warhistoryonline.com/war-articles/the-many-movie-mistakes-of-enemy-at-the-gates.html

Radzinsky, Edvard. 1996. *Stalin: The First In-Depth Biography Based on Explosive New Documents from Russia's Secret Archives.* New York: Doubleday.

Schwarzbaum, Lisa. 2001. "Enemy at the Gates." *Entertainment Weekly*, March 14, 2001. https://ew.com/article/2001/03/14/enemy-gates-2/

Thomson, David. 2010. *The New Biographical Dictionary of Film.* New York: Alfred A. Knopf.

Toland, John. 1976. *Adolf Hitler.* Garden City, NY: Doubleday.

Chapter 11

Flags of Our Fathers and *Letters from Iwo Jima* (2006)

An actor and filmmaker with a long and eclectic résumé, Clint Eastwood (1930–) directed and co-produced a pair of films on one of World War II's most storied battles, Iwo Jima. Each film looked at the battle with unique insights from different national perspectives. *Flags of Our Fathers*, released on October 20, 2006, was based on the best-selling book of the same name (2000) by American historians James Bradley (1954–) and Ron Powers (1941–). *Letters from Iwo Jima*, released in Japan on December 9 and the United States on December 20, 2006, was based on a 2005 best-selling Japanese account of the battle by Japanese author Kumiko Kakehashi (1961–). Her book, published in the United States as *So Sad to Fall in Battle: An Account of War*, was drawn from the wartime letters of Japan's commander on Iwo Jima, General Tadamichi Kuribayashi (1891–1945).

Steven Spielberg (1946–) and Robert Lorenz (1965–) co-produced both films, Paramount Pictures released *Flags of Our Fathers* in the United States, and Warner Brothers released it internationally. After *Flags of Our Fathers* underperformed at the box office, Paramount gave Warner Brothers distribution rights for *Letters from Iwo Jima* in the United States and Japan and retained them in other foreign markets. The two films were completed back to back and were meant to complement each other. *Letters from Iwo Jima* is the only major international film to offer a Japanese perspective on World War II aside from the segments of the Pearl Harbor dramatization, *Tora! Tora! Tora!* (1970), directed by Toshio Masuda (1927–) and Kinji Fukasaku (1930–2003).

Veteran Hollywood writer, director, and producer Paul Haggis (1953–) worked on the screenplays for both films. His collaborator on *Flags of Our*

Fathers, William Broyles Jr. (1944–), had contributed to the screenplay for *Saving Private Ryan* (1998); for *Letters from Iwo Jima*, Haggis worked with Japanese-American writer Iris Yamashita (1965–).

Eastwood chose to tell *Flags of Our Fathers* in a nonlinear fashion. He explained in a 2006 interview that "we had difficulty going into flashback, and then into flashbacks within the flashback, and then having to unwind and come back." He admitted that the format could be confusing, but "it seemed like the logical way to do it—James Bradley wrote his book as something like a detective story, going round and talking to people, and it's a big, sprawling book" (Newgen 2006).

Flags of Our Fathers focuses on three of the U.S. servicemen involved in raising the American flag at the summit of Mount Suribachi on Iwo Jima. They are Pharmacist's Mate John "Doc" Bradley (1923–1994), played by Ryan Phillippe (1974–); Corporal Rene Gagnon (1925–1979), played by Jesse Bradford (1979–); and Corporal Ira Hayes (1923–1955), played by Adam Beach (1972–). Eastwood cast lesser-known actors because he wanted them to appear to be the same age as the average 19- or 20-year old soldier on the front lines.

The film begins as the aged John Bradley awakens from a nightmare of being in combat on Iwo Jima. The post-traumatic stress image recurs throughout *Flags of Our Fathers*. Much of the film is structured around interviews with survivors in the 1990s, conducted by James Bradley, played by Tom McCarthy (1966–). Among the interviewees is retired Associated Press photographer Joe Rosenthal (1911–2006), played by Ned Eisenberg (1957–), who took the famous picture of the flag-raising on Iwo Jima's highest point, Mount Suribachi.

Although U.S. propaganda allowed the public to believe that the men in the photograph were the first to reach the summit and raised the flag while still under enemy fire, in reality, they were part of the second contingent up the mountain. The first flag had already been raised, and the second contingent was ordered to replace it with the Stars and Stripes seen in Rosenthal's impromptu photo shoot. "Plenty of other photos were taken but no one wanted them," Rosenthal tells Bradley in the film. He explains the iconic importance of his photo. "If you can get a picture, the right picture, you can win or lose the war."

Flags of Our Fathers zigzags between the 1990s when the author conducted interviews for his book, the battle for Iwo Jima, and the 1945 war bonds tour marketed around the heroism of Bradley, Gagnon, and Hayes. After the photograph of the flag-raising circulates throughout the American news media, the military sends the three men home to encourage audiences to buy bonds, but their flashbacks to the scene of battle are harrowing, and their memories differ from the official account. They are uncomfortable being singled out for attention. They insist that their fight was no more difficult than that of their comrades and are dismayed by the hollow excitement surrounding them.

Letters from Iwo Jima is built around two sets of characters representing Japan's class system, the highborn General Kuribayashi (played by Ken Watanabi, 1959–) and Baron Nishi (Tsuyoshi Ihara, 1963–) and the commoners, privates Saigo (Kazunari Ninomiya, 1963–), Kashiwara (Takashi Yamaguchi, 1936–), and Shimizu (Ryo Kase, 1974–). The enlisted men grumble and the officers are fatalistic, even as they work hard to build defenses on the island that will cost many American lives while only delaying the inevitable defeat.

Letters from Iwo Jima is a long flashback framed by the discovery of a cache of letters buried beneath Kuribayashi's underground headquarters, and although it includes several flashbacks within the flashback, its structure is more straightforward than *Flags of Our Fathers*. Several battle scenes in *Letters from Iwo Jima* fit together with scenes from *Flags of Our Fathers* like pieces of a puzzle.

Letters from Iwo Jima follows the experiences of its main characters from 1944 through their defeat in 1945. When Kuribayashi arrives to take command of the Iwo Jima garrison, he is immediately dissatisfied with the trenches his predecessor had ordered dug near the beaches. Kuribayashi begins an ambitious program of constructing a network of tunnels connecting concealed strongpoints that covered the island in crossfire from artillery and machineguns.

Kuribayashi's experience as military attaché in the United States during the 1920s is glimpsed in flashbacks. He is joined on Iwo Jima by an old friend, Baron Nishi, the equestrian champion at the 1932 Olympics in Los Angeles and now a lieutenant colonel. Both men have an accurate appraisal of the United States as a formidable enemy. When Nishi informs Kuribayashi that Japan lost most of its naval and airpower in recent defeats, the general realizes that he has no chance of victory but can only hope for an honorable defeat.

The lower ranks have no access to information beyond the censored Japanese media and have been educated to view Americans as weak and undisciplined. Despite the diet of lies fed to them, Saigo is cynical and gets in trouble for his unguarded remarks about the futility of the war. His friend Kashiwara is more conventionally patriotic. A newcomer to their unit, Shimizu, is viewed warily and suspected of being a spy for the Kempeitai, Japan's military police. A flashback shows that he was briefly in the Kempeitai but discharged after refusing to kill a dog.

Japanese defeat is inevitable once the United States landing begins. Kuribayashi and Nishi take their own lives in ritual suicide, and Kashiwara dies in the assault. U.S. Marines kill Shimizu in cold blood after surrendering. Only Saigo survives.

Critics generally hailed both films, but they often considered *Letters from Iwo Jima* the better of the two pictures. For example, *Entertainment Weekly* called *Flags of Our Fathers* "an honorable and rather plodding movie" offering "more earnestness than urgency" (Gleiberman 2006) but praised *Iwo Jima* as "profound, magisterial, and gripping" (Schwarzbaum 2006). Both had trouble finding large audiences at U.S. box offices, with *Letters from Iwo Jima* outperforming *Flags of Our Fathers*. Britain's *Guardian* newspaper praised *Flags of Our Fathers* and chided American audiences for failing to respond enthusiastically, calling it "a sombre and shrewd movie about America's war in the Pacific," adding that it "plays out in a haunting minor key—perhaps a little too haunting and minor for American cinemagoers who have received this movie coolly, perhaps now finding the subject of war uncongenial, and probably unready for a film that challenges the myths of the one war whose essential rightness is an article of faith" (Bradshaw 2006).

Despite mixed results in ticket sales, both films dominated Top 10 lists among critics. The National Board of Review named *Letters from Iwo Jima* as the top film of 2006 and included *Flags of Our Fathers* in its Top Ten (King 2006). Reflecting on the films of 2006, the *Chicago Sun-Times*' Roger Ebert tied *Flags of Our Fathers* and *Letters from Iwo Jima* at seventh place in his Top 10 list. "With masterful production planning, Eastwood is able to make the strategies of both sides clear, and we understand what is happening and how deadly it is, and how the famous photograph of the flag being raised over Iwo Jima does not represent what is assumed, or even show what it seems to show," he wrote (Ebert 2007).

Flags of Our Fathers was nominated for Academy Awards in Sound Mixing and Sound Editing but won neither. The Golden Globes nominated Eastwood for Best Director, but he lost to Martin Scorsese for *The Departed*. The awards season was more generous to *Letters from Iwo Jima*. It received four Academy Award nominations, including Best Picture, Director, and Screenplay, but won only for Best Sound Editing. *Letters from Iwo Jima* also earned a Golden Globe for Best Foreign Language Film as well as other trophies in the United States, Japan, and Europe.

Although neither film was a blockbuster, both have endured among history buffs and war movie fans. *Letters from Iwo Jima* was recently cited among the 20 best (Ross 2019) and the 12 best World War II movies (Adams 2019) with *Letters from Iwo Jima* and *Flags of Our Fathers* ranking together in a Top 30 World War II movie ranking (Verhoeven 2018).

HISTORICAL BACKGROUND

In the final weeks of 1941 and the opening months of 1942, the Allies were in retreat across East Asia and the Pacific. The British lost Hong Kong, Malaya, and Burma as the Japanese pressed toward the border of India. The Dutch East Indies (Indonesia) fell; the United States lost the Philippines and Guam. Australia would have been next, but the Japanese Imperial Navy decided to move instead against Midway Island, an American atoll located roughly midway between North America and Asia. They hoped to lure the U.S. Pacific Fleet into a decisive defeat and bring the United States to the peace table.

Their failure "marked the beginning of the end of the Japanese Empire," although at the time neither side realized that the Pacific war had reached a turning point (Costello 1981, 332). The Battle of Midway (June 4–7, 1942) was fought primarily by aircraft with secondary assistance from submarines. The big guns of the battleships and cruisers proved to be of no consequence. American determination overcame superior numbers, sinking four Japanese aircraft carriers and downing over 200 planes. The Japanese sank only one U.S. carrier. The Japanese achieved the secondary objective of the offensive when its forces seized Attu and Kiska in the Aleutian Islands, allowing them to raise the battle flag of the rising sun above a particle of mainland America. The Battle of the Aleutian Islands (June 1942 to August 1943) continued for many months by air and sea until the United States with Canadian assistance finally retook the islands.

After Midway, Admiral Chester Nimitz (1885–1966), commander of the U.S. Pacific Fleet, announced, "Pearl Harbor has now been partially avenged" (Potter 1976, 107). However, despite lack of radar on most of its ships, the Japanese navy remained stronger than the Pacific Fleet, and the Allied counterattack gathered momentum slowly during the next months. President Franklin D. Roosevelt (1882–1945) and his chief of staff, General George Marshall (1880–1959), prioritized the Atlantic convoy pipeline to Great Britain and the Soviet Union, and preparing for the liberation of Europe, over fighting the war in the Pacific. Also, U.S. commanders in the Pacific theater fought among themselves over priorities.

Although defeated at Midway, the Japanese remained on the offensive. On July 6, they landed at Guadalcanal in the British Solomon Islands and began constructing an airbase that could threaten Australia and enhance the defensive perimeter of fortified islands across the Pacific prepared by Japan in anticipation of an American counterattack. On August 7, U.S. Marines easily took part of the island from the "outnumbered Japanese, most of them construction troops." However, it "remained to be seen if they could hold the enclave they had seized" (Symonds 2018, 300).

Japanese air raids commenced almost immediately, and a naval squadron under Vice Admiral Gunichi Mikawa (1888–1981) set forth to disrupt the Allied operation. The ensuing Battle of Savo Island (August 8, 1942) was a humiliating blow for the Allies and, second only to Pearl Harbor, the worst defeat suffered by the U.S. Navy during the war. Three American and one Australian cruisers were among the losses. One of the surviving American commanders, Captain Howard Bode (1889–1943), took his own life after he was judged incompetent by a naval review. The U.S. government suppressed news of the defeat at Savo Island, allowing the *New York Times* to report that the Japanese were "thwarted" and "compelled to retreat" (Symonds 2018, 310).

The United States reinforced the 1st Marine Division on Guadalcanal by day, and the Japanese shuttled infantry onto the island by night. The resources that both sides hurled onto the island "had a significant impact on the global war"; the Japanese diverted warships from their planned incursion into the Indian Ocean, and U.S. troopships earmarked for the invasion of Europe were forced to remain in the Pacific (Symonds 2018, 326).

The marines on Guadalcanal were ill-informed about the island they were tasked with securing. The "grassy knoll" near the beach turned out to be a 1,500-foot mountain; a creek was actually a river too deep to ford. The dense rainforest turned much of Guadalcanal into a place of darkness even at noon. Wet layers of vegetation made climbing the island's hills difficult for men shouldering heavy packs. Around noon each day, "Tojo time" the marines called it, Japanese planes strafed the U.S. positions. At night, enemy warships used searchlights to find targets to bombard. As Private Sid Phillips (1924–2015) recalled, "The typical marine on the island ran a fever, wore stinking dungarees, loathed twilight and wondered whether the U.S. Navy still existed" (Ward and Burns 2007, 51). They felt abandoned.

Once the Japanese infantry attacked in earnest, the fighting was brutal and hand-to-hand. The battle for Guadalcanal received ample American press complete with war correspondents trailing behind the marines. The reporting softened the horror but represented the difficulty of subduing an enemy hidden in an alien landscape. *Life* magazine compared a platoon of marines advancing into the jungle to "a band of Western pioneers, or some gold prospectors, wary of Indians." The writer quoted a marine colonel who "learned respect for the Japs. What they have done is to take Indian warfare and apply it to the 20th Century" (Hersey 1942).

The deadlock prompted Admiral Isoroku Yamamoto (1884–1943), architect of the Pearl Harbor and Midway operations, to transport the 5,800 soldiers once earmarked for occupying Midway Island to Guadalcanal. His fleet clashed with American units through the last week of August in the Battle of the Eastern Solomons. Despite incurring heavy losses, the United States prevented a massive reinforcement of Japanese troops on Guadalcanal. The critical factor for the United States was holding the airstrip on the island against repeated enemy assaults and bombardments.

The ongoing struggle by air and sea continued. The Battle of the Santa Cruz Islands (October 26, 1942) unfolded according to a now familiar pattern with scout planes from both sides identifying enemy ships and calling for airstrikes; "the opposing attack formations actually passed each other en route to their targets" (Symonds 2018, 344). In a precursor to the kamikaze attacks late in the war, crippled Japanese planes crashed onto an American aircraft carrier, forcing the captain to abandon ship. Although the Japanese

> **ISOROKU YAMAMOTO (1884–1943)**
>
> Admiral Isoroku Yamamoto planned Japan's attack on Pearl Harbor (1941), a decision he did not support. As a young officer, he had studied at Harvard, was posted to Washington, D.C., as naval attaché, and visited the U.S. Naval War College. Unlike those who advocated drawing the United States into the war, Yamamoto was aware of America's size and potential strength. He did not care to arouse the sleeping giant.
>
> Through the 1930s, Yamamoto drew death threats from Japanese nationalists for criticizing the country's pact with Nazi Germany and opposing the invasion of China. According to some reports, Yamamoto's superiors ordered him to sea as commander of the Combined Fleet, the main ocean-going component of Japan's navy, to foil his assassination. Despite his political objections to the course of Japan's politics, Yamamoto was an early advocate of naval airpower and deemed the best tactician for a carrier-based strike against U.S. installations at Pearl Harbor. He also commanded the Combined Fleet in the Battle of Midway (1942), Japan's first defeat in the Pacific.
>
> The American military did not forgive him. In 1943, when U.S. codebreakers discovered Yamamoto's plans to inspect forward positions in the Pacific, a squadron of American fighters attacked his plane, which they shot down over the island of Bougainville, killing Yamamoto.

also suffered heavy losses, after the battle, the United States possessed only one operational, if badly damaged, carrier in the Pacific.

The Pacific war's outcome remained uncertain, and both sides invested their hope for victory in the outcome at Guadalcanal. In the Naval Battle of Guadalcanal (November 13, 1942), Japanese and American warships found themselves at close quarters in the dead of night. "The two fleets bled into each other and lost cohesion almost at once"; friendly fire was inevitable, but many ships were too close to fire anything but machine guns. The commander of the U.S. cruiser *Portland*, Captain Laurence Du Bose (1893–1967), recalled, "In the confused picture of burning and milling ships, it became impossible to distinguish friend from foe" (Symonds 2018, 366). The battle ended in another draw. The Americans lost 2 admirals and 700 sailors. The Japanese also suffered high casualties, including the loss of two battleships.

By the end of 1942, the Japanese high command concluded that Guadalcanal was no longer worth the cost. In February 1943, the Japanese evacuated the last starving soldiers by night from the island. The struggle cost over 30,000 Japanese and 7,100 American lives. "For all the heroic courage and sacrifice of the men on both sides who fought for six months in appalling conditions, the key to eventual Allied success was superior sealift protected by land-based air power" (Symonds 2018, 373). America's industrial capacity, located beyond the range of air raids, enabled the United States to outproduce its enemies in ships, planes, and other vehicles.

The expansion of American codebreaking capacity was also crucial. By 1943, the Joint Intelligence Center Pacific Ocean Area, staffed by more than 1,000 people, rapidly decoded and interpreted many Japanese messages. Codebreakers read Japanese orders to reinforce its forward base in New Guinea, the port of Lae, with convoys carrying 6,000 troops. In the Battle of the Bismarck Sea (February 1, 1943), American and Australian bombers swooped upon those convoys, bombing and strafing at low altitude. Both sides showed no mercy. The United States machine-gunned survivors in lifeboats, and the Japanese machine-gunned a crew parachuting from a crippled bomber.

The U.S. facility with codebreaking, coupled with the urge to avenge Pearl Harbor, claimed the life of one of Japan's top officers. After intercepting messages that detailed Admiral Yamamoto's flight plan, the United States sought out and shot down his plane in an aerial ambush over the Solomon Islands. His death "hit the Imperial Navy as severely as if one of its superbattleships had been sunk—a loss that was all the more keenly felt because they had been robbed of their leading naval strategist" (Costello 1981, 435).

By then, Japan's military leaders had realized that defeating the Allies was unrealistic. They planned instead to outlast their enemies. Japan saw no alternative but to defend "each of the Empire's outposts so fiercely that even as they fell one by one, the losses the Americans suffered in capturing them would erode their will to continue the war" (Symonds 2018, 409). The Japanese clung to the idea that their warrior spirit would triumph in the end as U.S. forces conducted amphibious landings across the Solomon Islands and an American-Australian expedition under Douglas MacArthur (1880–1964) pushed up the coast of New Guinea.

The struggle for Munda Point in New Georgia, the largest of the Solomon Islands, helped determine America's response to Japan's suicidal determination. The Japanese dug gun emplacements into coral, reinforced by logs and imperceptible from a distance of a few yards. "The defenders had to be pried out of each of their cleverly camouflaged pillboxes with tanks and flamethrowers" and hand-to-hand fighting at every strongpoint (Costello 1981, 447). It took 32,000 U.S. infantrymen and 1,700 marines five weeks to take Munda from 5,000 Japanese troops.

Afterward, the United States pursued the strategy of "island hopping," bypassing many fortified Japanese-held islands to conserve casualties and secure the most important stepping-stones on the way to Tokyo. Hundreds of thousands of Japanese personnel remained marooned on bypassed islands until the war's end.

The U.S. and Japanese navies played dangerous games of hide and seek in middle-of-the-night battles around the Solomons as summer of 1943 slipped into fall. The engagements did not alter the course of the war as America's momentum gained force despite ongoing conflict between MacArthur and his foremost opponent in the navy, Admiral Ernest King (1878–1956), over command of the Pacific theater and the direction of the war. MacArthur wanted to make good his promise to return to the Philippines. The navy favored an assault on the Gilbert Islands in the Central Pacific, a healthier climate for servicemen and closer to the Japanese home islands. The key to the Gilberts was Tarawa, an atoll surrounded by small islands. To take Tarawa, the United States organized the Fifth Fleet, the largest combat fleet America had ever assembled with 12 battleships and 20 aircraft carriers under Rear Admiral Raymond Spruance (1886–1969).

Tarawa was so distant from the nearest Allied base that maintaining an efficient resupply line was nearly impossible. The Fifth Fleet had to carry the entire contingent of troops and all of their equipment for the assault; "the invaders had to seize the whole of the island on the first try or fail entirely" (Symonds 2018, 491).

The attack on Tarawa began on November 2, 1943, with "the greatest concentration of aerial bombardment and naval gunfire in the history of warfare" (Alexander 1993, 9). The shellfire and bombs were expected to obliterate the defenders, but the Japanese installations withstood the assault. The terrain favored them. The atoll's coral reefs, submerged by only three feet at high tide, were treacherous for landing craft. The first wave of Marines came to shore riding "amphtracks" or "alligators," a landing craft fitted with tank treads, carrying 20 men. The Japanese held their fire until

DOUGLAS MACARTHUR (1880–1964)

Douglas MacArthur held virtually every position of importance in the U.S. Army, including Chief of Staff and Superintendent of West Point. During World War II, he commanded Allied forces against Japan as Supreme Commander Southwest Pacific. Accepting Japan's surrender in Tokyo harbor, he became the country's military governor with the title of Supreme Commander for the Allied Powers and took a leading role in writing the country's new constitution and reforming its social and economic life. During the Korean War, MacArthur became Commander-in-Chief United Nations Command, leading an international force against North Korea and China.

The most controversial U.S. general since the Civil War, MacArthur angered many when his troops broke up the "Bonus Army" veterans protest in Washington, D.C. (1932). His policy toward Occupied Japan involved sheltering the emperor from charges of war crimes. During the Korean War, President Harry S. Truman removed MacArthur from command due to insubordination.

MacArthur's handling of the Philippines defense was also controversial. He refused to believe that the Japanese would attack the islands in the immediate aftermath of Pearl Harbor, and some accused him of being ill prepared. In their rapid retreat to the Bataan, U.S. troops abandoned most of their supplies, which worsened conditions on the peninsula and gave Japan a speedier victory.

the vehicles were in close range. Some units suffered 70 percent casualties before reaching the beach.

With the aid of continual bombardment from navy vessels anchored close to the shore, 20,000 marines eventually overwhelmed the 4,800 Japanese defenders. Only 17 Japanese were taken alive. The United States suffered 1,000 dead and 3,000 wounded. "The Americans had secured their objectives, but the cost had been far beyond any of the pre-invasion projections." While casualties on Guadalcanal had been higher, "the slaughter on Tarawa took place in three days instead of six months, and in less than one square mile" (Symonds 2018, 495).

MacArthur used the slaughter as an excuse for demanding supreme command over all U.S. forces in the Pacific. Warner Brothers released a documentary drawn from combat footage, *With the Marines at Tarawa*, which displayed the difficulty faced by the United States as it advanced toward Japan. The film aroused public outcry for retribution against the Japanese and won an Academy Award for Best Documentary Short Subject.

Next stop for the United States was Kwajalein, a large atoll in the Marshall Islands 600 miles northwest of Tarawa. The American military learned lessons from its previous amphibious assault. The "amphtracks" were transformed into amphibious tanks with armor and a 37mm gun, and the navy practiced gunnery in Hawaii by shelling targets modeled after the Japanese fortifications on Tarawa. The invasion of Kwajalein on January 31, 1944, went swiftly with light American casualties.

The next objective was Saipan in the Marianas. Once the United States established bases there, U.S. B-29 Superfortress bombers could conduct raids on the Japanese home islands. As the lynchpin of a ring of defensive islands, the Japanese had to hold Saipan. Japan gambled its fleet in a bid to fend off the U.S. assault, but the Battle of the Philippine Sea (June 19–20, 1944) proved catastrophic. The Japanese lost 3 aircraft carriers and more than 400 planes, many of them piloted by inexperienced teenagers. The United States lost no ships and only 100 planes, many of them ditched in the ocean for running out of fuel. However, the Americans had a harder time on land in securing Saipan against suicidal resistance. The Japanese commanders killed themselves rather than surrender, and civilians died in mass suicide events as entire families hurled themselves from cliffs or blew themselves up with grenades (Symonds 2018, 552–553).

MacArthur successfully argued that the next target should be the Philippines, specifically the island of Leyte at the heart of the archipelago, but in preparation, the United States had to secure Peleliu, an island 600 miles to the west. On Peleliu, the Japanese retreated into a network of tunnels and caves impervious to naval guns or air raids. It took 10 weeks and 6,000 American casualties to capture the caves.

Meanwhile, the American invasion armada sailed for Leyte. On October 20, 1944, MacArthur fulfilled the pledge he had made when he fled the Philippines two and a half years earlier by wading ashore with camera crews waiting despite persistent sniper fire. "People of the Philippines, I have returned," he declared. Broadcasting on a radio rigged by the Signal Corps, MacArthur called on Filipinos to rise against the Japanese. By nightfall, the United States landed four infantry divisions on Leyte, and MacArthur received a hero's welcome across the chain of islands.

However, the United States had many months of hard fighting ahead, capped by the Battle of Manila (February 3, 1954, to March 3, 1945). By the time the Philippines' capital fell to the United States, most of the city was in ruins. Japan lost 16,000 dead and the United States 1,000. Nearly 100,000 Filipino civilians also died, "some hit by American artillery, many slaughtered by their retreating captors" (Ward and Burns 2007, 346).

The invasion of the Philippines triggered an immediate Japanese naval response. The Battle of Leyte Gulf (October 23–26, 1944) was among the largest naval engagements in history. The United States lost 3 carriers and 2 destroyers, but Japanese suffered heavier losses, including 4 carriers, 3 battleships, 10 cruisers, and 13 destroyers. The defeat marked the end of the Japanese navy as an effective combat force and hastened American victory. Japan faced other problems at sea. Emulating their German counterparts, 40–50 U.S. submarines patrolled the western Pacific in wolf packs, sinking Japanese transports, starving Japan's military of fuel by cutting the supply chain to the oil fields of Dutch East India, and threatening "to shut down the Japanese economy altogether" (Symonds 2018, 590).

On November 24, 1944, the U.S. 21st Air Force began bombing runs over Japan's cities from its new base on Saipan. The round trip of 3,000 miles was challenging for the B-29s, dropping their payloads from 30,000 feet in daylight runs. Accuracy was poor even if the damage to civilians was great. Having no fighter planes with sufficient range to provide escort, the Army Air Force searched their maps for a solution. Halfway between Saipan and Japan sat the island of Iwo Jima, close enough for fighter planes to join the bomber formations on their raids. Iwo Jima could also provide a more convenient airfield where damaged B-29s could land on the way home from missions. With the prodding of Air Force commanders, the United States deemed the conquest of the island to be its next strategic objective. Admiral King later complained that the "sole importance" of Iwo Jima was "the performance of the long range aircraft of the Army Air Corps" (King and Whitehill 1952, 596).

DEPICTION AND HISTORICAL CONTEXT

Clint Eastwood took care to accurately render most of the visual and locational details in both *Flags of Our Fathers* and *Letters from Iwo Jima*. Referenced in the dialogue is Iwo Jima's sulfurous stench and lack of good drinking water. Japanese stationed on the island suffered from diarrhea and other maladies as a result of those conditions (Kakehashi 2007, 7, 17). Both films give a realistic impression of the scale of the combat. The Battle of Iwo Jima (February 19, 1945, to March 26, 1945) lasted 36 days and pitted 75,000 marines against 22,000 Japanese troops. By the end, the United States had suffered 28,851 casualties, including 6,821 killed or missing. Twenty-seven marines were awarded the Medal of Honor for their courage on Iwo Jima, 13 posthumously (Ross 1985, xiii). As shown on film, some marines fell to friendly fire (Bradley and Powers 2000, 195). Victorious U.S. forces captured only 200 Japanese alive.

Eastwood shot *Flags of Our Fathers* in a corner of Iceland, whose bleak landscape resembles the terrain of Iwo Jima with its black surface of soft volcanic stone. Civilian access to Iwo Jima is severely limited; the island is a U.S.-Japanese cemetery and serves as a naval and air base for Japan's Self-Defense Force, but Eastwood obtained permission to film portions of *Letters from Iwo Jima* on the island.

The film of *Flags of Our Fathers* conforms closely to the book. The primary screenwriter, Paul Haggis, handled the material sympathetically, condensing *Flags of Our Fathers* into a two-hour production that dramatizes essential characters and episodes. The film also explores the author's theme of heroism, a word greatly overused as the twentieth century ended. The men Bradley spoke with, who faced death at Iwo Jima, did not consider themselves heroes (Bradley and Powers 2000, 353). Like the characters in the film, they did the job they were trained to do.

"The real heroes of Iwo Jima are the guys who never came back," John Henry Bradley said to his son James, who wrote *Flags of Our Fathers* to try to piece together what actually happened when six servicemen were photographed hoisting an American flag on a makeshift pole over Mount Suribachi (Bradley and Powers 2000, 4). Like many World War II veterans, John Henry said little about his wartime experiences.

The book and the film version also tell a story about the American public's reaction to news of the fighting on Iwo Jima. Recent battles for Tarawa and Guadalcanal left Americans with the profound and accurate impression that the United States fought the war in the Pacific against an enemy determined to destroy itself if necessary and kill as many American GIs as possible in the process. As a voiceover in the film declares, "People were becoming cynical, tired of war."

Until the appearance of Rosenthal's photograph, the news from Iwo Jima had been disheartening. Four days into the invasion, a *New York Times*' headline read, "Marines Halted on Iwo," and the newspaper's reporting amplified the alarm. "Now the Marines have come to their hardest battle, a battle still unwon. Our first waves on Iwo Jima were almost wiped out; 3,650 Marines were dead, wounded or missing after the two days of fighting" (Bradley and Powers 2000, 219). The public wanted hope and heroes, and the U.S. government, aided by the news media, gave them the "historic flag-raising photograph made atop Mount Suribachi [which] was to etch the monumental combat into American history alongside Antietam and Gettysburg" (Ross 1985, xiii).

Both films reenact the attack on Iwo Jima with accuracy. Some controversy was generated when director Spike Lee criticized the films for lack of African American actors. One black face is briefly visible aboard one of the troopships. Eastwood responded, correctly, that the Marine Corps was segregated at the time. The only black servicemen on Iwo Jima were in a support company, and none were involved in raising the flag over Suribachi (Dawson 2008). The naval and air bombardment was intense as shown with thousands of tons of explosives fired or dropped onto the eight-and-a-half-square mile island. The marines waiting on the decks of the troopships and landing craft "watched and wondered how any Japanese could survive" (Ross 1985, 61). If anything, *Letters from Iwo Jima* underplays the impact of the shelling, especially from the big guns of the battleships, on the Japanese waiting in their underground strongholds. "It was all so quiet at first," Private Donald Howell recalled. "When the landing gate dropped I just walked onto the beach. I was confident. Everyone was milling around. I thought this would be a cinch" (Bradley and Powers 2000, 151).

As marines advanced up the slopes, "smoke and earsplitting noise suddenly" erupted (Bradley and Powers 2000, 155). Machine guns emerged from the narrow slits of hidden blockhouses, mortar squads and light artillery emerged on the heights, and heavy guns embedded in Suribachi opened fire. Eastwood visualized many scenes with details straight from eyewitness accounts. Private Robert Leader (1924–2006) recalled the fate of an amphtrack. "There was this enormous blast and it disappeared. I looked for wreckage and survivors, but nothing. I couldn't believe it. Everything just vaporized (Bradley and Powers 2000, 156).

For Rosenthal, who landed with the first wave of marines, "not getting hit [by Japanese fire] was like running through rain and not getting wet" (Bradley and Powers 2000, 157). Somehow, individual valor and team cohesion kept the marines moving forward in the face of terrible, gruesome casualties.

Flags of Our Fathers reconstructs the flag-raising as described in Bradley's book. On day five of the battle, a platoon made it to the top of Suribachi, rigged a flagpole from a piece of Japanese metal pipe, and hoisted the Stars and Stripes at the summit. Photographers documented this "original flag raising," but their pictures were overlooked. When the marines on the beach spotted the flag, thousands erupted in cheers, and the ships offshore blew their bellowing horns in triumph. Although the platoon did not ascend the mountain under heavy fire, as some press reports claimed, Japanese stragglers sniped at them before the United States fully secured the summit (Bradley and Powers 2000, 294–208).

From the shore, the Secretary of the Navy, James Forrestal (1892–1949), witnessed the flag-raising and told the marines' commanding officer, General

Holland M. Smith (1882–1967), that he wanted the flag as a souvenir. The order did not sit well further down the line. Colonel Chandler Johnson (1905–1945) insisted that the flag belonged to his battalion and ordered that the marines raise a second substitute flag on Suribachi. The marines strung the new flag to a 100-pound drainage pole, which accounts for the sense of struggle in the famous photograph that Rosenthal snapped.

In his book, Bradley identifies the six men handling the second flag as Ira Hayes, Rene Gagnon, John Henry Bradley, Mike Strank (1919–1945), Franklin Sousley (1925–1945), and Harlon Block (1924–1945). The latter three were killed in action within days as fighting continued. By the time of the "second flag raising," the danger from snipers at Suribachi's summit had passed. That second flag-raising was a casual affair. "No one else on the summit paid much attention to what was going on. The action had all the significance of a new football being tossed into a game in progress" (Bradley and Powers 2000, 210).

The Marines Corps' battlefield report for February 23 mentioned only the first flag-raising. Many photographs from both flag-raisings by other cameramen were wired to the United States, but Rosenthal's was the one that instantly caught the eye of newspaper editors and was splashed on front pages across America. The picture was a moment in time captured in a hurry with no thought of posterity, yet it embodied the American public's heroic aspirations for triumphing over the enemy (Bradley and Powers 2000, 212).

Because of the publicity surrounding the photo, the three surviving flag-raisers, Hayes, Bradley, and Gagnon, were sent stateside to support a campaign that may have been more vital than the capture of a small Pacific island. Much of the money to pay for the unprecedented wartime industrial production and the enormous military needed to fight on all fronts was raised by selling bonds. Altogether, the United States borrowed $185 billion in bonds purchased by banks, corporations, and private citizens to pay for the war. To drum up sales, traveling "bond tours" featured popular music and screen stars for events resembling a cross between a country fair and an Independence Day parade. On one tour, actress Hedy Lamarr sold kisses for $25,000 each (Ward and Burns 2007, 90).

With a goal of raising $14 billion, the Seventh Bond Tour starred the "heroes of Iwo Jima," the three surviving men identified from Rosenthal's photograph, and reached 33 cities across the United States. As in the film, they traveled by train accompanied by a Marine Corps officer, whose job was to keep the boys on message and out of trouble. As in the movie, Chicago police nearly arrested Hayes for a drunken disturbance shortly before the trio mounted a replica of Suribachi at Soldier Field (Bradley and Powers 2000, 282–290). The three men sometimes doubted their role and the image they represented. "It took everyone on that island and the men on the ships offshore to get that flag on Suribachi," Bradley told the press at one stop (Bradley and Powers 2000, 285).

Embarrassed by Hayes's public drunkenness, the Marine Corps ordered him back to the Pacific theater during the bond tour. He was denied permission to visit his mother in Arizona on the way back (Bradley and Powers 2000, 290–291). The other two men completed the tour.

Bradley's attempt to set the record straight about Rosenthal's photograph took an unexpected turn after the film's release. The Marine Corps, using photo-enhancement technology, began to question the identity of the six men in the photo. Bradley conceded that his taciturn father, who seldom spoke of the war, was involved in the "original" but not the "second" flag-raising on Suribachi. "I'm not so disappointed that he's not in the second photo. I was trying to write a factual book about the heroes of Iwo Jima," Bradley said, satisfied that the new technology clarified the confused historical record (Gibbons-Neff 2016). The revelation that the men in Rosenthal's photo might have been misidentified might explain their sense of unease for the credit they received, evident in Bradley's book and on film.

In *Letters from Iwo Jima*, the three protagonists among the enlisted men were fictional but not unrealistic representations of ordinary Japanese soldiers on the island. The characters, like many of the men actually stationed there, were conscripts in their twenties and thirties torn from jobs and families to buttress Japan's faltering war effort (Kakehashi 2007, xi).

The two officers were accurately drawn from Japanese accounts. Baron Nishi and General Kuribayashi were upper-class gentlemen who had lived in the United States. Kuribayashi was in America from 1928 to 1930 as part of the military attaché staff. As glimpsed in the film's flashbacks, he delighted in traveling the country by car and enjoyed the friendship of American cavalry officers. Nishi was the toast of American high society after winning the gold medal for horse riding at the 1932 Los Angeles Olympics. Neither man underestimated America's industrial capacity or its military potential. Japanese commentators have suggested that their knowledge of America might also have led them to believe that, given the country's limited appetite for war, massive casualties might bring the United States to the peace table (Kakehashi 2007, 37, 47, 113).

The movie's timeline is correct. Kuribayashi arrived on Iwo Jima in June 1944 and Nishi shortly thereafter. Both men are correctly characterized as worldly and benign in contrast to the narrow-minded brutality of many of their colleagues. They ate the same rations as their men and ended harsh corporal punishment. Upon arrival, the first thing Kuribayashi did was "to inspect every inch of the island so he could get a firm grip on the topography." As seen in the film, he toured the island on foot (Kakehashi 2007, 25, 29–30).

Letters from Iwo Jima summarizes Kuribayashi's strategy. He orders the civilians to be evacuated to Japan and did not allow "comfort women," the Japanese euphemism for prostitutes, on the island (Kakehashi 2007, 33–34). The only women in the film are the unseen recipients of the soldiers' letters.

The general led the rapid construction of the island's elaborate underground defense system. "It was Kuribayashi's staunch leadership that pulled together an ill-equipped bunch of randomly cobbled-together units and enabled them to put up such a heroic fight" (Kakehashi 2007, 11). He had to overcome resistance to his plans from several hidebound army and navy officers. Even in the final hours, there was some disobedience. Kuribayashi ordered no "banzai charges," deeming them a waste of manpower, but some junior officers launched suicide assaults regardless.

Eastwood made a few digressions from the historical record for the sake of visual interest. The film shows Kuribayashi with a pearl-handled Colt pistol at his hip. However, he usually went about armed with only a wooden cane. Nishi may have ridden one of the handful of horses left behind on Iwo Jima but would not have been able to transport his personal steed to the island under wartime conditions (Kakehashi 2007, 29, 70).

The climax of *Letters from Iwo Jima* is fiction based on probabilities. Kuribayashi's body was never identified, but he is thought to have died in battle, as in the movie, on March 26, the final day of battle (Kakehashi 2007, xvi).

FURTHER READING

Adams, Dave. 2019. "12 Best World War II Movies Every History Buff Should Watch." The Archive, January 30, 2019. https://explorethearchive.com/best-world-war-2-movies

Alexander, Joseph H. 1993. *Across the Reef: The Marine Assault on Tarawa*. Washington, D.C.: Marine Corps Historical Center.

Bradley, James, and Ron Powers. 2000. *Flags of Our Fathers*. New York: Bantam.

Bradshaw, Peter. 2006. "Flags of Our Fathers." *The Guardian*, December 22, 2006. https://www.theguardian.com/film/2006/dec/22/drama.actionandadventure

Costello, John. 1981. *The Pacific War*. New York: Rawson, Wade.

Dawson, Jeff. 2008. "Dirty Harry Comes Clean." *The Guardian*, June 5, 2008. https://www.theguardian.com/film/2008/jun/06/1

Ebert, Roger. 2007. "The Best Movies of 2006." Roger Ebert's Journal, RogerEbert.com November 22, 2007. https://www.rogerebert.com/rogers-journal/the-best-movies-of-2006

Gibbons-Neff, Thomas. 2016. "'Flags of Our Fathers' Author Now Says His Father Was Not in the Iconic Iwo Jima Photo." *Washington Post*, May 3, 2016. https://www.washingtonpost.com/news/checkpoint/wp/2016/05/03/flags-of-our-fathers-author-now-says-his-father-was-not-in-iconic-iwo-jima-photo/

Gleiberman, Owen. 2006. "Flags of Our Fathers." *Entertainment Weekly*, October 18, 2006. https://ew.com/article/2006/10/18/flags-our-fathers-2/

Hersey, John. 1942. "The Battle of the River." *Life*, November 23, 1942. From *Reporting World War II, Part One: American Journalism, 1938–1944*. 1995. New York: Library of America, 402.

Kakehashi, Kumiko. 2007. *So Sad to Fall in Battle: An Account of War Based on General Tadamichi Kuribayashi's Letters from Iwo Jima*. New York: Ballantine.

King, Ernest, and Walter Muir Whitehill. 1952. *Fleet Admiral King: A Naval Record*. New York: W. W. Norton.

King, Susan. 2006. "Board of Review Names 'Iwo Jima' Top Movie." *Los Angeles Times*, December 7, 2006. https://www.latimes.com/archives/la-xpm-2006-dec-07-wk-national7-story.html

Newgen, Heather. 2006. "Clint Eastwood on *Flags of Our Fathers*." the drifter, October 13, 2006. http://www.leatherneck.com/forums/archive/index.php/t-35660.html

Potter, Elmer Belmont. 1976. *Nimitz*. Annapolis, MD: Naval Institute Press.

Ross, Bill D. 1985. *Iwo Jima: Legacy of Valor*. New York: Vanguard Press.

Ross, Graeme. 2019. "Second World War in Film: 20 of the Best War Movies Ever Made." *The Independent*, June 6, 2019. https://www.independent.co.uk/arts-entertainment/films/second-world-war-best-dday-films-war-movies-british-a8946901.html

Schwarzbaum, Lisa. 2006. "Letters from Iwo Jima." *Entertainment Weekly*, December 31, 2006. https://ew.com/article/2006/12/31/letters-iwo-jima/

Symonds, Craig L. 2018. *World War II at Sea: A Global History*. New York: Oxford University Press.

Verhoeven, Beatrice. 2018. "30 Classic World War II Movies, from 'Battleground' to 'Dunkirk.'" The Wrap, November 11, 2018. https://www.thewrap.com/world-war-ii-movies-d-day-photos/

Ward, Geoffrey C., and Ken Burns. 2007. *The War: An Intimate History, 1941–1945*. New York: Alfred A. Knopf.

Chapter 12

Dunkirk (2017)

Dunkirk celebrated its world premiere on July 13, 2017, at London's Odeon Leicester Square, a cinema that survived the German blitz on the city, and Warner Brothers Pictures released the film worldwide on July 21. British-born filmmaker Christopher Nolan (1970–) wrote and directed *Dunkirk*, which details the story of the Battle of Dunkirk (May 26, 1940, to June 4, 1940) and the famous British evacuation of the French port city. Nolan co-produced *Dunkirk* with his wife and longtime collaborator, Emma Thomas (1971–).

Although *Dunkirk*'s cast includes familiar faces to moviegoers such as Mark Rylance (1960–) as the boat owner Mr. Dawson, Tom Glynn-Carney (1995–) as his teenage son Peter, James D'Arcy (1975–) as Colonel Winnant, Tom Hardy (1977–) as the RAF pilot Farrier, and Kenneth Branagh (1960–) as Commander Bolton, the story is the star, not the actors. Several recurring characters are never named. Their bravery is collective as well as individual. Nolan's decision to shoot *Dunkirk* on IMAX 65mm film stock provides a richly immersive experience, whose drama is heightened by his use of period airplanes and boats, thousands of extras, and minimal deployment of computers. It's a story about one of history's turning points and a film best appreciated on a big screen.

Nolan shows the fighting around the French coastal town of Dunkirk (Dunkerque) and the evacuation of British and French troops from three perspectives: *Dunkirk* shifts back and forth between British troops on the ground, Royal Air Force units trying to stave off attacks by the Luftwaffe, and the efforts by the Royal Navy, eventually augmented by a fleet of civilian vessels, to rescue as many troops as possible. With the action ongoing, Nolan provided a sense for the simultaneous unfolding of events.

The British soldier Tommy (Fionn Whitehead, 1997–), a private who survives a German ambush, makes his way to the coast of the English Channel and is characteristic of the remnants of British forces he meets on the beach of Dunkirk. The troops assembled on the beach, hoping for evacuation while dodging German air strikes. However, embarking on a ship is no insurance for returning home. The first ship Tommy boards is sunk by German bombers, forcing him back to shore. Eventually, Tommy and his mates make it to England, where they read Churchill's defiant proclamation, promising to fight Nazism by land, air, and sea until Britain's eventual triumph.

Farrier and other RAF fighter pilots battle superior numbers of German aircraft to provide a fragile dome of shelter for the men below. After downing several enemy planes over the English Channel, Farrier's Spitfire runs out of fuel. He makes a soft landing on the Dunkirk shore but is captured by the Germans, who by then have secured the beach.

Mr. Dawson, his son Peter, and a local boy, George (Barry Keoghan, 1992–), respond to the call for civilian boats. On the way to Dunkirk, they rescue a soldier clinging to the wreckage of a sunken ship. The soldier, played by Cillian Murphy (1976–), is shell-shocked and kills George in a senseless altercation. After a minesweeper is sunk by Luftwaffe planes, Dawson rescues sailors. During the course of the movie, Bolton and Winnant have brief exchanges discussing the status of evacuation plans.

Produced on a budget of $100 million, *Dunkirk* sold over $525 million in tickets. After edging out *Saving Private Ryan* (1998) in most nations except the United States, it became the highest grossing World War II film ever made (Brace 2017). It received sterling reviews in Commonwealth countries. According to Canada's most-read newspaper, the *Toronto Star*, *Dunkirk* was "a tremendous and thoughtful examination of a signal drama of the Second World War" (Howell 2017). Britain's prestigious *The Guardian* newspaper called *Dunkirk* "a powerful, superbly crafted film with a story to tell, avoiding war porn in favour of something desolate and apocalyptic, a beachscape of shame, littered with soldiers zombified by defeat, a grimly male world with hardly any women on screen" (Bradshaw 2017).

Most American critics agreed. For the *Los Angeles Times*, "the surpassing accomplishment of 'Dunkirk' is to make us feel an almost literal fusion with its story. It's not so much that we've seen a splendid movie, though we have, but as if we've been taken inside a historic event, become wholly immersed in something real and alive" (Turan 2017). The *New York Times* called *Dunkirk* a "tour de force of cinematic craft and technique" (Dargis 2017). The reviewer for rogerebert.com gave a more mixed assessment, criticizing "the persistent anonymity of the characters; just because a gambit is a conscious part of the film's design doesn't mean it always works, and there are moments you may wonder whether treating supporting players as something other than glorified cannon fodder might have resulted in a film as emotionally powerful as it is viscerally overwhelming" (Seitz 2017).

Because many characters speak no more than a dozen lines in the entire film, *Dunkirk* was ineligible in many of the major motion-picture awards categories. It received nominations for eight Academy Awards, winning for Best Sound Editing, Best Sound Mixing, and Best Film Editing. *Dunkirk* likewise received eight nominations at the British Academy Film Awards but won only for Best Sound. Although it remains too early to measure its historical legacy, *Dunkirk* occupies a place in several top movie lists and was named one of the 100 best British films by London's *Time Out* magazine (Calhoun 2018).

HISTORICAL BACKGROUND

After Germany invaded Poland on September 1, 1939, Great Britain and France declared war on the aggressor and, instead of rushing to the rescue of their Eastern European ally, waited for the expected German assault on the Western Front. The press dubbed it the "Phoney War." Unless a peace settlement was reached, there was no doubt that the assault would come. At the conclusion of the Polish campaign, Germany "immediately began to turn its victorious divisions westward" to man its line of border fortifications, dubbed the Siegfried Line or the West Wall, "and prepare for a campaign against the British and French" (Keegan 1989, 47).

However, months passed in anticipation, tension, and even boredom on the Western Front. French troops waited inside the Maginot Line, a 300-mile long complex of underground fortifications studded with gun turrets that made the border from Switzerland through Luxembourg virtually impregnable, while other units massed at encampments across the country. Meanwhile, the British Expeditionary Force began to assemble on the Belgian-French border. Skirmishes occurred between the Allies and the Germans on land and air, but the world's attention was focused on the Winter War (November 30, 1939, to March 12, 1940), an ill-planned Soviet invasion of Finland that revealed the vulnerability of Soviet forces.

On April 9, 1940, Germany moved north instead of west, subduing Denmark after a brief fight and battling with French and British forces for control over neutral Norway, important as a transit route for Swedish iron ore and for its ports on the North Atlantic. Norway fell to the Nazis, who established a puppet regime under a notorious collaborator, Vidkun Quisling (1887–1945). Norway's King Haakon (1872–1957) managed to escape the country and continued the fight from London exile. One month later, on May 10, Germany ended the Phoney War on the Western Front by launching its blitzkrieg against the Netherlands, Belgium, Luxembourg, and France.

In the years leading up to the German attack, British prime minister Neville Chamberlain (1869–1940) pursued a policy of appeasing Hitler in the hope of averting another war. With the support of France, Chamberlain made concession after concession until it became clear with the invasion of Poland that Hitler's appetite could not be satisfied. "No British politician of any stripe wanted to precipitate another world war"; the country's three parties agreed on a strategy based on "a large air force and navy, a reliance on economic power, and no great army to be sucked into the trenches of another Western Front" (Todman 2016, 133). As a French historian and veteran of the 1940 campaign later complained, Britain "trusted entirely to the French army" to carry the heavy burden of the land war (Benoist-Mechin 1963, 26).

The British strategy was reasonable on paper. By May 1940, the French had mobilized over 3 million men and 3,500 tanks, many of them better than the German panzers. Their air force was smaller than the Luftwaffe but reasonably well equipped. But despite its apparent advantages, France crumbled within six weeks of the German attack. Although a recent historian called it "a catastrophe still inexplicable nearly eighty years later" (Hanson 2017, 248), various explanations contribute to a picture of the French defeat, starting with "the general defensive mentality instilled by the Maginot Line," blamed for dampening the military's offensive spirit (Hanson 2017, 249).

Also blamed was the fossilized thinking of the country's top commanders. "It was still a marching army, its pace of manoeuvre determined by the age-old rhythm of soldier's stride and horse's walk" (Keegan 1989, 60). The French army was categorized as "a piecemeal collection of divisions and units, good, indifferent and plain bad" with divisions culled from reluctant reservists called "militarily inept and even plain insubordinate" (Keegan 1989, 62). Among the best units were cavalry and tank contingents along with colonial troops recruited from Algeria, Senegal, and Vietnam, who often fought the Germans with something approaching hatred.

While the French had more and better tanks than the Germans, France had only three fully formed armored divisions. Germany had 10 and Britain mustered only 1 understrength division. The Allies had no solid mass of armor to blunt the panzer assault.

Germany enjoyed a unified chain of command with Hitler at the top, working through a skilled general staff and disciplined ranks of subordinate officers. The Allies lacked that advantage. The British Expeditionary Force (BEF) under General John Vereker (1886–1946), an aristocrat who was usually called by his title, Lord Gort, supposedly reported to the French commander of the country's northeast region, General Alphonse Joseph Georges (1875–1951), and to the French commander-in-chief, General Maurice Gamelin (1872–1958). In reality, Gort preferred to take orders from London, not Paris, and sometimes acted on his own. Authority over British aircraft was divided between Gort and Bomber Command in London (Keegan 1989, 63). Allied coordination was also hindered by the tenacious claims of neutrality by Belgium and the Netherlands. The military advisor to Belgium's King Leopold III (1901–1983), Lieutenant General Raoul van Overstraeten (1885–1971), was wary of the French and British. Not without cause, he believed the Allies were interested in his country only as a forward battleground, an expendable piece on the chessboard (Keegan 1989, 66).

When the fighting finally began, the Allies were taken aback by Germany's battle plan. The Germans divided their forces into three army groups. Army Group C faced the Maginot Line to prevent a counter thrust into Germany. Army Group B rolled across the Low Countries and drove toward the English Channel. What the Allies did not anticipate was Army Group A, which rushed through the hilly Ardennes forest in Belgium and across the border into France. The Allies deemed the Ardennes impossible for mechanized forces. The Germans proved them wrong. Among the bold-thinking German panzer commanders in the campaign were General Heinz Guderian (1888–1954), who distinguished himself the following year on the Eastern Front, and General Erwin Rommel (1891–1944), later acclaimed as the "Desert Fox" for commanding the Afrika Korps in Libya.

The German assault was closely coordinated with Stuka dive bombers, shrieking as they flew low over their targets, and involved other innovative tactics. On the opening day of the campaign, fewer than 100 German troops landed in gliders on top of Belgium's Fort Eben-Emael. The supposedly impregnable stronghold guarding a key crossroads was subjugated by the small contingent using concrete-piercing charges that shattered its cement and steel shell. The fortress's fall was demoralizing, but Belgium wasn't out of the war just yet. With support from French and British forces, the Belgians fought a brave rearguard action until Leopold, despairing of Allied victory, surrendered on May 28. The Netherlands fell more quickly. German airborne forces hopscotched over the country's network of defensive canals and leveled the center of Rotterdam in an air raid. On May 13, Queen Wilhelmina (1880–1962) left for London on a British destroyer and formed a government-in-exile. With an army of fewer than 1,000 men, Luxembourg fell within one day, but its head of state, Grand Duchess Charlotte (1896–1985), fled to London as the head of a government-in-exile.

In France, Army Group A crossed the River Meuse and took Sedan, the city where Napoleon III surrendered to the Prussians in 1870. The fall of Sedan was a resounding blow to French morale as their forces reeled under the assault from panzers and Stukas. "The atmosphere was that of a family in which there had been a death," recalled a staff officer at General Georges's headquarters (Keegan 1989, 70). The Germans cut across the country, encircling much of the French army and the entire BEF. Roads crowded with fleeing refugees, and poor communications hampered Allied counteradvances. German units were equipped with radios while Allied commanders relied on the French telephone system.

The British formed their expeditionary force hastily and assembled it from the country's five regular divisions and by calling up units of the Territorial

Army, Britain's equivalent to the National Guard. They numbered 300,000 and were often "high in enthusiasm but low in experience and skill" (Keegan 1989, 62). Aside from colonial contingents scattered across the empire and the British-led Indian Army, the BEF represented virtually all of the country's ground forces. Loss of the BEF would have left Britain hard-pressed to repel a German invasion of their islands.

Despite facing superior forces, the BEF was not without accomplishments in the field. On May 21, British tanks surprised the German 7th Panzer Division, "causing panic out of all proportion to their number" because German anti-tank guns were unable to penetrate the tanks' thick armor. But with his usual agility, Rommel improvised and discovered that the German anti-aircraft cannon, the 88mm, was the war's best anti-tank weapon (Todman 2016, 333).

Gort has been criticized as brave but unimaginative, yet his refusal to obey the Imperial General Staff's orders to retreat to Amiens, north of Paris, saved the BEF from destruction. Instead of blocking the road to Paris, he withdrew to Dunkirk, only 47 miles across the choppy English Channel from Dover. "Gort displayed a realistic appreciation of the dire circumstances without giving in to despair like his French counterparts" (Todman 2016, 334).

The German assault had an immediate political effect in Britain, where Chamberlain had already endured increasing criticism for his handling of the war. On May 10, Labour Party leader Clement Attlee (1883–1967) rebuffed Chamberlain's bid to include him in a national unity government. Realizing that his support in Parliament was unsustainable, Chamberlain promptly offered his resignation to King George VI (1895–1952). The leading critic of Chamberlain's policy of appeasement within his own Conservative Party, Winston Churchill (1874–1965) was invited to form a government. Churchill became prime minister and minister of defense and divided other key positions among members of the Conservative, Labour, and Liberal parties. Despite the show of unity, British politics remained divisive until the peril to the home islands grew too clear to ignore. In his first speech to Parliament as prime minister (May 13), Churchill promised "blood, toil, tears and sweat" in the struggle against Nazism and called for "victory, however long and hard the road may be." Labour parliamentarians cheered, but many members of the Conservative Party sat silent (Todman 2016, 319–320). Churchill's May 13 speech stands alongside the Gettysburg Address as history's most famous speech. A recent historian wrote that its power at the time and its enduring fascination "derived from its moral purity, its courage, its rash gamble for victory" (Wilson 2005, 385).

In recent decades, some have questioned the "Churchill myth," but unlike many legends of the past, the mountains of documentation surrounding Churchill's conduct and their results more than sufficiently support the well-established story. At the war's end, even Soviet leader Josef Stalin (1878–1953) was moved to say that he "could think of no other instance in

> **WINSTON CHURCHILL (1874–1965)**
>
> Winston Churchill exemplified the role of "great men" in making history while embodying the flaws of even the greatest leaders. Churchill's stubbornness prevented Great Britain from seeking peace with Nazi Germany, and his dynamism sustained the nation during its darkest hours.
>
> Churchill was a remarkable man by any measure. An articulate speaker and prolific Nobel Prize-winning writer, Churchill was an adventurer as a young man. While in the army, he fought hand-to-hand in India and in a cavalry charge in Sudan. As a war correspondent during the Boer War (1899), he escaped from a prison camp and trekked 300 miles to British lines. The fame gained from that led to his long career in Parliament and various cabinet offices, including First Lord of the Admiralty as World War I began. When Churchill's amphibious assault against Turkey at Gallipoli (1915) proved catastrophic, he resigned and redeemed his reputation by rejoining the Royal Army and serving on the Western Front.
>
> As a member of Parliament between the world wars, his short-sighted stand on colonial policies helped doom British rule in India, but he was also among the first to warn of the threat posed by Hitler. When World War II began, he was appointed First Lord of the Admiralty, and faced with defeat at German hands, Parliament chose him as prime minister. His perseverance enabled Britain to hold on until the United States joined the war.
>
> Popular in war, he was less popular in peace. In July 1945, two months after Germany surrendered, Churchill was turned out of office in an election defeat. He coined the term "Iron Curtain" to describe Soviet rule over Eastern Europe and returned as Prime Minister in 1951, stepping down into a rapidly changing world four years later.

history where the future of the world depended on the courage of one man" (Moran 1966, 244).

Unlike the hapless Chamberlain or his French counterparts, Churchill brought dogged energy as well as resounding eloquence to the war effort. His confident belligerence contributed to saving the day, and his determined spirit was behind the evacuation at Dunkirk, one of history's greatest examples of snatching victory from the jaws of defeat. The evacuation from the French coastal town saved nearly 340,000 British, French, and other Allied troops from German captivity.

DEPICTION AND HISTORICAL CONTEXT

Christopher Nolan was determined to get the history correct and to tell the story from the perspective of ordinary participants on the ground, at sea, and in the air. As a result, *Dunkirk* is a World War II movie unlike any other. No generals are shown huddled around maps plotting strategy; there are no sentimental *Saving Private Ryan*-style conversations among the troops as the enemy closes in. There is no strategy beyond figuring out survival and not much talk beyond "bloody hell!" Except for a brief blur at the end, the Germans are invisible, apparent only for the markings on the planes they fly: the swooping Stuka dive bombers, lumbering Heinkel bombers circling like vultures, and the swift Messerschmitt fighters engaging in dogfights with the handful of British flyers who sally forth to thwart their attacks.

Although *Dunkirk* doesn't show how German and British strategy was planned, the results of the tactics adopted by political and military leaders are accurately represented as experienced by the men on the beach. On May 24, the Germans halted their advance on Dunkirk at Hitler's order. The decision was made in part to allow infantry and logistical support to catch up to the panzers and because the canals and rivers near Dunkirk were hard terrain for tank warfare (Keegan 1989, 78). Hitler also counted on the Luftwaffe, whose commander, Reichsmarshal Hermann Goering (1893–1946), boasted that airpower could prevent the evacuation and force Allied survivors at Dunkirk to surrender.

The film captures the uncertainty of British soldiers on the beach who knew only what they saw. On May 26 and 27, only 8,000 of the nearly 340,000 Allied troops at Dunkirk were evacuated, and air support appeared to be minimal (Keegan 1989, 80–81). "Where's the bloody air force?" one of *Dunkirk*'s anonymous soldiers complains.

Bolton explains to Winnant that the thinking in London was to conserve ships and planes for the next battle, the Battle of Britain. Plans shifted rapidly when the British war cabinet grasped the possibility of saving its army through an improvised rescue of unprecedented scale. Churchill had been stingy in committing the Royal Air Force to the Battle of France, but now every fighter squadron was devoted to relieving pressure on the troops by intercepting Luftwaffe attackers. Reinforced by Canadian and French warships, the Royal Navy launched a rescue mission called Operation Dynamo. Organized by Rear Admiral Bertram Home Ramsay (1883–1945), who watched developments through a telescope from his headquarters in the high tower of Dover Castle, the navy rapidly assembled a flotilla of 900 ships and boats; more than 200 of them were private craft. Unlike the legend that grew up around Dunkirk, most civilian boats were requisitioned by the navy and manned by naval personnel. However, *Dunkirk*'s depiction is not wrong. Several boat owners like Mr. Dawson slipped out of port on their own initiative, determined to do their bit (Todman 2016, 334–335). As in the film, ships making the passage across the English Channel were subject to Luftwaffe attack. Twenty-eight Royal Navy warships were sunk or badly damaged during the operation. Dunkirk depicts air attacks by the Luftwaffe on Operation Dynamo but ignores the threat posed by the German navy. German E-boats, equivalent to the swift American PT boats, sniped at the convoys with torpedoes and sank several ships.

The confusion displayed by the troops in *Dunkirk* was real. For many enlisted members of the BEF, their campaign was a baffling sequence of advances and retreats across Belgium and northern France. Many units never lost a pitched battle. For some soldiers on the way to Dunkirk, "it was days before they realized that they had been heading backwards, let alone that they were about to be evacuated" (Todman 2016, 335). As seen in the movie, they were short of water and food and "enthusiastically made off with whatever they could find from the houses and shops they passed" (Todman 2016, 336). Dunkirk shows that some units withdrew to Dunkirk in good order while others crumbled, leaving their men to straggle alone or in small parties to the beach. Private Joe Catt recalled, "When you realize the people you are supposed to obey don't know what they're doing, that's when you begin to get worried." He added, "Can you imagine the feeling of panic when officers ordered us to make our own way to Dunkirk? Most of us had no idea where it was, or even what it was" (Akin 2000, 161).

Luftwaffe raids destroyed all of Dunkirk's piers and jetties, forcing the masses of troops to evacuate in the dangerous and clumsy manner shown in the film. Thousands of troops lined up single file on the "mole," a breakwater made of boulders and covered with narrow wooden planks to serve as a makeshift pier. They were easy targets for low-flying German planes. The purpose-built landing craft that later played a vital role in the war's amphibious assaults naval vessels did not exist in 1940, and warships could not closely approach the shore through the shallow water. As a result, the small boats seen in the film touched the beach, retrieved as many soldiers as they could hold, and ferried them to the larger ships offshore.

Once they made it to Dunkirk beach, they were subjected to continual air raids as visualized in the film. Captain Alan Macdonald of the Royal Artillery recalled "lying flat on the sand listening to the shriek of the bombers and the crack of explosions" (Akin 2000, 175). Within days, the BEF had evidence that they were not forgotten as the vast flotilla began to shuttle back and forth across the English Channel. On May 28, 19,000 troops were rescued by sea; the number jumped to 47,000 on May 29, and on May 31, Gort departed along with 68,000 of his men (Keegan 1989, 80–81). The BEF left behind most of its equipment, but the men were saved.

Dunkirk portrays the air war faithfully. Nolan pressed into service several authentic Supermarine Spitfires, the fast and highly maneuverable fighter plane that became crucial in defeating the Luftwaffe during the Battle of Britain. As depicted in the film, the Spitfire's greatest limitation was range.

Working with British historian Joshua Levine, Nolan interviewed veterans of Dunkirk in preparation for the film and derived several scenes from their conversations (Nolan 2017). As much as possible, Nolan filmed on the Dunkirk beach but set the opening street-skirmish scene in nearby Malo-les-Bains because the town of Dunkirk was largely destroyed in 1940. Nolan was meticulous in recreating the uniforms, manufacturing them in Pakistan. Thousands of extras were recruited in France (Sexton 2017). Several retired warships from various fleets were refurbished to replicate Royal Navy ships present at Dunkirk. Two dozen fishing boats and yachts that participated in the events of 1940 were also used. Visible errors in military equipment and insignia were minor and of no consequence to the action.

Dunkirk shows the initial resistance by the British to evacuating their French allies but gives no clue that most of the 110,000 French troops rescued at Dunkirk were sent back to Normandy and Brittany to rejoin the French army in the field. Many were killed or captured in the weeks ahead (Keegan 1989, 81). The British government gambled until the end that France would somehow hold out, but the French leadership had lost hope. On June 22, France, now governed by Marshal Henri Petain (1856–1951), signed a harsh armistice with Germany, dictated on Hitler's terms.

CONCLUSION

History has traditionally focused on "great men" whose actions and character determined the course of events. In the past century, historians began to invest greater importance in everyday men and women whose actions and beliefs, as individuals and in mass, also shaped the direction of history. With the events of 1940 fresh in mind, British philosopher-pundit Isaiah Berlin (1909–1985) wrote that in the crisis of those months, ordinary Britishers were "clad in the fabulous garments appropriate to a great historic event" that even "transformed cowards into brave men" (Berlin 1949, 29). With *Dunkirk*, Christopher Nolan amplifies Berlin's observation in his retelling of a pivotal moment that helped determine the outcome of World War II. In *Dunkirk*, a mass of individuals acting in concert were decisive in the outcome of events. His depiction is correct but incomplete. The outcome at the Battle of Dunkirk was guided and directed by the determination of one great figure, Winston Churchill. To fully understand Britain's refusal to surrender or seek peace with Nazi Germany in 1940, *Dunkirk* should be watched back to back with a film released in the same year, *Darkest Hour* (2017). British actor Gary Oldman (1958–) earned an Academy Award for his gripping depiction of Churchill and his efforts to persuade defeatists within his own political party to stand up against Hitler.

FURTHER READING

Akin, Ronald. 2000. *Pillar of Fire: Dunkirk, 1940*. London: Sidgwick & Jackson.
Benoist-Mechin, Jacques. 1963. *Sixty Days That Shook the West: The Fall of France, 1940*. New York: G.P. Putnam's Sons.
Berlin, Isaiah. 1949. *Mr. Churchill in 1940*. London: John Murray.

Brace, Samuel. 2017. "*Dunkirk* Becomes the Highest Grossing WWII Film of All Time." flickeringmyth.com, September 12, 2017. https://www.flickeringmyth.com/2017/09/dunkirk-becomes-the-highest-grossing-wwii-film-of-all-time/

Bradshaw, Peter. 2017. "Christopher Nolan's Apocalyptic War Epic Is His Best Film So Far." *The Guardian*, July 18, 2017. https://www.theguardian.com/film/2017/jul/17/dunkirk-review-christopher-nolans-apocalyptic-war-epic-is-his-best-film-so-far

Calhoun, Dave. 2018. "The 100 Best British Films." timeout.com, September 10, 2018. https://www.timeout.com/london/film/100-best-british-films

Dargis, Maholia. 2017. " 'Dunkirk' Is a Tour de Force War Movie." *New York Times*, July 23, 2017. https://www.nytimes.com/2017/07/20/movies/dunkirk-review-christopher-nolan.html

Hanson, Victor Davis. 2017. *The Second World Wars: How the First Global Conflict Was Fought and Won*. New York: Basic Books.

Howell, Peter. 2017. "*Dunkirk*'s Disorienting Brilliance Is a Victory for Christopher Nolan." *Toronto Star*, July 20, 2017. https://www.thestar.com/entertainment/movies/2017/07/20/dunkirks-disorienting-brilliance-is-a-victory-for-christopher-nolan-review.html

Keegan, John. 1989. *The Second World War*. London: Hutchinson.

Moran, Lord. 1966. *Churchill Taken from the Diaries of Lord Moran: The Struggle for Survival, 1940–1945*. London: Constable.

Nolan, Christopher. 2017. "Spitfires, Flotillas of Boats, Rough Seas and 1,000 Extras: Christopher Nolan on the Making of *Dunkirk*, His Most Challenging Film to Date." *Daily Telegraph*, July 10, 2017. https://www.telegraph.co.uk/films/2017/07/08/spitfires-flotillas-boats-rough-seas-1000-extras-christopher/

Seitz, Matt Zoller. 2017. "Dunkirk." RogerEbert.com, July 21, 2017. https://www.rogerebert.com/reviews/dunkirk-2017

Sexton, David. 2017. "*Dunkirk*: Everything You Need to Know about the Cinematic Event of 2017." *London Evening Standard*, July 26, 2017. https://www.standard.co.uk/go/london/film/dunkirk-everything-you-need-to-know-about-the-cinematic-event-of-2017-a3587021.html

Todman, Daniel. 2016. *Britain's War: Into Battle, 1937–1941*. New York: Oxford University Press.

Turan, Kenneth. 2017. "Christopher Nolan Puts Audiences in the Middle of WWII in the Intimates and Epic 'Dunkirk.'" *Los Angeles Times*, July 20, 2017. https://www.latimes.com/entertainment/movies/la-et-mn-dunkirk-review-20170720-story.html

Wilson, A.N. 2005. *After the Victorians: The Decline of Britain in the World*. New York: Farrar, Strauss and Giroux.

Bibliography

World War II on Film is of necessity a hybrid project for its examination of the political and military complexity of the war through the productions of a movie industry more concerned with profitability and entertaining its audience than with historical accuracy. But despite obstacles, many directors and screenwriters have done honest work in their representation of the most all-encompassing conflict in world history.

Because of its hybrid nature, the sources for *World War II on Film* range widely. They include standard accounts of the war alongside standard accounts of Hollywood; they include biographies of filmmakers and stars along with biographies of generals and political leaders. For the sake of providing context, the sources include old travelogues of battlegrounds, analysis of cultural issues, and histories that seek for the roots of World War II in the years before 1939. The sources span continents, albeit the prominence of Hollywood inevitably determines that a book of this kind concentrates on Anglo-American sources. When applicable, the author has tried to include work reflecting on the German, Russian, Italian, and Japanese experiences.

Akin, Ronald. 2000. *Pillar of Fire: Dunkirk, 1940*. London: Sidgwick & Jackson.
Alexander, Joseph H. 1993. *Across the Reef: The Marine Assault on Tarawa*. Washington, D.C.: Marine Corps Historical Center.
Alexievich, Svetlana. 2017. *Unwomanly Face of War: An Oral History of Women in World War II*. New York: Random House.
Ambrose, Stephen E. 1994. *D-Day: June 6, 1944: The Climactic Battle of World War II*. New York: Simon & Schuster.

Andelman, David A. 2008. *A Shattered Peace: Versailles 1919 and the Price We Pay Today*. Hoboken, NJ: John Wiley & Son.
Anders, Curt. 1966. *Fighting Airmen*. New York: G.P. Putnam's Sons.
Anderton, David A. 1981. *The History of the U.S. Air Force*. New York: Crescent Books.
Axelrod, Alan. 2006. *Patton: A Biography*. New York: Palgrave Macmillan.
Balakian, Peter. 2003. *The Burning Tigris: The Armenian Genocide and America's Response*. New York: HarperCollins.
Balio, Tino. 1987. *United Artists: The Company That Changed the Film Industry*. Madison: University of Wisconsin Press.
Balkoski, Joseph. 2004. *Omaha Beach: D-Day, June 6, 1944*. Mechanicsburg, PA: Stackpole Books.
Barker, A.J. 1969. *Pearl Harbor*. New York: Ballantine Books.
Basche, James. 1971. *Thailand: Land of Freedom*. New York: Caplinger.
Becker, Lucille. 1996. *Pierre Boulle*. New York: Twayne.
Beekman, Scott. 2005. *William Dudley Pelley: A Life in Right-Wing Extremism and the Occult*. Syracuse, NY: Syracuse University Press.
Bell, Leland V. 1973. *In Hitler's Shadow: The Anatomy of American Nazism*. Port Washington, NY: Kennikat Press.
Benoist-Mechin, Jacques. 1963. *Sixty Days That Shook the West: The Fall of France, 1940*. New York: G.P. Putnam's Sons.
Berlin, Isaiah. 1949. *Mr. Churchill in 1940*. London: John Murray.
Bishop, Chris. 2006. *Kriegsmarine U-Boats, 1939–45*. London. Amber Books.
Bix, Herbert P. 2000. *Hirohito and the Making of Modern Japan*. New York: HarperCollins.
Blumenson, Martin. 1985. *Patton: The Man behind the Legend, 1885–1945*. New York: William Morrow.
Boulle, Pierre. 1964. *The Bridge over the River Kwai*. New York: Time.
Bradley, James, with Ron Powers. 2000. *Flags of Our Fathers*. New York: Bantam.
Brinkley, Alan. 1982. *Voices of Protest: Huey Long, Father Coughlin, and the Great Depression*. New York: Alfred A. Knopf.
Brown, Anthony Cave. 1975. *Bodyguard of Lies*. New York: Harper & Row.
Bullock, Alan. 1992. *Hitler and Stalin: Parallel Lives*. New York: Alfred A. Knopf.
Burleigh, Michael. 2000. *The Third Reich: A New History*. New York: Hill and Wang.
Burrin, Philippe. 1996. *France under the Germans: Collaboration and Compromise*. New York: The New Press.
Carlson, John Roy. 1943. *Under Cover: My Four Years in the Nazi Underworld of America—The Amazing Revelation of How Axis Agents and Our Enemies within Are Now Plotting to Destroy the United States*. New York: Dutton.
Chuikov, Vasili. 1963. *The Beginning of the Road*. London: McGibbon & Kee.
Clark, Alan. 1965. *Barbarossa: The Russian-German Conflict, 1941–1945*. New York: William Morrow.
Clarke, Thurston. 1991. *Pearl Harbor Ghosts: A Journey to Hawaii Then and Now*. New York: William Morrow.
Cole, Wayne S. 1974. *Charles A. Lindbergh and the Battle against American Intervention in World War II*. New York: Harcourt Brace Jovanovich.

Collingham, Lizzie. 2012. *The Taste of War: World War II and the Battle for Food*. New York: Penguin Press.
Conquest, Robert. 2007. *The Great Terror: A Reassessment, 40th Anniversary Edition*. New York: Oxford University Press.
Costello, John. 1981. *The Pacific War*. New York: Rawson, Wade.
Cousins, Mark. 2004. *The Story of Film*. New York: Thunder's Mouth Press.
Craig, William. 1973. *Enemy at the Gates: The Battle for Stalingrad*. New York: Reader's Digest Press/E.P. Dutton.
Cremer, Peter. 1982. *U-Boat Commander: A Periscope View of the Battle of the Atlantic*. Annapolis, MD: U.S. Naval Institute.
Curtis, Michael. 2002. *Verdict on Vichy: Power and Prejudice in the Vichy France Regime*. London: Weidenfeld & Nicholson.
Day, A. Grove. 1955. *Hawaii and Its People*. New York: Duell, Sloan and Pearce.
Dennis, Lawrence. 1936. *The Coming of American Fascism*. New York: Harper & Bros.
Doenecke, Justus D., and John E. Wilz. 1991. *From Isolation to War, 1931–1941*. Arlington Heights, IL: Harlan Davidson.
Doherty, Thomas. 1999. *Projections of War: Hollywood, American Culture, and World War II*. New York: Columbia University Press.
Ellis, John. 1993. *The World War II Data Book: The Essential Facts and Figures for All the Combatants*. London: Aurum Press.
Erickson, John. 1984. *The Road to Stalingrad: Stalin's War with Germany*. Boulder, CO: Westview Press.
Fest, Joachim C. 1970. *The Face of the Third Reich: Portraits of Nazi Leadership*. New York: Pantheon.
Fishgall, Gary. 2002. *Gregory Peck*. New York: Scribners.
Fleming, Samuel P., and Ed Y. Hall. 1992. *Flying with the "Hell's Angels": Memoirs of a B-17 Flying Fortress Navigator*. Spartanburg, SC: Honoribus.
Friedman, Lester D., and Brent Notbohm, eds. 2008. *Steven Spielberg: Interviews*. Jackson: University of Mississippi Press.
Gabler, Neil. 1994. *Winchell: Gossip, Power and the Culture of Celebrity*. New York: Alfred A. Knopf.
Gaskin, Hilary. 1990. *Eyewitnesses at Nuremberg*. London: Arms and Armour.
Gilmour, David. 2011. *The Pursuit of Italy: A History of a Land, Its Regions, and Their Peoples*. New York: Farrar, Straus and Giroux.
Glantz, David M. 2002. *The Battle for Leningrad: 1941–1944*. Lawrence: University Press of Kansas.
Goodman, Walter. 1968. *The Committee: The Extraordinary Career of the House Committee on Un-American Activities*. New York: Farrar, Straus and Giroux.
Gröning, Erich. 1966. *Die deutschen Kriegsschiffe, 1815–1945*. Munich: J. F. Lehmanns Verlag.
Gross, Raphael. 2007. *Carl Schmitt and the Jews: The "Jewish Question," the Holocaust, and German Legal Theory*. Madison: University of Wisconsin Press.
Hague, Arnold. 2000. *The Allied Convoy System, 1939–1945*. Annapolis, MD: U.S. Naval Institute.
Hanson, Victor Davis. 2017. *The Second World Wars: How the First Global Conflict Was Fought and Won*. New York: Basic Books.

Harmetz, Aljean. 2002. *The Making of "Casablanca": Bogart, Bergman, and World War II*. New York: Hyperion.
Haskell, Molly. 2017. *Steven Spielberg: A Life in Films*. New Haven, CT: Yale University Press.
Heberer, Patricia, and Jürgen Matthaus, eds. 2008. *Atrocities on Trial: Historical Perspectives on the Politics of Prosecuting War Crimes*. Lincoln: University of Nebraska Press.
Heller, Mikhail, and Aleksandr M. Nekirch. 1986. *Utopia in Power: The History of the Soviet Union from 1917 to the Present*. New York: Summit Books.
Higham, Charles. 1985. *American Swastika*. Garden City, NY: Doubleday.
Hitler, Adolf. 1943. *Mein Kampf*. Boston, MA: Houghton Mifflin.
Hofman, Reto. 2015. *The Fascist Effect: Japan and Italy, 1915–1952*. Ithaca, NY: Cornell University Press.
Horne, Gerald. 2006. *The Color of Fascism: Lawrence Dennis, Racial Passing, and the Rise of Right-Wing Extremism in the United States*. New York: New York University Press.
Hoyt, Edwin P. 1988. *The Death of the U-Boats*. New York: McGraw-Hill.
Ickes, Harold. 1954. *The Secret Diaries of Harold Ickes*. Vol. 3. New York: Simon & Schuster.
Isenberg, Noah. 2017. *We'll Always Have* Casablanca: *The Life, Legend, and Afterlife of Hollywood's Most Beloved Movie*. New York: W. W. Norton.
Jeansonne, Glen, with David Luhrssen. 2006. *A Time of Paradox: America since 1890*. Lanham, MD: Rowman & Littlefield.
Jeansonne, Glen, with David Luhrssen. 2016. *Hoover: A Life*. New York: New American Library.
Jeansonne, Glen, and David Luhrssen. 2016. *War on the Silver Screen: Shaping America's Perception of History*. Lincoln, NE: Potomac Books.
Joestring, Edward. 1972. *Hawaii: An Uncommon History*. New York: W. W. Norton.
Johnson, Paul. 1991. *Modern Times: From the Twenties to the Nineties*. New York: HarperCollins.
Jones, James. 1974. *Viet Journal*. New York: Delacorte Press.
Judt, Tony, with Timothy Snyder. 2012. *Thinking the Twentieth Century*. New York: Penguin Press.
Kahn, David. 1991. *Seizing the Enigma: The Race to Break the German U-Boat Codes, 1939–1943*. Boston, MA: Houghton Mifflin.
Kakehashi, Kumiko. 2007. *So Sad to Fall in Battle: An Account of War Based on General Tadamichi Kuribayashi's Letters from Iwo Jima*. New York: Ballantine.
Kanfer, Stefan. 2011. *Tough Guy without a Gun: The Extraordinary Life and Afterlife of Humphrey Bogart*. New York: Alfred A. Knopf.
Kauffman, Bill. 1995. *America First! Its History, Its Culture, and Politics*. Amherst, NY: Prometheus Books.
Keegan, John. 1989. *The Second World War*. London: Hutchinson.
Kershaw, Ian. 1998. *Hitler, 1889–1936: Hubris*. New York: W. W. Norton.
Kershaw, Ian. 2000. *Hitler, 1936–1945: Nemesis*. New York. W. W. Norton.
Kershaw, Ian. 2007. *Fateful Choices: Ten Decisions That Changed the World, 1940–1941*. New York: Penguin Press.

Keynes, John Maynard. 2007. *The Economic Consequences of the Peace*. New York: Skyhorse Publishing.
King, Ernest, and Walter Muir Whitehill. 1952. *Fleet Admiral King: A Naval Record*. New York: W. W. Norton.
Kinvig, Clifford. 1992. *River Kwai Railway: The Story of the Burma-Siam Railroad*. London: Brassey's.
Koch, Howard. 1973. Casablanca: *Script and Legend*. Woodstock, NY: Overlook Press.
Kotkin, Stephen. 2017. *Stalin Waiting for Hitler, 1929–1941*. New York: Penguin Press.
Lacouture, Jean. 1991. *De Gaulle: The Rebel, 1890–1944*. London: W. W. Norton.
Levy, Shawn. 1998. *Rat Pack Confidential: Frank, Dean, Sammy, Peter, Joey & the Last Great Showbiz Party*. New York: Doubleday.
Lindbergh, Anne Morrow. 1980. *War Within and Without: Diaries and Letters of Anne Morrow Lindbergh, 1939–1944*. New York: Harcourt Brace Jovanovich.
Lochery, Neill. 2011. *Lisbon: War in the Shadows of the City of Light, 1939–1945*. New York: PublicAffairs.
Lomax, Eric. 1995. *The Railway Man: A POW's Searing Account of War, Brutality and Forgiveness*. New York: W. W. Norton.
Longerich, Peter. 2019. *Hitler: A Biography*. New York: Oxford University Press.
Luhrssen, David. 2015. *Secret Societies and Clubs in American History*. Santa Barbara, CA: ABC-CLIO.
Mackenzie, S.P. 2017. *Flying against Fate: Superstition and Allied Aircrews in World War II*. Lawrence: University Press of Kansas.
McAuley, Mary. 2019. *Remembering Leningrad: The Story of a Generation*. Madison: University of Wisconsin Press.
McGilligan, Patrick. 2003. *Alfred Hitchcock: A Life in Darkness and Light*. New York: Regan Books/HarperCollins.
McGuire, Melvin W., and Robert Hadley. 1993. *Bloody Skies: A 15th Army Air Force Combat Crew*. Las Cruces, NM: Yucca Tree.
Miller, Frank. 1992. Casablanca *as Time Goes by . . . 50th Anniversary Commemorative*. Atlanta, GA: Turner Publishing.
Mitchell, William. 1960. *Memoirs of World War I: "From Start to Finish of Our Greatest War."* New York: Random House.
Montefiore, Simon Sebag. 2004. *Stalin: The Court of the Red Tsar*. New York: Alfred A. Knopf.
Moody, A. Donald. 2014. *Ezra Pound: A Portrait of the Man and His Works, Volume II: The Epic Years 1921–1939*. New York: Oxford University Press.
Moran, Lord. 1966. *Churchill: The Struggle for Survival*. London: Constable.
Morrison, Samuel Eliot. 1947. *Operations in North African Waters*. Boston, MA: Little, Brown.
Osborne, Richard E. 2011. *The* Casablanca *Companion: The Movie Classic and Its Place in History*. Indianapolis, IN: Riebel-Roque Publishing.
Paxton, Robert O. 1975. *Vichy France: Old Guard and New Order, 1940–1944*. New York: W. W. Norton.
Payne, Stanley G. 1995. *A History of Fascism, 1914–1945*. Madison: University of Wisconsin Press.

Pelley, William Dudley. 1935. *No More Hunger*. Ashville, NC: Pelley Publishing.
Pelley, William Dudley. 1939. *The Door to Revelation*. Ashville, NC: Pelley Publishing.
Persico, Joseph E. 1994. *Nuremberg: Infamy on Trial*. New York: Viking.
Pfaff, William. 2004. *The Bullet's Song: Romantic Violence and Utopia*. New York. Simon & Schuster.
Phillips, Gene D. 2006. *Beyond the Epic: The Life and Films of David Lean*. Lexington: University Press of Kentucky.
Potter, Elmer Belmont. 1976. *Nimitz*. Annapolis, MD: Naval Institute Press.
Radzinsky, Edvard. 1996. *Stalin: The First In-Depth Biography Based on Explosive New Documents from Russia's Secret Archives*. New York: Doubleday.
Reporting World War II, Part One: American Journalism, 1938–1944. 1995. New York: Library of America.
Reporting World War II, Part Two: American Journalism, 1944–1946. 1995. New York: Library of America.
Rode, Alan K. 2017. *Michael Curtiz: A Life in Film*. Lexington: University Press of Kentucky.
Rooney, Andy. 2000. *My War*. New York: PublicAffairs.
Ross, Bill D. 1985. *Iwo Jima: Legacy of Valor*. New York: Vanguard Press.
Sands, Philippe. 2016. *East West Street: On the Origins of "Genocide" and "Crimes against Humanity."* New York: Alfred A. Knopf.
Santas, Constantine. 2012. *The Epic Films of David Lean*. Lanham, MD: The Scarecrow Press.
Sarantakes, Nicholas Evan. 2012. *Making Patton: A Classic War Film's Epic Journey to the Silver Screen*. Lawrence: University of Kansas Press.
Sarris, Andrew. 1998. *"You Ain't Heard Nothin' Yet": The American Talking Film, History and Memory, 1927–1949*. New York: Oxford University Press.
Schaller, Michael. 1989. *Douglas MacArthur: The Far Eastern General*. New York: Oxford University Press.
Schlesinger, Arthur, Jr. 1960. *The Age of Roosevelt: The Politics of Upheaval*. Boston, MA: Houghton Mifflin.
Schumacher, Michael. 1999. *Francis Ford Coppola: A Filmmaker's Life*. New York: Crown.
Sharp, Harold S. 1977. *Footnotes to American History*. Metuchen, NJ: Scarecrow Press.
Sheward, David. 2008. *Rage and Glory: The Volatile Life and Career of George C. Scott*. New York: Applause.
Showalter, Dennis. 2009. *Hitler's Panzers: The Lightning Attacks That Revolutionized Warfare*. New York: Berkley Caliber.
Sklar, Robert. 2002. *Film: A World History*. New York: Abrams.
Sloan, John S. 1946. *The Route as Briefed: The History of the 92nd Bomb Group, USAAF, 1942–1945*. Cleveland, OH: Argus.
Speer, Albert. 1970. *Inside the Third Reich: Memoirs*. New York: Macmillan.
Spoto, Donald. 1978. *Stanley Kramer: Film Maker*. New York: G.P. Putnam's Sons.
Steinberg, Cobbett. 1980. *Film Facts*. New York: Facts on File.

Strong, Donald S. 1941. *Organized Anti-Semitism in America: The Rise of Group Prejudice during the Decade 1930–1940*. Washington, D.C.: American Council on Public Affairs.
Symonds, Craig L. 2018. *World War II at Sea: A Global History*. New York: Oxford University Press.
Tenney, Lester I. 1995. *My Hitch in Hell: The Bataan Death March*. Washington, D.C.: Brassey's.
Thomson, David. 2008. *"Have You Seen . . . ?": A Personal Introduction to 1,000 Films*. New York: Alfred A. Knopf.
Thomson, David. 2010. *The New Biographical Dictionary of Film*. New York: Alfred A. Knopf.
Thomson, David. 2012. *The Big Screen: The Story of the Movies*. New York: Farrar, Straus and Giroux.
Todman, Daniel. 2016. *Britain's War: Into Battle, 1937–1941*. New York: Oxford University Press.
Toland, John. 1976. *Adolf Hitler*. Garden City, NY: Doubleday.
Truffaut, Francois, with Helen G. Scott. 1983. *Hitchcock*. New York: Simon & Schuster.
Tusa, Ann, and Tusa, John. 1986. *The Nuremberg Trial*. New York: Atheneum.
Underbrink, Robert L. 1971. *Destination Corregidor*. Annapolis, MD: U.S. Naval Institute.
Ward, Geoffrey C., and Ken Burns. 2007. *The War: An Intimate History, 1941–1945*. New York: Alfred A. Knopf.
Williamson, Gordon. 2002. *Kriegsmarine U-Boats, 1939–45*. London: Osprey Publishing.
Wilson, A.N. 2005. *After the Victorians: The Decline of Britain in the World*. New York: Farrar, Strauss and Giroux.
Wright, John M., Jr. 1988. *Captured on Corregidor: Diary of an American P.O.W. in World War II*. Jefferson, NC: McFarland.
Wright, Theon. 1972. *The Disenchanted Isles: The Story of the Second Revolution in Hawaii*. New York: Dial Press.
Wyatt, David K. 1984. *Thailand: A Modern History*. New Haven, CT: Yale University Press.
Yahil, Leni. 1990. *The Holocaust: The Fate of European Jewry*. New York: Oxford University Press.
Yoshitake, Oka. 1992. *Konoe Fuminato: A Political Biography*. Lanham, MD: Madison Books.

Index

Alison, Joan, 17
All Quiet on the Western Front, 119
Ambrose, Stephen, 117, 120
America First, 10–11, 13, 24
Annaud, Jean-Jacques, 131
Anti-Semitism, 10, 13, 25–26
Arsenal of Democracy, 1. *See also* Roosevelt, Franklin D.
Atlantic Charter, 51
Atlantic Wall, 125–126, 127. *See also* Rommel, Erwin

Band of Brothers, 119
Barlett, Sy, 31–38, 41
Bataan, 62, 63–66, 68, 153
Bates, Michael, 100
Beach, Adam, 146
Bergman, Ingrid, 18
Bletchley Park, 111
Block, Harlon, 158
Bogart, Humphrey, 18, 20
Borgnine, Ernest, 44
Bormann, Martin, 138
Boulle, Pierre, 59, 62, 67, 68
Bradford, Jesse, 146
Bradley, James, 145, 146, 156, 158, 159
Bradley, John Henry "Doc," 146, 156, 158–159
Bradley, Omar N., 91, 101, 122, 124

Branagh, Kenneth, 163
Brandt, Willy, 75, 98
Bridge on the River Kwai, The, 59–72, 117
Bridge over the River Kwai, The, 59
Brokaw, Tom, 119
Broyles, William, 146
Bryce, Ian, 117
Buchheim, Lothar-Günther, 103
Bulge, Battle of, 93, 100
Burnett, Murray, 17
Burns, Edward, 118

Capra, Frank, 126
Casablanca, 18–30
Casablanca Conference, 19
Chamberlain, Neville, 165–166, 168, 169
Chiang Kai-shek, 49
Churchill, Winston, 104, 120, 168, 169; as wartime leader, 19, 22, 51, 129, 140, 164, 170, 172
Clift, Montgomery, 43, 74, 75
Cohn, Harry, 44
Cohn, Ronald, 103
Communist Party, 8, 21, 59, 133, 136
Coppola, Francis Ford, 91, 92, 94, 98, 101
Corregidor, 63–66. *See also* MacArthur, Douglas

Coughlin, James, 10
Craig, William, 131, 141
Cummings, Robert, 1
Curtiz, Michael, 17–18

D'Arcy, James, 163
D-Day, 23, 36, 93, 97, 121–124; film, depiction in, 117–120, 124–129
Damon, Matt, 118
Das Boot, 103–115
Davies, Jeremy, 118
De Gaulle, Charles, 21–24, 27, 28, 67, 78. *See also* Free French
Dennis, Lawrence, 12–14
Diesel, Vin, 118
Donald, James, 60
Dönitz, Karl, 80, 82, 84, 109, 110, 114
Doolittle, James, 37
Dunkirk, 163–173
Dunkirk, Battle of, 163–164, 169–173

Eastwood, Clint, 145, 146, 155, 156, 157, 160
Eden, Anthony, 78. *See also* Churchill, Winston
Eisenberg, Dwight D., 99, 122, 123
Eisenberg, Ned, 146
Empire of the Sun, 118
Enemy at the Gates, 131–144
Enigma, 111
Epstein, Julius J., 17
Epstein, Philip G., 17
Everybody Comes to Rick's, 17

Farago, Ladislas, 91
Fascism, American, 1–14
Fiennes, Joseph, 131
Fifth Column, 1, 4, 11
Flags of Our Fathers, 145–161
Ford, Henry, 8, 10
Foreman, Carl, 59, 62
Forrestal, James, 157–158
Franck, Hans, 80, 82
Free French, 24, 27, 28, 67, 78. *See also* De Gaulle, Charles
Frick, Wilhelm, 80
From Here to Eternity, 43–58. *See also* Pearl Harbor

Gagnon, Rene, 146, 158
Garland, Judy, 74, 75
Geneva Convention, 60, 68, 71
German-American Bund, 8–9
Glynn-Carney, Tom, 163
Godard, Alain, 131
Goebbels, Joseph, 79, 137
Goldberg, Adam, 118
Gordon, Mark, 117
Göring, Hermann, 36, 80, 83, 138
Great Depression, 10
Great Escape, The, 103
Greatest Generation, The, 119
Greenstreet, Sydney, 18
Grönemeyer, Herbert, 104
Guadalcanal, 149–151, 156
Guinness, Alec, 60, 61, 62, 70

Haggis, Paul, 145–146, 156
Hanks, Tom, 118
Hardy, Tom, 163
Harris, Ed, 131
Harrison, Joan, 3
Hawkins, Jack, 61
Hayakawa, Sessue, 60, 61, 62
Hayes, Ira, 146, 158–159
Henreid, Paul, 18
Hess, Rudolf, 80, 85
Himmler, Heinrich, 79
Hirohito, 51
Hitchcock, Alfred, 1, 2, 4, 10, 14
Hitler, Adolf, 5, 6, 7, 13, 36, 82, 87, 104, 112, 136, 138; conquest, plans for, 133; Japan, alliance with, 49, 80; Jews, persecution of, 20; meetings with Americans, 9, 12; racism, 133; war leader, as, 21, 84, 92, 95, 97, 108, 110, 113, 121, 134, 135, 137, 139–140, 166
Holden, William, 60, 62
Holocaust, 22, 74, 76–77, 80, 85, 132, 138
Hoover, Herbert, 48
Horne, Geoffrey, 61
Hoskins, Bob, 131
Houseman, John, 3

Ihara, Tsuyoshi, 147
Isolationism, 3, 10–12, 24, 25, 56
Iwo Jima, 145–148, 155–161

Jackson, Robert H., 77, 78, 81, 82
Jagger, Dean, 31, 33
Japanese-Americans, internment of, 4, 14
Jodl, Alfred, 81, 82, 133
Jones, James, 43, 54, 55, 56
Judgement at Nuremberg, 73–90

Kakehashi, Kumiko, 145
Kase, Ryo, 147
Kasserine Pass, 92
Keitel, Wilhelm, 80, 82, 83
Kellogg, John, 32
Kennedy, John F., 11, 43
Keoghan, Barry, 164
Kerr, Deborah, 44
Khruschev, Nikita, 131, 142
Kimmel, Husband E., 53, 55, 56
King, Ernest, 153, 155
King, Henry, 31
Klemperer, Werner, 73
Koch, Howard, 17, 20
Kramer, Stanley, 73, 74, 76
Kruger, Alma, 2
Kruger, Otto, 2, 4
Kuhn, Fritz, 8
Kuribayashi, Tadimichi, 145, 147, 159, 160
Kursk, 139–140

Lancaster, Burt, 44, 74
Lane, Priscilla, 2
Lauterpacht, Hersch, 77
Laval, Pierre, 22, 23, 24. *See also* Petain, Henri Philippe; Vichy French regime
Law, Jude, 131
Lay, Bernie, 31, 38, 40, 41
League of Nations, 46, 48
Lean, David, 59
Leder, Erwin, 105
Lee, Spike, 157
LeMay, Curtis, 39
Lemke, Raphael, 77
Leningrad, 135, 137

Letters from Iwo Jima, 145–161
Levine, Joshua, 171
Levinsohn, Gary, 117
Lindbergh, Anne Morrow, 12
Lindbergh, Charles, 10–11, 13
Lloyd, Frank, 3
Lloyd, Norman, 1
Long, Huey, 10
Lord Haw Haw, 39
Lorenz, Robert, 145
Lorre, Peter, 18

MacArthur, Douglas, 13, 53, 122, 152, 153; Philippines, in, 63, 64, 154–155
"Magic," 56
Maginot Line, 21, 134, 165, 166, 167
Malden, Karl, 92
Manilla, Battle of, 155
Mann, Abby, 73, 75
Mao Zedong, 49
Marlowe, Hugh, 32
Marshall, George C., 96, 118, 120, 149
Marshall-Thomson, Gabriel, 131
"Massie Affair," 54–55
McCarthy, Tom, 146
Mein Kampf, 133
Merrill, Gary, 32
Meyer, Torben, 75
Midway, Battle of, 149, 150, 151
Mitchell, Millard, 32
Mitchell, William "Billy," 35
Molotov, Vyacheslav, 133
Montgomery, Bernard Law, 93, 96, 99, 100, 122
Morgenthau, Henry, 50
Munich Conference, 49
Murphy, Cillian, 164
Mussolini, Benito, 5, 6, 67, 136

Nimitz, Chester, 149
Ninomiya, Kazunari, 147
Nolan, Christopher, 163, 169–172
North, Edmund, 91
Nuremberg Laws, 79, 80, 87. *See also* Holocaust
Nuremberg War Crimes Tribunal, 73, 76–86

Ober, Philip, 44
Omaha Beach, 122–127

Papen, Franz von, 80, 84
Parker, Dorothy, 3
Patten, Robert, 32
Patton, 91–102
Patton, George S., 17, 91–102, 120, 122
Paulus, Friederich, 135, 138, 139
Pearl Harbor, 1, 8, 10, 11, 17, 24, 51, 96, 110, 118, 145, 149, 150, 153; Japanese attack on, 35, 37, 43–45, 52–57, 62, 63, 64, 151
Peck, Gregory, 32, 33
Pelley, William Dudley, 6–8
Pepper, Barry, 118
Pershing, John J., 34, 35
Petain, Henri Philippe, 21, 22, 23, 24, 28, 172. *See also* Laval, Pierre; Vichy French regime
Petersen, Wolfgang, 103, 106
"Phoney War," 165
Powers, Ron, 145
Prochnow, Jürgen, 104
Pyle, Ernie, 123

Quezon, Manuel L., 63, 64

Raft, George, 18
Rains, Claude, 18
"Rape of Nanking," 49
Ray, Aldo, 43
Reagan, Ronald, 18, 118
Reed, Donna, 44, 45
Reville, Alma, 3
Ribbentrop, Joachim von, 81, 83, 133
Ribisi, Giovanni, 118
Rodat, Robert, 117
Rommel, Erwin, 92, 96, 97, 126, 167. *See also* Atlantic Wall
Rooney, Andy, 127
Roosevelt, Franklin D., 13, 77; Allies, support for, 1, 24, 109–110; diplomacy of, 23, 49, 50, 51, 140; Japanese-Americans, internment of, 14; right-wing, opposed by, 8, 9, 13; wartime leader, as, 19, 36, 53, 149
Roosevelt, Theodore, 46

Rosenberg, Alfred, 81, 138
Rosenthal, Joe, 146, 156–158, 159
Rylance, Mark, 163

Saboteur, 1–15
Sakall, S. Z., 18
Sander, Otto, 104
Saving Private Ryan, 117–129, 132, 142, 164, 170
Scapa Flow, 108–109
Schaffner, Franklin J., 91, 101
Schell, Maximilian, 73, 74, 75
Schmitt, Carl, 87–88
Schofield, John D., 131
Scott, George C., 92, 93, 94, 98
Segregation in U.S. military, 118, 157
Selznick, David O., 3
Shatner, William, 74
Silver Shirts, 5–8
Sinatra, Frank, 44, 45
Sizemore, Tom, 118
Skirball, Jack H., 3
Smith, Gerald L. K., 10
Sousley, Franklin, 158
Speer, Albert, 41, 81, 82, 83–84, 85
Spiegel, Sam, 59
Spielberg, Steven, 62, 117–119, 124, 142, 145
Stalin, Josef, 134, 136, 137, 138, 140, 142
Stalingrad, 131–132, 135, 138–143
Strank, Mike, 158
Streicher, Julius, 81, 85
Sturges, John, 103
Suribachi, 146, 156–158, 159

Taradash, Daniel, 43, 45
Tarawa, 153–154, 156
Tehran Conference, 140
Tojo, Hideki, 52
Tora! Tora! Tora!, 56, 145
Tracy, Spencer, 74, 75
Truman, Harry S., 153
Twelve O'Clock High, 31–42

Vandenberg, Hoyt, 33
Veidt, Conrad, 18
Versailles, Treaty of, 36, 95, 108

Vichy French regime, 21, 22, 24, 26, 27, 28, 29, 50, 67, 99, 120. *See also* Laval, Pierre; Petain, Henri Philippe
Viertel, Peter, 3
Vogler, Karl Michael, 100

Wallis, Hal, 3, 17, 18
Warner, Jack, 18
Watanabe, Ken, 147
Weisz, Rachel, 132
Whitehead, Fionn, 164
Widmark, Richard, 74

Wilson, Dooley, 18
Wilson, Michael, 59, 62, 71
Winchell, Walter, 11

Yamaguchi, Takashi, 147
Yamamoto, Isoruku, 46, 52, 150, 151, 152. *See also* Pearl Harbor
Yamashita, Iris, 146

Zaitsev, Vasily, 131–132, 141–142
Zhukov, Grigori, 137
Zinnemann, Fred, 41, 45

About the Author

DAVID LUHRSSEN is the author of *Secret Societies and Clubs in American History*, *Mamoulian: Life on Stage and Screen*, and *Hammer of the Gods: The Thule Society and the Birth of Nazism* and coauthor of several books including *Encyclopedia of Classic Rock*, *Elvis Presley: Reluctant Rebel*, and *A Time of Paradox: America Since 1890*. He is a contributor to *100 People Who Changed 20th-Century America*, *Women at War*, American National Biography Online, and the Grove Dictionary of Music and has written for *Historically Speaking*, *History Today*, the *Journal of American History*, and other publications.

Luhrssen received graduate and undergraduate degrees in history from the University of Wisconsin-Milwaukee and taught at Milwaukee Institute of Art and Design and Milwaukee Area Technical College. He is managing editor and film critic for Milwaukee's weekly newspaper, the *Shepherd Express*, and has written about music and film for *Billboard*, the *Milwaukee Journal*, and other newspapers and magazines. He is also a regular commentator on film for Milwaukee's NPR affiliate.

www.ingramcontent.com/pod-product-compliance
Lightning Source LLC
Chambersburg PA
CBHW070255230426
43664CB00014B/2539